JAMAA

A Charismatic Movement in Katanga

JOHANNES FABIAN

Northwestern University Press
Evanston 1971

Johannes Fabian is Assistant Professor
of Anthropology at Northwestern University

TO THE MEMORY OF
PAUL SCHEBESTA

Contents

Figures and Tables

Foreword

This is a splendid piece of work, to which I am proud to add a few prefatory words. Johannes Fabian has been "my student" in only the most formal sense. Together with colleagues at the University of Chicago, it was my duty to impose upon him the usual academic requirements, but throughout he remained an autodidact, his own man, as every serious and creative scholar must. He has educated himself, synthesizing his European intellectual formation with ideas drawn from contemporary social-cultural anthropology to forge the kit of intellectual tools which he applies here in a fascinating and convincing analysis of an African "charismatic movement."

In a continent which has produced many such movements, this is one of an uncommon sort; to my knowledge it resembles, even broadly, only one other: the Balokole ("the Saved") of East Africa. Both arose out of a reconversion, or renewal of faith, through crucial encounter between European and African Christians. Both remain, if sometimes precariously, within the mission church—Anglican in the case of the Balokole, Roman Catholic in the case of the Jamaa. Both are radically interethnic. The differences perhaps reflect in part the different ecclesiastical environments in which the two movements have grown: set in a "broad-church" Anglican milieu, the Balokole have been more revivalist in a Wesleyan sense, stressing personal morality and salvation. Their worship is more "enthusiastic." The adherents of Jamaa, while remaining attached to the sacraments of the church, are somewhat more doctrinal in orientation, and their doctrine springs from a quite explicit attempt to translate Christianity into Bantu culture. Their extraecclesiastical worship is more instructional.

Further comparison must wait upon a study of the Balokole comparable in depth and sensitivity to the present one.

This will not be easy, for research into these movements presents a considerable challenge to the anthropological craft. Movement members are scattered over wide areas and are minorities within their communities. They represent a substantial diversity of cultural and linguistic traditions, hence the standard anthropological methods of participant observation and intensive interviewing within localized social microcosms become unworkable. The persuasiveness of Fabian's work under these conditions represents a very considerable achievement and one which helps point the way for colleagues who are increasingly extending their researches to sociocultural units other than local communities.

On a more theoretical plane, Fabian's study of the Jamaa bears upon what is perhaps the most central and enduring problem in social science: the relationship between thought and action or, in more anthropological language, between the social and the cultural—a preoccupation with which he and I share. The Weberian formulation, with which we both begin, is easy to state: men in society create ideas which render meaningful their changing social situations; the logic of these ideas, in turn, leads them into novel social action. This notion of a continuing dialectic between the cultural and the social, however, is more easily set forth programmatically than put into practice in empirical study. One reason is a certain asymmetry in the state of the art of research in the two domains brought together by the formulation. In general, our conceptual tools for understanding social structure and organization remain better developed than those for analyzing cultural systems. This imbalance is being rectified, as this book shows. But in my view it is crucial that the many new developments now afoot in cultural theory be kept in contact with social theory so that we may avoid repeating the endless cycles of polemic between cultural and social reductionisms that have characterized so much of the discussion of these matters in the past.

Fabian would, I am sure, agree; but, perhaps in part because of the nature of his subject and in part in reaction to the past neglect of culture, in this study cultural analysis dominates the scene. In a spirit of continuing discussion of an important subject, I should like to raise a few questions about this emphasis.

The Jamaa doctrine is here seen as a means of conferring meaning, for Congolese workers, upon the new industrial, intertribal social situation of the mining camps. But this social situation itself is dealt with rather cursorily, as are the social consequences of the Jamaa in reshaping the lives of its adherents outside the microcosm of the movement itself. Fabian argues, essentially, that the movement's charismatic vision, far from summoning them to struggle against their situation, instead makes them passive, sober, reliable workers. The evidence presented, such as it is, is plausible, and indeed this is one sort of social consequence of the logic of culture. But the "definition of the situation" which the Jamaa doctrine presents, as Fabian himself seems to suggest from time to time, is not the only definition relevant to a full sociocultural analysis. Among others are those of non-Jamaa residents of the mining camps and of Fabian himself. How far would these coincide? How might they differ?

Again, I have some questions about the contribution of formal semantic analysis to Fabian's understanding of Jamaa doctrine, an understanding which, I may say, I find convincing. As he says, the logic of culture is not the grammar of language. Neither do words stand in one-to-one correspondence with concepts. Would Fabian now say that his understanding of the concepts *derives* in some sense from the formal analysis, or that it provides a check upon understandings arrived at in other ways?

This, then, is a fine book—one worth reading, pondering, and arguing with for the insights it provides and the questions it raises about contemporary African life, indeed about social life in general and about the nature of our efforts to understand it.

LLOYD FALLERS

The University of Chicago
June, 1970

Acknowledgments

The Jamaa movement is an attempt at religious innovation. It was chosen as an object for observation and analysis in terms of the author's interests in problems of cultural change. Scientific motivations and scientific analysis, however, do not relieve the social scientist of a grave ethical problem. Involved readers—critics and supporters of the Jamaa—may interpret the results of this study as pronouncements about an alleged heretic or sectarian character of the movement. In a situation as unique and precarious as the coexistence of the Jamaa with the mission church, this may have consequences for which the researcher cannot take responsibility. It was decided not to disclose the identity of some of the events, informants, and actors in order to avoid misunderstandings. To all of them, especially to those who introduced him to the common language of Katanga and to the teaching of the Jamaa, the author owes his deepest gratitude.

Professors Lloyd Fallers and Fred Eggan of the University of Chicago offered valuable criticism during the first stages of writing. Many others have contributed with suggestions to its final version. Without their help and without the support of the Wenner-Gren Foundation, New York, the Department of Anthropology and the Committee on African Studies of the University of Chicago, and the Program for African Studies of Northwestern University this project could not have been carried out.

J. F.

Evanston, Illinois
August, 1970

JAMAA
A Charismatic
Movement
in Katanga

❧ INTRODUCTION

WORDS AND DEEDS

While probably all social scientists would agree that their task is the study of social reality in the broadest sense, there has always been considerable disagreement as to what that reality consists of and how it presents itself to the observer. Not long ago, an eminent member of the discipline distinguished two major tendencies, one characteristic of British, the other of French, anthropology. According to V. W. Turner, it is typically British to be concerned with "social relations" as they appear in the "ritual situation," i.e., in sequences of acts. French anthropologists tend to start with "the vernacular text" and concentrate on myths, beliefs, and concepts (cf. Third International African Seminar, *African Systems of Thought* 1965:9). As we proceed in this study of an "African system of thought," it will become clear that our own inclinations lean toward the "French" approach. But we would argue that our choice is not only determined by cultural preferences. It has grown out of the specific problems we had to face when we made the attempt to enter the world of the Jamaa movement.

When "social reality" presents itself in a political, social, and cultural situation of violent sudden change, of disorder and loss of orientation—as in Katanga since 1960—the prospective master of the situation and the analyst of the situation may be in a strikingly similar position. For neither of them is there hope of settling down quietly and trying to bring order and organization into his environment. This study is written with the assumption that the master of the anomic situation is the prophetic-charismatic leader with a vision of meaning in a world that has become meaningless. It is also written with the assumption that a theory and method able to understand the emergence and function of charisma must concentrate on, and take as its point of departure, meaning, that is, conscious perception and interpretation of the human situation which then guides action. Throughout this study we will refer to the charismatic leader as the prophet, "the one who speaks out," as it should be translated literally. He is the formulator of meaning. "Words" as carriers of meaning, their formulation and integration into a system of thought, are taken to be of primary importance in the explanation of such "deeds" as are represented by a charismatic movement: therefore the emphasis we put on the intellectual climate in which the founder formulated, and his followers accepted, the charismatic message of the Jamaa (Part I of this study); therefore the attempt to present "the vernacular text" directly and to analyze it as a system with boundaries and an internal logic and as a depository of meaning shared by a group of people (Part II).

However, it should be clear that the emphasis on "words" in our theoretical approach does not imply a metaphysical statement on the relative importance of ideas over actions. We are aware of the fact that meaning, embodied in words and other symbolic sources of orientation, does not fully account for human behavior; innate or acquired physiological and psychological mechanisms induce people to actions that cannot be accounted for by their expressed convictions. We only maintain that *if* one wishes to confront phenomena of rapid sociocultural change, such as charismatic movements, one must approach them through the material which lends itself most easily to methods of anthropological investigation; and these are the "words," the manifest ideology of such a movement.

CHARISMA AND SOCIOCULTURAL CHANGE

In contemporary social science the concept of charisma and the name of Max Weber have become inseparable. Divergence of opinion and undeniable difficulties of operationalization, however, cannot be blamed on Max Weber. He did not invent the term, as Talcott Parsons once thought (1961:564, note 5), but took it from a long tradition of theological thinking about the difference and relative importance of the institutionalized and the free, "spiritual" aspects of Christianity (Weber 1964:160). For Weber, the starting point was a valid *logical opposition* between forms of authority based on fully developed institutions and others apparently independent from such institutions but nevertheless effective. Yet in many of his formulations he sounds as if he had also accepted the *theological,* if not magical, ingredients of the thinking of his predecessors. "Charisma," in the early Christian tradition, means a special gift of grace. This aspect of the special, supernatural gifts of the charismatic leader remained a problem that neither Weber nor his followers were able to solve or to reformulate in such a way that it could be tested empirically. Of course, Weber did not believe in supernatural powers in an individual. He speaks of the *perception* of such powers among the followers of a leader (Weber 1964:179). The study of the perception of extraordinary personal qualities obviously is a legitimate aim for research. Unfortunately, concern with this aspect of the issue has tended to neutralize the analytical power of Weber's initial step. It will be remembered that charisma was part of a typology of authority. As an admittedly residual category it was meant to handle the questions arising, so to speak, at the borderlines of established traditional or rational forms of authority: the rise of new leaders, the emergence of new groups and alliances. Parsons, like most interpreters of Weber, remained on the whole fascinated by the "personal-power" aspect of charisma. However, he did touch on what should be considered Weber's most important contribution when he remarked:

> It . . . was one of the theoretical functions of the concept of *charisma* to serve as a conceptualization of the source of new orientations on which the process of rationalization is conceived to operate [1963:502, note 9; cf. also Weber 1964:187].

Because of its relation to processes of rationalization, charisma implies a historical, developmental perspective. Weber pointed to this when he said:

> Charisma is *the* great revolutionary force in tradition-bound epochs. This distinguishes charisma from the force of *ratio,* which works either from the outside—changing the conditions and problems of life and, therefore, the attitudes towards these conditions and problems, or through intellectualization. Charisma *can* be a transformation starting from the inside, born from necessity or inspiration. As such, it may cause a change in the central tendencies of belief and

action; it may result in a completely new orientation of all attitudes to all particular phenomena of life and to the "world" as such. In pre-rationalist epochs, tradition and charisma divide between each other almost all orientations of action [1964:182].[1]

Quite obviously, this statement fits the situation in which most African "movements" operate as well as the function which they fulfill for their respective societies.

But the fact that a concept such as charisma permits an intelligent grasp of certain situations and phenomena is still far from making it an operational tool for the description and analysis of movements. Our own gradual explication and differentiation of the concept will be done throughout this study as we struggle with the material presented by the movement under consideration. In this introduction we can only indicate the major lines of our argument.

1. The man in the center of a charismatic movement is, as Weber pointed out (1964:159), neither the "boss," with rational-bureaucratic authority, nor the "lord," who has inherited traditional authority, but the *leader*. In an earlier attempt to construct a framework for the analysis of charismatic movements, I postulated that leadership is "the fundamental area of comparability" between the movements and, therefore, the given point of departure for the understanding of a particular movement (Fabian 1963:780). I insisted on the *prophetic* function of the charismatic leader (*ibid.*, 797–803), that is, his role as the formulator and "speaker" of orientations. Chapter 1 of this study will deal with these questions.

2. Emphasis on the intentional, orientational character of charismatic authority has two methodological corollaries. One is the concept of the "situation," in both the more concrete sense of the "colonial situation" as used by Mannoni (1950), Balandier (1955, 1957), and Gluckman (1963) and the analytical use of action theory (Parsons and Shils).[2] One of the necessary tasks in the analysis of charisma is to present, not the total society, culture,

---

1. All translations of passages quoted from German, French, Dutch, and Swahili are my own, unless a published translation is listed in the Bibliography.

2. "Situation" as an analytical concept in a theory of action is defined as follows: "It is the part of the external world which means something to the actor whose behavior is being analyzed. It is only part of the whole realm of objects that might be seen. Specifically, it is that part to which the actor is oriented and in which the actor acts. The situation thus consists of objects of orientation" (Parsons and Shils 1959:56).

economy, and so forth, but the specific configuration, or the specific segment of reality, in which the leader and his followers find themselves. This is why, in our description of the sociocultural background of the Jamaa movement, we concentrate on the very particular world of the urban and industrial centers of south Katanga (Chapter 2).

Emphasis on the orientational character of charisma implies a second methodological step. When Weber talked of "faith" in charisma (1964:159) and of unconditional allegiance, he left two alternatives for further reasoning. One of them would be to concentrate on the emotional and enthusiastic identification of followers with their leader. The other alternative seems to be more promising for research. It is the fact that this so-called unconditional faith means acceptance of a *total system* of orientation. A charismatic leader does not gain influence by giving piecemeal advice in particular situations. He has his impact because he offers an all-embracing definition of the situation. It is because his message is total and "logical" that the behavior of his followers is not erratic and "curious" (as movements appeared to many observers not long ago) but consistent and observable as a *distinct social reality*. Chapter 3 presents the message of the charismatic leader as a total system. The emphasis will be not on specific propositions but on its internal structural integration. In Chapter 3 this study ends where an action- rather than language-centered approach would have started: in the "ritual situation." It is an attempt to show how the movement's message is internalized, shared, and enacted by its members.

3. Emphasis on orientational aspects, finally, puts an analysis of charisma in the context of problems of sociocultural change.[3]

---

3. Recently the problem of social change has received new attention, e.g., in F. Barth's address to the American Anthropological Association (Barth 1967). We certainly share his discontent with dominant theories and concepts in social anthropology, most of which are designed to deal with static referents and thus are unable to serve as tools for an analysis of change. We whole-heartedly subscribe to his postulate: "If we want to understand social change, we need concepts that allow us to observe and describe *events* of change" (*ibid.*, 661). This is our rationale for choosing such an "event" as the rise of a charismatic movement as a problem for explanation. But we cannot accept his pessimistic conclusion, "There is no way to observe and describe an event of change, except perhaps in the field of legislation" (*ibid.*, 662). Barth does not tell us why the "field of legislation" should be excepted, but obviously he points to the same sort of change that is represented by, and may be observed

Revived interest in the study of orientational systems, or ideologies, goes together with a spreading discontent with some of the precon- ceptions of the "classical" structuralist-functionalist approach in anthropology and sociology.[4] Its difficulties are best illustrated by the way in which Parsons had to struggle with the problem of the relative importance of the "cultural" *vs.* the "social." In the con- clusions to his main work, he distinguished three classes of "theo- retical systems": "systems of nature, action, and culture" (1961: 762). Only the first two of these occur in space and/or time, whereas culture exists only "in the minds" of actors, "or 'embodied' in systems of symbols the 'understanding' of which implies a mind" (*ibid.*, 763, note 2). Therefore, only they are "systems of *empirical* scientific theory" (*ibid.*, 762); culture "occupies a special status" (*ibid.*). Because of this special status, a study of cultural systems cannot serve the "causal understanding of events" (*ibid.*). But, undoubtedly under the influence of Max Weber, he admits:

> From the causal point of view we must grant to them the relation to action, a certain *Eigengesetzlichkeit*. A thought process which *is* a process of action is canalized by logical considerations. The system of logic, a culture system, is a causal element in the concrete result [1961:764, note 3].[5]

---

in, other symbol systems directly guiding action—such as the doctrine of a charismatic movement. We believe a study of the orientational content of social action may allow us to perceive both the event and the direction of sociocultural change. In this sense, our attempt could complement Barth's propositions to adopt a basically quantitative approach to social behavior ("al- location of time and resources"). In this context also belongs Gluckman's essay defending the equilibrium model (and the structural-functional method based on it) for the study of social change. He tries to introduce a dynamic aspect into this basically static view by postulating a structure-immanent time called "structural duration" (1968:221)—the time necessary for an institution to become a full-grown structure, as it were, and also the time necessary for the analyst to "work out" such a structure. Of course he is right if he implies that the absolutely unextended in time could not be the object of anthropo- logical analysis. But I fail to see what this has to do with the study of social change.

4. Cf. Geertz's article on "Ideology as a Cultural System" in Apter (1964). An impression of the importance of the study of ideology (up to 1960) is given by the bibliography by Birnbaum (1960).

5. At a later stage Parsons tried to solve this contradiction by declaring that cultural systems are action systems on the same analytical level as the social and personality systems and that their content—and meaning—aspects are to be handed over to the "formal disciplines such as logic, mathematics, structural linguistics . . ." (Parsons, Shils, *et al.* 1961:II, 964). While pur-

It is on this line that we intend to follow the development and impact of Jamaa doctrine. We by no means claim that the movement we study has sprung full-grown from the head of its founder. On the contrary, if one looks at its various elements separately, every one of them can probably be traced to sources or models in the sociocultural environment. But we do insist on the fact that the *specific integration* of these elements cannot be reduced to the exigencies of the social and personality systems involved. It must be taken as a causal factor in the explanation of change in the limited area of the urban-industrial centers of Katanga.[6] But we shall not be able to pursue this last aspect of a theory of charisma to its full extent. In order to make visible not only the fact but the direction of change, it would be necessary to observe its development over a longer period of time and in a broader comparative context. It would also imply not only a formal analysis of the doctrine as a system but an ideological critique of the major ideas and propositions. At this time, these tasks must remain projects for future work.

THE JAMAA MOVEMENT:
A BRIEF DESCRIPTIVE DEFINITION

The *Jamaa* (Swahili for "family") began as a small group in a miners' settlement near Kolwezi, an urban-industrial center in Katanga. Placide Tempels, a Franciscan missionary known as the author of *Bantu Philosophy* (first published in 1945) had found

---

suing this line of his thought, he pointed to an important connection between these problems of the scientific status of the cultural system and the processes of *social change:* "The impetus to a process of change may perfectly well originate in the development of a cultural configuration, such as the development of a science or of religious ideas" (1963:493).

Furthermore, he stated: "Of the two [i.e., value orientation and belief systems], by far the more obvious case is that of belief systems. Here there seems to be no doubt that there is an inherent factor of directionality which was classically formulated by Max Weber in what he called 'process of rationalization'" (*ibid.,* 399).

6. I have tried to lay the theoretical foundations for these assumptions in my paper "Ideology and Content" (Fabian 1965a). Examples of a revived interest in the study of charisma may be found in one of the recent numbers of *Daedalus* (summer, 1968); cf. especially the contribution by Tucker (1968). An attempt to use the concept in an African context is the work by Dow (1968; cf. also Dow 1969).

enthusiastic response to his preaching of the Christian doctrine, re-
formulated in terms of his discoveries of Bantu categories of
thought and speech. The core of his message was the idea of the
human dignity of adult and free Christians, symbolized in the concept of *umuntu* ("being man"). Clearly, his thinking reflected an
increasing self-consciousness and a drive to its liberation among
the masses in the industrial centers during the last years of the colonial regime. However, by linking the doctrine of human dignity to
"three basic aspirations of the ancestors"—life/force, fecundity/
filiation, and union in love—Tempels also provided a sense of
identity and continuity for his followers. Initially his ideas were
formulated in Swahili, which is spoken as a lingua franca in the
cities of south Katanga. They spread rapidly among the workers
of the Union Minière, the mining trust which controlled most industrial and commercial operations in this part of the Congo. The
troubles and upheavals following Congolese independence and the
secession of Katanga in 1960 sharply increased the mobility of
workers and resulted in a spectacular spread of the movement in
Katanga, the Kasai province, neighboring Ruanda, and most large
cities throughout the Congo Republic. The propagation of the
movement was not centrally directed or organized. Followers who
had received their initiation into the Jamaa from the founder or one
of his disciples in turn assembled a group which they instructed in
the new doctrine. The great majority of adherents were recruited
among Catholic-mission Christians. Typically, Jamaa groups are
intertribal, except, of course, in rural regions with a homogeneous
population. Unlike many prophetic-charismatic movements in
Africa, the Jamaa is all but invisible to the occasional outside observer. The members do not carry any insignia. The weekly meetings of the local group take place on the premises of the parish and
are very inconspicuous.

Lack of overt patterns of organization, official records, and so
forth makes it very difficult to assess the numerical importance
of the movement. During the period of my field work in Katanga
(1966–67), almost all practicing Catholics were either members
of, or somehow in contact with, the Jamaa. In Kolwezi, the population of which was estimated at 130,000, about 1 per cent, according to my observations, were active members. It is possible that in
the thoroughly Christianized Kasai the percentage is much higher.

The founder left the Congo in 1962 and, for reasons of health, never returned. From all available evidence, one must conclude that this did not influence the development of the Jamaa, partly because Tempels continues to give directions in letters, partly because, from the beginning, the dominant pattern of organization was one of self-supporting segmentary lineages of spiritual kinship. Initiation into the movement is conceived of as a birth into a unit of spiritual *kizazi* (generation/filiation).

As a rule, Jamaa members faithfully participate in the ritual of the church, and, because of the somewhat amorphous, segmentary character of the movement, they have been able to maintain a delicate coexistence with the official hierarchy of the Catholic missions. The Jamaa is, as yet, not a sect or a separatist church.[7]

THE NEW AND THE OLD:
THE SOCIOCULTURAL BACKGROUND

If one claims that a charismatic movement derives its impact from the fact that it offers new orientation in a situation of anomie, one has the task of showing what is "old" and to what extent it has lost its orientational functions. Part of this task we shall try to handle in Chapter 2, when we describe the miners' settlement and the orientational problems it poses for potential recruits to the Jamaa. We have chosen this approach because it seems to be the only way to localize the extremely diffuse and complex factors involved in a manageable unit of observation. But the great majority of Jamaa members were not born and brought up in these settlements, and even those who are second-generation workers for the mining company have not severed their ties with their villages and countries of origin. These ties are sometimes economic but always social and ideological. They are centered around traditional

7. Recent information (summer, 1969) indicates that the hierarchy of the church has radicalized its attitude to the movement. Reactions vary between outright prohibition (in south Kasai) and certain regulations for the clergy involved in the Jamaa (at Lubumbashi). Since the consequences of this change cannot be assessed from a distance, the reader should keep in mind that our observations are recorded in an "ethnographic present" and are valid only for the time of our field work.

conceptions of kinship, sacred authority vested in elders, chiefs, and ancestors, and a total conception of reality.

Jamaa members, asked why they were attracted by Tempels, would invariably come up with two reasons: he had a new message, different from the one preached by other white missionaries, and "he touched our hearts, because he knew the ways of our forefathers."

What are the ways of the forefathers? Is it possible to give a consistent picture of the elements of traditional culture and society in the world view of the members of the Jamaa? In Chapter 2 we argue that a typical Jamaa group reflects the ethnic composition of the population in the miners' settlements. Official statistics of the Union Minière listing fourteen major tribal subdivisions are not beyond doubt. How complicated and confusing the situation really is may be exemplified by the ethnography of tribal affiliations around Kolwezi, the immediate area of field work. According to the best source available, the former colonial administrative unit, "Territoire Kolwezi," is occupied by:

1. *Kaonde,* in the (former) chiefdoms of Mushima and Kiombela; in the chiefdom of Musokatanda they are "Lunda-ized," and in Kazembe Mumba they are "mixed with Lunda" (Boone 1961: 65).

2. *Luba-Katanga* and *Ndembo* in the chiefdom Mwilu (*ibid.,* 133).

3. *Lunda,* "also called *Ndembo,*" in the chiefdoms Kawewe and Mwene Kasanga (*ibid.,* 162).

4. *Ndembo* in the (former) chiefdoms Kawewe, Mwene Kasanga, and Mafunga Lumbwe (*ibid.,* 190).

All this suffices to show that we shall not be able to trace the traditional background to a single unified culture such as Sundkler (1961) was able to do for separatist churches with Zulu background and Andersson (1958) for Simon Kimbangu's origins in the Bakongo tradition. The fact that Tempels had "learned" his Bantu philosophy among the Luba in central Katanga will occasionally allow us to point to the specific source of some of his ideas. But there must also be an explanation for the acceptance of his message by followers with a different ethnic background.

Most of the ethnic groups represented in the settlements of the Union Minière were included by Baumann and Westermann in the "Southern Congolese Culture Circle," the distinctive trait of which was the formation of states (1948:170).[8] We need not go into particulars of this history; as the most important point, we should retain the following observation by J. Vansina:

> The crucial event in the earlier history of Central Africa has been not the creation of a Luba kingdom by Kongolo and Kalala Ilunga, but the introduction of Luba principles of government into Lunda land under Cibinda Ilunga and their transformation by the Lunda. The new political pattern, which evolved around 1600 in the Lunda capital, could be taken over by any culture. Its diffusion was to condition until 1850 the history and the general cultural evolution of a huge area [1966:97].

We must conclude, then, that these large political entities were able to impose, or to cultivate, certain cultural universals within a remarkable social and cultural diversity. Following the latest ethnographic synthesis by Vansina (n.d. [1966]), we shall point out some of the general characteristics relevant for our purpose:

1. The Luba-Lunda area is not divided by any major linguistic boundary; hence there is a facility of everyday communication and of long-term diffusion of cultural elements (*ibid.,* 164). The open savanna in which all these cultures are located further facilitated frequent contacts.

2. The development of political systems covering vast areas must not be taken to imply centralization. As Vansina points out for the Luba-Katanga:

> The political ideology of the Luba-Katanga was very complex and intensely sacralized. There were titles, insignia, rites, innumerable magic charms; and the system made it possible for every leader of a *kisaka* [the maximum kinship unit] to participate. But participation was dangerous because power was cruel and brutal, especially in

---

8. Concerning the general ethnographic background for the Luba-Lunda region, I refer to the classic studies by Colle (1913), Verhulpen (1936), and Burton (1961). Useful bibliographies are contained in the ethnographic atlas by Boone (1961) and in a recent compilation from secondary sources by Verstraelen (1964). Most helpful, however, for direct use in this study I found the writings of Vansina (n.d. [1966]) and, above all, Theuws (1962). I should also mention the Kiluba dictionary by van Avermaet and Mbuya (1954), an invaluable source of ethnographic detail. Theuws and van Avermaet, together with the writings of Tempels (cf. bibliography), are of chief importance in identifying the elements of traditional culture to which Jamaa doctrine addresses itself or which it incorporates.

military competitions and in human sacrifices to the power charms. Furthermore, one must not forget that the territorial organization was very fluid and very decentralized [*ibid.*, 169].

In the phase of development in which colonial rule "froze" the situation, the *village* was the focus of cultural, political, and economic activities for a vast majority of the population.

3. A further characteristic of the entire area is the importance of very strongly organized, albeit shallow, segmentary kinship units. Almost all major systems of descent and alliance were in use (e.g., Luba-Katanga: patrilineal; Lunda: "basically" matrilineal but in some groups bilineal or with double descent; Tshokwe-Ndembo: matrilineal). This resulted in local diversity in transmission of political power, land tenure, residence, and marriage rules. But the basic ideological components of all these systems have been the same everywhere. Most important among them is an emphasis on the vertical aspect of kinship relationships, even though the kinship units ("lineages") usually were not much deeper than three living and a few preceding generations. *Generation/filiation,* which was to become one of the central themes of the Jamaa, was always deemed more important than collateral links, and this to such an extent that political (chief-subject) or magicoreligious (initiating-initiated) ties were expressed in terms of parent-child relationships.

4. Religious beliefs and their ritual-symbolic expressions appear to have been equally uniform. A more or less remote "high God" and creator is known throughout the area (Nzambi, Vidye Mukulu, Efile, Kalunga, Cinaweezy, etc.; cf. *ibid.,* 169, 182, 196); sometimes he was conceived of as the first ancestor, sometimes he was associated with cosmic or meteorological phenomena (lightning, rain). Ancestors, usually distinguished as "near" or "remote," were venerated. They were regarded as the proprietors of the land and as the source of life (and sometimes death) for the living.

An important trait in terms of our study is the conception of *bwanga* (cf. van Avermaet and Mbuya 1954:24–26), usually translated as "magic medicine" or "charm." We are using here the Luba term; the referend is known and used throughout the cultural area we are trying to characterize. As we shall show in Chapter 4, *bwanga,* materialized, symbolized force, became one of the elements which Tempels transformed and incorporated into his message. One reason why his ideas became socially effective, i.e., why they resulted so easily and rapidly in the formation of a group of followers, must probably be sought in the particular character of the traditional Luba conception of "magic." [9]

SCOPE AND APPROACH

Observations to be presented and analyzed in this study were collected between January, 1966, and May, 1967. Interviews with the founder of the movement and other persons who are now living in Europe preceded the period of field work in Katanga; these were continued late in 1967 and were resumed in July, 1969.

As already mentioned, the Jamaa has spread from Katanga to other regions in the Congo. The empirical basis on which we shall draw in this book is a fairly complete survey of groups and activities in south Katanga and Kinshasa. For practical and methodological reasons it was impossible to include the Kasai. The Kasai province has been the most extensively missionized rural region of the Congo. The Jamaa has spread to it only during the past five or six years. There the movement still is in its "virulent" stage, spreading like a bushfire from village to village. Reports indicate that in the process of this rapid spread it has more and more departed from the original form and even shows antimission or antiwhite tendencies, otherwise unknown in the Jamaa. Clearly, such a situation is highly interesting, but it is not favorable to the sort of research we were trying to carry out—research emphasizing ideology, its origins, development, manipulation, ritualization.

The most promising solution to these problems of limitation seemed to be to concentrate on the cities of Kolwezi and Lubumbashi as the original and still the most important ideological centers of the movement. Such concentration was called for, above all, by problems of communication. It goes without saying that work on the doctrinal aspects of a charismatic movement presupposes com-

9. Vansina makes the following remarks concerning the *buyanga,* an association of hunters among the Baluba Katanga which will have our attention in Chapter 4: "The *buyanga* was not really an association because it was a *bwanga.* There were no collective rites, except for the initiation of new members and the funeral dances in honor of a deceased member. But it must be said that many other associations were, in fact, not more than that. *Bwanga and association very often went together*" (*ibid.,* 170; my italics; cf. also van Avermaet and Mbuya 1954:26).

mand of the language. Swahili, as the language spoken in the industrial centers and as the "original" language used by Tempels, was the obvious choice.

Further limitation to a few local groups and regions became necessary since participation and daily contact proved to be the only ways to get firsthand information. During the whole period of field work the closest contact was maintained with the Jamaa group of Musonoi (see Chapter 2), a miners' settlement near Kolwezi. Personally or via informants, about sixty local groups were reached.[10]

The high value placed by the Jamaa on personal relationships and friendship made it necessary to proceed very carefully in preparing interviews, especially taped interviews. Usually through several visits, informants had to be accustomed to the tape recorder and convinced of the researcher's good intentions. An attempt to collect detailed statistical information on the Jamaa group at Musonoi had to be booked as a failure. Taking down names, ages, etc., on prepared forms was considered a hostile act by some of the leaders. Even after the matter had been explained, they insisted that charisma must not be measured, registered, or analyzed. This is entirely in the spirit of the founder, Placide Tempels, who reacts in his writings and in interviews in much the same way. Most difficulties of this kind, however, were amply compensated for by the eagerness of Jamaa people to talk in less formal situations about the movement, its doctrine, and their personal problems.[11]

On the other hand, there is the fact that speaking about Jamaa doctrine is subject to a code of rules regarding appropriate style, content, and level of instruction. These rules are, as we shall see in the final chapter, linked to stages in a formal initiation. For ethical

10. Most important among them were those at Kinshasa (formerly Léopold-ville); Luluabourg (Kasai), Lukalaba-Bakwanga (Kasai); Musonoi, Kapata, Ruwe, Luilu, Metalkat, Kolwezi, Kipushi (all miners' settlements near Kolwezi and Lubumbashi); Camp B.C.K. Lubumbashi, C.E.C. Lubumbashi, Camp Sogechim Jadotville, C.E.C. Kolwezi (communities not run by the Union Minière); and the villages and towns of Pwene, Mpala, Kasaji, Dilolo, San-doa, Samutoma, Muteba, Kamina, Luabo, Luena, Bukama, Kikondja, Malemba-Nkulu (all in southwest Katanga).

11. In many respects I encountered the same problems on which H. W. Turner comments in his paper on "Problems in the Study of African Independent Churches" (1966). But, judging from my experience with the Jamaa, I tend to think that communication through language is a more important access than participation in ritual.

as well as practical reasons (normally, preparation for each of the three degrees takes one or two years), I made no attempt to undergo the ritual. Is the noninitiated anthropologist, therefore, missing essential information? Our treatment of the problem of initiation will make it clear that this is not the case. Initiation is centered upon the experience of being "born" into the movement rather than on the transmission of doctrinal content. Most of what is kept "secret" the researcher can learn indirectly (provided he has command of the language and the time to learn where his "blind spots" are). The rest must be regarded as "secret" because it touches on personal matters that should not be told to a third person.

Finally, I should briefly comment on the wider relevance of this study. When my work on the Jamaa began, the movement was still virtually unknown to anthropologists and experts on charismatic-prophetic phenomena in Africa.[12] Meanwhile, it has received attention in at least one major study (Barrett 1968) and has become a "case" in this growing field of specialization. Even though I recognize its significance in a comparative perspective (cf. Fabian 1969a,b), I choose to concentrate in this study on a monographic presentation. I feel justified in doing this because, at this stage of elaboration, an attempt to be "comparative" could only result in recording redundant parallels. I reserve my opinions concerning the position of the Jamaa in the ethnography of African movements for a time when it will be possible to draw on an adequate documentation and analysis of the *content* of its doctrine.[13] Formal organizational resemblances among movements are easily stated and incorporated in typologies (and I am not denying the usefulness of typologies for the classification of an enormous bulk of ethnographic descriptions). But in the work on the Jamaa I pursue a different and more ambitious aim. I want to understand the intellectual, ideological process which led to its emergence and which makes it a force in the postcolonial development of an African country. At this point I am more interested in the Jamaa as the concrete *result* of a historical process than as a *case* serving verification of a general theory of movements.

12. Even though Theuws's paper had appeared in 1961 and the study by De Craemer had just been published at what was then still Léopoldville (1965).
13. A volume documenting Jamaa teaching through a selection of original texts (in Swahili and an English translation) is being prepared for publication at Northwestern University Press. See the Epilogue to this book.

PART I

The Movement

1 ❦ THE FOUNDER

A prophet's personality and life story provide important keys to the understanding of his message and the movement he initiated. Yet, in introducing this chapter, we will limit ourselves to the bare essentials of his career. We do this out of respect for the right of a living person in his own life. We can combine such necessity with reasons stemming from our theoretical orientation. Rather than through "deeds," we intend to approach the Jamaa through "words," through objectivations of an intellectual process. Tempels' writings will be the evidence on which we shall base our arguments.

Placide Tempels was born in 1906 near Hasselt in the Flemish-speaking Limburg province of Belgium. His father was the local stationmaster. In 1924 he began his studies for the priesthood with the Franciscans at Hasselt. He became a member of the order and was ordained priest in 1930. He then pursued his studies and also taught at the college at Turnhout. After that he was sent as a missionary to Katanga. His first assignment, in 1933, was to Luabo, an important mission among the Baluba Shamba. Between 1933 and 1945 he worked at several mission posts: on Lake Moero, at Kamina, and at others. From 1945 till 1949 he stayed in Belgium, more or less forced into exile after the publication of *Bantu Philosophy*.[1] In 1949 he was back in Katanga, first on several posts in Luba country (Kayeye, Kabondo-Dianda); then, in 1953, he was appointed pastor in a miners' settlement at Ruwe, near Kolwezi. In 1957 he was transferred to Musonoi, also near Kolwezi, where he stayed until 1962. Since then he has been living in the Franciscan monastery of his home town.

1. To be exact, Tempels left the Congo on a regular leave. But he was prevented from returning on orders from his superiors, due to an intervention by Msgr. de Hemptinne at the Vatican.

Occasionally Father Tempels has traveled and participated in international meetings (e.g., in 1946 in Vienna), the most important of which was perhaps a conference organized by the Présence Africaine in Abidjan, Ivory Coast, in 1961. But much more remarkable is his ability to adapt to the particular place assigned to him by the exigencies of his work or the circumstances of his career as a "prophet" of Bantu thought.

I made his acquaintance in Hasselt at a time when he had been suffering from a grave illness. He is a rather short and heavily built man, and a long white beard makes his appearance grave and solemn. But in conversation he turns out to be a person of great charm and warmth. His friends in the Congo described him as a passionate hunter and fisherman and as an excellent cook. He loved music and was an exceptionally gifted photographer and amateur painter. His ability to create a friendly and humane atmosphere made him a center of attention among both his confreres and the European community at Kolwezi. His contacts with the Congolese were deep and personal, beyond the demands of his function as a missionary. He had an excellent command of the languages (Kiluba and Swahili). Tempels was also known as an inspiring preacher. In his philosophical and theological opinions, he seemed to have been neither conservative nor progressive but, rather, independent, following his own ideas. Contrary to his claims (cf. 1962: 36), he was apparently not a great reader, although a few books did influence him deeply.

His attitude toward me was one of defensive benevolence. He was willing to cooperate by giving me information, but obviously he was more interested in "testimony" for his ideas and his movement than in their scientific dissection.

THE UNCOMFORTABLE MISSIONARY

A Climate for Rebellion

It is not easy to reconstruct the situation which made a charismatic leader out of a missionary. Tempels and the people who influenced him during his years in Africa are still too close to us in time to be researched extensively and critically. But since this study is written with the assumption that charismatic leadership emerges as a solution for problems of orientation, we may try to picture the situation in the former Belgian Congo as it appears in accessible documents.

Tempels has made it abundantly clear that, at a certain moment in his career as a missionary in the bush of Katanga, sometime in the early forties, he had come to a point where the ideas he had grown up with and the things he was doing proved a failure in the face of the realities they were supposed to define and to handle. He arrived as a "white man to a colonized Africa, above all, as the carrier of a divine message" (1962:36). But he confesses that he adopted the attitudes of the "white master" when he traveled through the bush and tried to organize his church (*ibid.*). This is how he describes what happened to him when he came to realize his limits:

> During ten years . . . I always had my eyes on my manual. I tried all the methods, all the schemes in order to make people understand, accept, and practice Christian religion. I had followed scrupulously all directions but, nevertheless, the machine would not work. It was only then that, for the first time in ten years, I gave up consulting manual, catechism, and doctrine. I had a surprised and intrigued look at the machine that refused to work, at the man I had never noticed. I never had been interested in him, his thinking, his aspirations, but only in the religion whose propagator I was [*ibid.*, 36 f.].

With this confession, Tempels gives us insight into the sort of traumatic experience that preceded his "conversion," marked by *Bantu Philosophy*. The process that led to his discovery of the Bantu world was, of course, not entirely endogenous. He did not react merely to a personal failure to communicate with Africans. What he had to say was part of a discussion that went on in the colony. He talked because he started to feel uncomfortable in the intellectual climate that reigned in the Congo, especially in Katanga. Tempels began to question, or to "forget," as he likes to put it, some of the most cherished principles of the missionary and colonial endeavor. This was bound to get him into trouble with the "official" ideology, whose eloquent and domineering spokesman was Monsignor de Hemptinne, at that time apostolic vicar of Elisabethville. In 1967, seven years after independence, I met oldtimers in Elisabethville (now Lubumbashi) who talked about de Hemptinne with almost religious devotion. And even Congolese paid tribute to his

powerful personality by calling him—wrongly but significantly—
"the child of Leopold II," i.e., of the founder of the Congo as a
colonial entity.[2]

It cannot be our task to attempt an analysis of de Hemptinne's
numerous pronouncements. We shall have to resort to a somewhat
impressionistic method of characterizing his "style" of dealing with
people whom he considered enemies of the true interests of the
colony. A short pamphlet ("La Politique des missions protestantes
au Congo") represents his reaction to a program of the Protestant
missions, published in Léopoldville in 1929.

From a religious leader one might expect a discussion of the
religious issues raised in the program. Instead, de Hemptinne
launches an attack on "foreign intruders" (most of the Protestant
missionaries came from Anglo-Saxon or Scandinavian countries)
and does not hesitate to point out similarities between certain mod-
erate ideas on social improvement in the Congo and "Moscow":
"Coincidences, you may say. Coincidences which call imperiously
for prudence and force" (1929:31).

He also indulges in some ironic comments on the fact that Protestant missionaries, many of them without adequate education in
philosophy and theology, claim to act upon inspiration by the Spirit.
There are other spirits besides the Holy Spirit, de Hemptinne argues,
and he urges: "It is for the government, responsible for public security, to discern the spirits" (*ibid.*, 22). This will suffice to show
the opposition someone would have to face who dared to disagree
with de Hemptinne's ideas about the aims and methods of mission
and colonization.

Since Tempels actually did write *Bantu Philosophy* against those
views, let us seek further background information by taking a brief
look at the minutes of the Permanent Commission for the Protection
of Natives. This institution dates back to Leopold II's Free State
and came to play, in the course of its history, the precarious double
role of the "moral ombudsman," as Young called it (1965:26), acting as the conscience of the colonial administration and as a pressure

2. B. Fetter, of the University of Wisconsin, collected a strange but highly
interesting document, the *Vocabulaire de ville de Elisabethville*. In this "history" of the city, written for an organization of former houseboys (in Swahili), de Hemptinne is listed in the genealogy of the religious leaders as:
"Mupe Jean Hemptine Felixise, yule ni mtoto wa Mfaleme Leopold II"
(Father Jean-Felix de Hemptinne; he is the child of Leopold II).

group for the Catholic mission, represented by de Hemptinne and several other prelates.

De Hemptinne's influence is reflected in the proceedings of the 1923/24 meetings of the commission in Léopoldville as compared to those of the subcommission for Katanga, which met in Elisabethville in December–February, 1923/24. Both commissions agree that "assimilation" of the native population to European culture is the final aim of colonization (Guebels 1952:253 f., 299), but the documents differ considerably in tone and emphasis.

The gentlemen in Léopoldville advocate protection of the "respectable institutions" of native society because they believe that "this shall confer a particular character on Congolese civilization, which will not be just a poor imitation of our European civilization but the fruit of a happy union of the two *génies*" (*ibid.*, 250). They refuse to pronounce for or against the theory of indirect rule (*ibid.*, 253). They are content to express their aversion for any preconceived theories of colonization, reminding the administration that politics is "l'art des réalisations" (*ibid.*, 254).

The subcommission in Elisabethville is much more outspoken in its opposition to

> certain doctrines which tend to maintain, protect, or even reconstitute native customs and institutions. Fully applied, such a policy would result in a profound separation of an autonomous white civilization and a native society, artifically kept on an inferior level. . . . This policy is certain to fail because the evolution of native customs is the inevitable "fatal" result of our occupation, and it would also be against the moral and material interests of the natives [*ibid.*, 299 f.].

Nor does the subcommission envisage the final goal of the colonial endeavor to be the happy union of the two cultures. It is stated flatly that one should follow "the traditional policy, which consists of favoring the evolution of native customs and institutions toward the superior civilization, which is ours" (*ibid.*, 299).

The subcommission at Elisabethville met for a second time in 1936/37. Again it formulated a number of general principles for colonial policy which, in 1938, were adopted by the commission in Léopoldville (*ibid.*, 535). They reflect a changed situation, above all the fact that some "natives" had been ordained Catholic priests —"ce couronnement de l'effort civilisateur" (*ibid.*, 441). They had to be accepted as assimilated and therefore equal to Europeans. At the same time, the documents express concern over "subversive movements" among the natives, utilized by "troublemakers" for their dubious goals. These movements should be severely repressed (*ibid.*, 442). In other words, the commission had to face the fact that the natives were starting to move toward liberty and equality and that they desired assimilation. But, by and large, such moves were still looked upon as a "ridiculous parody" of the white man's ways (*ibid.*, 442).

In any case, the theory of assimilation now had to be redefined in order to retain its usefulness as an ideology of colonization and domination. The subcommission recommended:

1. The assimilation of the natives should remain the goal of our policy, defying the principle of a color bar and of inequality exclusively based on racial difference, which would result in unavoidable political and social dualism.

2. This assimilation of the population [*race*] placed under our tutelage should be effected with utmost prudence, without losing sight of the inferiority of almost the entire native population.

3. The government should put an end to all propaganda and all attempts to push the native toward premature emancipation.

4. The government should, as much as possible, grant the natives access to positions which correspond to their degree of evolution.

5. Those few natives who deserve it should find in the Eruopean society equality, based on their complete assimilation [*ibid.*, 442 f.].

The implementation of these ideas proved to be a failure, unless one has to assume that the talk about "assimilation" was but a Machiavellian device to deny equality to Africans. This is suggested by the "immatriculation" issue, i.e., the bureaucratic procedure that was to establish the degree of assimilation in every individual case (cf. Young 1965:75–87). The moral and intellectual demands were set at ideal European levels. Certainly, most of the Europeans living in the Congo would not have been able to meet these standards (cf. Guebels 1952:484–89, 536–39).

It is not our task to sort out the honorable and less honorable motivations which determined the recommendations of the commission. We are trying to sketch the general climate during Tempels' formative years as a missionary. That the Machiavellian element was indeed strong can be demonstrated by two quotations which speak for themselves. They clearly bear the stamp of de Hemptinne and depict quite vividly his attitudes toward free expression of opinion. A fortiori, they indicate what an independent mind, directly or indirectly under the prelate's jurisdiction, would have to face if he dared to speak up against "official" policy.

In 1936/37, the subcommission said, regarding the role of the press in the colony,

> The indisputable power of the press, both for good and for evil, is a commonplace. In a colony where the native population will be, for a long time, incapable of being seriously critical about what they read, the authorities should be prepared to exercise a rigorous surveillance [*ibid.*, 481].

The commission in Léopoldville was even more explicit about

> the inconvenience created by the sometimes inopportune intervention of the press in questions of political and social planning regarding the natives. Our pupils [*pupilles*] are not sufficiently educated to be aware of the exaggeration which is used when the press criticizes, insinuates, or attacks. . . .
>
> Certainly, in Europe it is sometimes useful that the newspapers appeal to public opinion and give support to certain causes in order to ameliorate certain situations in the public interest. We grant that the press intervenes in everything and does not hesitate before any subject. The journalist knows everything; at least, he is supposed to know everything and pronounce his opinion on everything. His zeal, as someone who inspires and offers criticism, may be worthy of praise in civilized countries, where the readers know what to think about the competence of each journalist in the matter under consideration. In the colony, such untimely zeal may prove awkward and intolerable, even dangerous for the maintenance of public order. Therefore, in the colony, all articles which could disturb the native conceptions should rigidly be removed from the columns of the newspapers [*ibid.*, 600 f.].

Announcing Rebellion

The paternalistic, or rather totalitarian, control of public opinion and the news media advocated by the commission did not come into effect, at least not to the desired degree. About five years after the recommendations just quoted, Tempels started to publish his views.

As far as our interests are concerned, he entered the discussion with an attack on one of the favorite ideas held by assimilationists: abolition of polygamy as the major obstacle on the road to higher civilization. He argued as follows:

1. The colonizers started out by projecting their own legalistic ideas about marriage onto native society. However, "matrimonial life is, for the Bantu, the cooperation of the superior forces of life with the aim of creating new life; or, more exactly, according to their mentality, it is an expansion, transmission, and continuation of their own life" (1944–45:267). In other words, Bantu marriage must be seen within a very large context of ideas and beliefs about the essence of life.

2. Because marriage has to do with their central values, Bantu will be inclined to preserve and expand their "vital force" whenever social, economic, or other reasons prevent monogamous marriage from having the desired results. Tempels then gives a list of these reasons (*ibid.,* 268 f.). But if, in customary law, there is anything like our marriage contract, it is between a man and his first wife; his other "wives" are concubines in European legal terms.

3. The colonizer committed a grave error when he took for customary law what for the Bantu was a necessary and regulated evil. Therefore, Tempels argues, "Nous avons institué la polygamie" (*ibid.,* 270).

4. Thinking that monogamous marriage was a European import to Africa, the administration created a false problem. The aim cannot be to replace customary-law marriage by civil-code marriage because "it would be absurd first to destroy customary monogamous marriage in order to introduce the monogamous marriage of written law" (*ibid.,* 270).

The argument can be summed up as follows: the colonizer is bound to fail in his efforts of assimilation because he starts with a false conception of the points of departure.

The same sort of reasoning can be found in another article written by Tempels for *L'Essor du Congo.* Interestingly enough, it appeared under the title "La philosophie de la rebellion" (Rubbens 1945: 17–23). But Tempels is not concerned, as one might expect, with a philosophy *for* a rebellion. Rather, he predicts rebellion and attributes it to the failure of the colonizers to communicate effectively with the Africans (and the other way around). The reason is to be sought in the lack of a philosophical foundation on which intercommunication might be based. The gap between the views of the world held by the colonizers and those of the colonized is such that "we destroy each other metaphysically" (*ibid.*, 19).[3]

In summary, Tempels sensed "rebellion" and "destruction" in the colony. What is more, he was not content to point to particular events (e.g., the mutinies in the garrison of Luluabourg; cf. Young 1965:77). Nor did he attribute the difficulties to "subversive" activities among the natives and to errors on the side of the administration. He maintained that there was something *basically and intrinsically wrong* in the way the colonizer related to the colonized, implying that things could not improve unless the fatal error was discovered and eliminated.

The Gods Dethroned: Tempels' "Disturbing" Discovery

Tempels' articles in *L'Essor du Congo* herald the manifesto of his thinking: *Bantu Philosophy*, written (first in Dutch) between June, 1944, and June, 1945, and published, first in French, in 1945, and then in English in 1959.

Bantu Philosophy undoubtedly is the most important document for the history, or prehistory, of what became the ideology of the Jamaa movement.[4] It will claim our attention on all levels of our analysis, but in this section we are trying to reconstruct the situation, social and intellectual, in which Tempels conceived his ideas. We are not yet concerned with the specific content of his message. What we are looking for at this stage are the problems and orientational needs that made Tempels reconsider his positions as a missionary and colonizer. We seek to grasp his motivations, attitudes, and aims.

3. "La philosophie de la rebellion" first appeared anonymously in *L'Essor du Congo* (August 31, 1944). The paper had acknowledged incidents of Congolese rebellion since the beginning of May, 1944, but almost always indirectly, in short releases mentioning the success of the colonial government in controlling the outbursts and punishing the leaders (through execution). To my knowledge it published only one article describing in some detail what happened ("L'assassinat des auxiliaires indigènes de Masisi, par Bushiri," by A. Bribosia, the local *administrateur territorial*, June 10, 1944). Clearly, Tempels' contribution was to express reactions which the censors did not permit to be linked directly to the reported incidents. This supports our view that the ideas of *Bantu Philosophy* were formulated in an atmosphere of general fear and political uncertainty.

4. This argument is developed more fully—and in response to a recent critique of *Bantu Philosophy* (Boulaga 1968)—in Fabian 1970b.

Let us start with a quotation from *Bantu Philosophy* which expresses what Tempels himself thought about the importance and consequences of his discovery. After what has been said in the preceding section, it needs no explicit comment to recognize against whom he is arguing.

The discovery of Bantu philosophy is a disturbing event for all those who are concerned with African education. We have had the idea that we stood before them like adults before the newly born. In our mission to educate and to civilize, we believed that we started with a *"tabula rasa,"* though we also believed that we had to clear the ground of some worthless notions, to lay foundations in a bare soil. We were quite sure that we should give short shrift to stupid customs, vain beliefs, as being quite ridiculous and devoid of all sound sense.

We thought that we had children, "great children," to educate; and that seemed easy enough. Then all at once we discovered that we were concerned with a sample of humanity, adult, aware of its own brand of wisdom and moulded by its own philosophy of life. That is why we feel the soil slipping under our feet, that we are losing track of things, and why we are asking ourselves, "What to do now to lead our colored people?" [1959:110 f.]. The gods are dethroned, the disinherited stand before us as equals [*ibid.*, 110].

Tempels felt that, in order to get out of this unbearable situation, the colonizers would have to start with a "general confession" (*ibid.*, 20), accepting the fact that most efforts had failed to produce any change in the natives. Search for a solution would have to start with the admission: "Something is lacking. There must be something wrong somewhere" (*ibid.*, 119). He himself admits to having committed grave errors in his career (cf. *ibid.*, 20 f.), until finally he discovered that he was wasting his time (cf. *ibid.*, 21).

The thing that was "wrong" was that the colonizers did not care to understand, from *their* point of view, the primitive peoples they were ruling (cf. *ibid.*, 20, 63). Nor did they bother to look for "the one and only key" (*ibid.*, 15; cf. 23, 24) to native thought: the set of beliefs and ideas that govern their actions. Tempels speaks of this basic system of orientations as "philosophy," "ontology," or "metaphysics" because those were the terms familiar to him from his education in Thomistic philosophy and theology and because he thought that they would best reflect his main concern: to reach the depths of the Bantu "soul."

Tempels likes to stress that *Bantu Philosophy* is a "systematic study" (*ibid.*, 25) and a contribution to anthropological knowledge in the technical sense of the term. On the other hand, he does not conceal the fact that the discovery he wishes to communicate came to him as a deeply personal experience. He tells us that his insights stem from an "intimate human contact" (*ibid.*, 28) with the people he studied. In fact, his kind of understanding is "far more a matter of experience and intuition than of study" (*ibid.*, 29). Consequently, he asks the reader of *Bantu Philosophy*

> to put out of his mind while reading it both his western philosophical thought and any judgments which he may have already made concerning Bantu and primitive peoples. I ask him to abandon received ideas and to apply his mind to getting hold of the significance of what is here said, trying to grasp Bantu thought from within and not allowing himself to be diverted into criticism of my way of setting it out or of my choice of terms [*ibid.*, 30].

Another important trait that pervades *Bantu Philosophy* is Tempels' concern with the reaction to his insights among Africans and Europeans. One outward sign of this is the fact that, in the English edition, he quotes twelve positive and admiring letters (from, among others, Melville Herskovits, Jacques Maritain, and Cardinal Lienart).

In the introductory chapter of *Bantu Philosophy* there is a passage in which Tempels reveals his own aims and motives and which makes it understandable why the reaction of others was so important to him:

> We do not claim, of course, that the Bantu are capable of formulating a philosophical treatise. . . . It is our job to proceed to such systematic development. It is we who will be able to tell them, in precise terms, what their inmost concept of being is. They will recognize themselves in our words and will acquiesce, saying, "You understand us: you now know us completely: You 'know' in the way we 'know.' "
>
> More than that, if we can adapt our teaching of true religion to what is worthy of respect in their ontology, we shall hear, in the same way in which it was given to me, such testimony as was given to me. "Now you deceive yourself no longer, you speak as our fathers speak, it always seemed to us that we must be right" [*ibid.*, 25].

Two important points should be retained from this quotation, since they announce, in a way, the basic issues of the following chapters:

1. The (re)discovered Bantu philosophy will serve to enlighten the Africans about their own profound conceptions.
2. The discovery will prove its validity by "testimony," i.e., enthusiastic response from the Africans.

What, in summary, was it that the "uncomfortable missionary" was looking for? Understanding! *Bantu Philosophy* was Tempels' attempt to make, first for himself and then for others, a foreign culture intelligible and, therefore, accessible. But careful examination of certain statements in his book reveals that, even at that stage of his thinking, he sought more than intellectual insights. Perhaps "recognition" could be the word to express his constant striving for two goals: to recognize in the other culture that which is "human" and valuable, and to be recognized by others as someone who shares their deepest human aspirations.

THE MISSIONARY TURNED PROPHET

"Man among Men"

In his essay "Stages in the Life of a Missionary" (1962:35–40), Tempels reports that he made the first step toward his "conversion" when he discovered that he knew almost nothing about the people he was trying to Christianize. He responded with a study of Bantu "philosophy." At that time, he tells us, he made an effort to understand how "the machine" (i.e., Bantu personality) worked in order to apply his insights to his work as a missionary; deeper knowledge of the Bantu should result in a more effective method of Christianization and colonization. But then something quite different happened:

> I thought that, having discovered Bantu personality, I would become once more the pastor, the boss, the doctor, now that I had mastered a technique, a language adapted to "teaching" Christianity. But all of a sudden I realized that, through this *encounter* between man and man, soul and soul, being and being, we had progressed from mutual knowledge toward sympathy and, finally, love: and it was exactly at that moment that Christianity was born and had already begun [*ibid.*, 38].

In other words, the communication of the Christian message did not come as the result of preconceived methods of indoctrination nor as any sort of transmission of a given content. Rather, it was experienced as an *event,* springing from a union of human beings.

The basic document for this section of our discussion is Tempels' "Catéchèse bantoue." First published in 1948, this short essay is the application of the findings of *Bantu Philosophy*. It is in two respects closer to our theme than the latter. First, it describes much more explicitly Tempels' personal involvement. Second, it already contains the core of what later became Jamaa doctrine; in some instances, formulae of the Swahili version recorded in the field are clearly recognizable.

Before we direct our attention to particular issues, I should like to point out a general difference between *Bantu Philosophy* and the "Catéchèse bantoue." It is a difference in emphasis rather than principles. But it is significant enough to indicate that the "origin" of the Jamaa, if it can be fixed at all historically, must be sought in the years prior to 1948. *Bantu Philosophy* revolves around the "concept of being" (vital force) as a key to Bantu ontology and as a point of departure for an understanding between the two cultures in the colony. The discovery of a "rational" system of values and ideas and the recognition of the Bantu's right to live according to their own philosophy was presented mainly as a matter of intellectual honesty. In "Catéchèse bantoue" this relatively detached view is superseded by an unabashed call for *love* and personal encounter between the white man and the African:

> It does not matter whether one does or does not accept *Bantu Philosophy* as an adequate interpretation of the soul of the Africans. At any rate, our attitude toward them must be one of true, positive, and total human love [1948:5].

> Thanks to his numerous failures, so to speak, the missionary will come to a view [*intuition*] of the ideal missionary life. And that must be love, nothing else. And true love cannot have anything for its object but the life of one's fellow man; it cannot be but totally human and concrete; it must love the other such as he is in his real life, his total life, and, therefore, in his ideas, his profoundest sentiments and aspirations [*ibid.,* 4].

In *Bantu Philosophy* Tempels saw himself as an "educationist" and felt the ground slipping beneath his feet as a result of his new insights. Now he is on firm ground. The first six pages of "Catéchèse bantoue" are filled with statements reflecting the fact that he has found a new and successful approach to the "soul" of the African. This is no longer "education" but the "testimony" of love (cf. 1948:2).

In a similar way, a shift of emphasis has occurred as far as the aim of his work is concerned. The missionary's task cannot be to convert the other to his own ideas and conceptions (*ibid.*, 1). The Africans should reach for Christ by means of a way of thinking "they have in themselves" (*ibid.*, 5). In *Bantu Philosophy* Tempels proclaimed that the students of their philosophy would be able to tell the Bantu what their "inmost concept of being" is (1959:25). Now he postulates: "They themselves must make the discovery" (1948:7). No longer is the white man the only one who, with deep respect but, nevertheless, from a superior position, leads the African to "true civilization" (cf. 1962:18). He, too, has to learn from his dialogue with the African. In the process of discussing the basic issues of life, both will become more "conscious of the vital force to which they aspire" (1948:7).

Another change becomes visible in "Catéchèse bantoue." Tempels no longer talks of projects and programs for action. He has found the "secret" of success: Love for the African, love which does not impose itself in order to dominate the other. It is a changed and "reformed" missionary who writes at the end of the introduction to "Catéchèse bantoue":

> It is this initial contact, this first identification with the soul of the pagans, such as they are and as they think, that I tried to make visible in these pages. It is simply this "being man among men" which has to come before the priest speaks and which is the first testimony of Christian love, even before one says a single word about "Christianity" [*ibid.*, 5 f.].

Clearly, Tempels still thinks of himself as a missionary, as a representative of Christ in a pagan world. But he has gone through an important experience; he has found the "secret of success": it was not the fact that he was an authorized teacher of a doctrine that made him reach the "soul" of the Africans; their response was due to his willingness to open himself up for a profound *personal encounter* on an equal basis.

In a somewhat different but related sense Max Weber defined

"personal" vocation as the distinctive criterion of a prophet (1964: 346). Since we are interested in understanding the change which made the missionary Tempels the prophetic-messianic focus of the Jamaa movement, we shall now take a closer look at those few statements in "Catéchèse bantoue" in which he speaks about his experience.

The Prophetic Event

Prophetic-charismatic leadership, as opposed to other forms of access to power, somehow carries the connotation of a "happening," of something that "clicks" between the prophet and his followers. It is a process so little extended in space and time, so little explicit in terms of the factors involved, that it is often thought of as something dramatic and mysterious. All this is echoed in one of Tempels' statements:

> The solution cannot be found in theories or formulae, but simply in the soul of living man, be he white or black, because the kingdom of Christ must be founded in men as they are. *You must leap headlong into the life of your fellow man and accept it as it is* [1948:3; my italics].

Love (*charité*) is the driving force behind this leap into the darkness, and love cannot exist without *response:* "This love, true, total, and perfectly human, irresistibly will produce a response on the side of our fellow man" (*ibid.,* 4).

What will this response be? "Unfailingly," someone approached by such love will be moved to rediscover inside himself his basic human values (*ibid.,* 5). Tempels never tires of stressing the importance of this response. Any statement that reflects his own view of the "prophetic" role is of great importance for our analysis. Thus we quote two passages from "Catéchèse bantoue":

> In the dialogue with the Africans one should not look for a complete outline of the doctrine. Nor should one be concerned with a theory or method to be proved and defended. The spontaneous and fervent response from the Africans alone can be the "sign" that will convince us. It will convince us against all doubts and objections, for it is the sign that Christ himself gave us: the sign of love. Once we see that our attitude toward the Africans makes love bud and grow in their

hearts, then this will be the proof. Once we see that, thanks to our attitude, the Africans become "alive"; once we see that they have accepted Christianity as something that belongs to them; once we see that, acting on an impulse from inside, they want to go to their fellow Africans to bring to them this new life: then we shall recognize the tree from its fruits. When the Africans manage to leave their egoistic paganism, rigid as it is and without regard for the stranger, and when they start to love one another, then we have the final proof: we have succeeded in "converting" them [*ibid.*, 6].

Only the missionary who has had this experience knows what it means to a man to discover himself in this way, to reveal his intimate being to a true friend. There is a sudden transformation in such a man, erupting from the subconscious; his supreme desire becomes more intense. Under the effect of his own words, the African will exclaim, "Yes, this is what we want in the innermost part of our heart; for that, we are ready to do anything." And the missionary is not going to stay indifferent, seeing how human the African is, much closer to himself than he had ever thought. From now on they will be friends; and, finally, they will be able to talk about the things that matter to both of them, the black and the white [*ibid.*, 7 f.].

Let us sum up the crucial points we have tried to document from "Catéchèse bantoue":

Tempels underlines the personal effort, the motivations, and the attitudes on the side of the missionary (i.e., on his own side). *Personal involvement* is dramatized to such an extent that, for lack of a better term, we call the role envisaged by him "prophetic."

The thing that makes personal involvement "prophetic" is, of course, its *direction toward communication*—love for fellow man, as Tempels puts it.

This takes us to the core of the problem, because we now have to ask: communication of what? If the term "prophet" (i.e., "the one speaking out") is to have any meaning at all, the message proclaimed by him should be an important aspect. But exactly on this point Tempels' "testimony" seems to contradict our assumptions. We saw that "conversion," the advent of Christianity, comes as an "event," not as a result of indoctrination. On the other hand, our document does not leave any doubts as to the final aim of encounter in love: it is *discovery, or rediscovery, of the fundamental human, i.e., Christian, values.* As can be seen in the second part of "Catéchèse bantoue," Tempels did formulate a message, a doctrinal system.

But we are still short of one essential criterion—the "congregation," in Weber's terms. In fact, in "Catéchèse bantoue" Tempels seems to suggest that the encounter which leads to the prophetic event is strictly between individuals, "from soul to soul." As we shall see in the course of our analysis, "the entirely personal" is an obsession with Tempels. But it should be kept in mind that this idea is part of his prophetic message which attracted his followers.

In "Catéchèse bantoue" Tempels talks much about the "initial contact" and the inevitable "response." He is not concerned with the social consequences of such response. But, at that stage of his development, he must have known about those consequences. It will be our task for the rest of this part of our study to inquire about his assumption of the role of prophetic leader.

"Response" at Ruwe

Drawing on information gathered in the field, I shall now try to trace the "social consequences," i.e., the origin of the Jamaa movement, as far as this can aid our understanding of the change that made a "prophet" out of a missionary.

In 1953 Tempels was appointed pastor at Ruwe, a mining settlement near Kolwezi. Here he took on teaching duties at a nearby trade school run by the Franciscan missionaries for the Union Minière (cf. De Craemer 1965:2). As we may infer from his writings, he had always sought close contact with his African parishioners. His findings in *Bantu Philosophy* reflect endless conversations and "palavers" through almost ten years in Luba country. It is, therefore, understandable that his colleagues did not pay any special attention to his informal meetings with Africans at the parish hall or in his office at the school. Tempels had now begun to employ a tape recorder and was very enthusiastic about collecting traditional songs, folk tales, dreams, and so forth. After discussing with the group the ways of the *bankambo* (the ancestors), he would then go on to talk about his view of Christianity, probably in much the same way as described in "Catéchèse bantoue." The first Jamaa group seems to have gathered in a very natural way: the people who came to Tempels' informal meetings and recording sessions became friends and identified themselves as "Jamaa" (family).

S. Mutombo, a muLuba-Katanga from the region of Bukama, was working at the time in Ruwe as an elementary school teacher. He describes the formation of the first group as follows: [5]

> We started in our household, husband and wife. Once we had come to understand each other, we began to inquire about these matters. We began to discuss: How are we going to live our Christian religion? How shall we be in our marriage? But then we didn't want to be alone with these thoughts. So we had an encounter [*kupatana*] with our priest. We received him [lit., "put him"] in our group. We began to talk to him and show him how we were living our marriage, our Christian religion, and told him everything we did. Then he started to explain to us, "Listen, Christianity is like this. . . ." So we began to have an encounter and understand one another. We explained to him the ways of the ancestors, the way we used to live in our country. We told him about our problems with marriage, our problems with Christian religion. He knew all our marriage problems. . . . So he came to know us and started to explain. . . . He knew the customs of the ancestors. And then he began to tell us about his priesthood, about God, and how he progressed in his work. Thus, we had an encounter. A small group was formed, and then we began to explain those things to our brothers [i.e., fellow Africans] [T 36].

Clearly, this account *post factum* is highly stylized and not very rich as a historical source. But it is typical of the sort of information Jamaa people would give about the beginnings of the movement, and it is highly interesting in that it reflects, on the side of the Bantu, exactly Tempels' views of the prophetic event: "encounter"—"receiving one another," the literal translation of *kupatana*—was the essential factor in the formation of the first group.

In a similar way, we recognize Tempels' contempt for "manuals" and preconceived methods of Christianization in the remarks of another member of the original group, L. Mujanshi. He recalls the reaction of the first followers when they saw Tempels occupied with the usual bureaucratic duties of a pastor:

> We saw him with books and pencil, and all sorts of things, being busy writing the names of Christians. . . . Then we told him: "This

5. Concerning interviews and doctrinal texts taped in the field, see the section "Jamaa Doctrine: Inventory and Evaluation of Sources and Documents," in Appendix III. References marked by a capital T and a number are to tape recordings.

is not your real work. If you try to get a group together, your real work will be to come to a mutual understanding with the *bababa* and *bamama* [i.e., the adult, married people] so that you will be 'one thing' with them" [T 51].

Tempels' aversion to "teaching" and any sort of indoctrination has been discussed earlier. In fact, some formulations in "Catéchèse bantoue" seem to suggest that any transmission of a message, i.e., of doctrinal content, was an unimportant factor in the process of Christianization. But the informants from the first group at Ruwe make it quite clear that he started with regular and obviously preplanned instruction in the new doctrine at a very early stage. The fact that formulae of later Jamaa doctrine can be found in "Catéchèse bantoue" can only mean that Tempels, despite everything he says against indoctrination, had a "message" which was at least premeditated, if not prefabricated.

Some remarks should be made about Tempels' role during the first period of expansion of the Jamaa, sometime between 1953 and 1960. This is the general picture as it appears from many interviews with Jamaa members:

The word about the *"mon père* at Ruwe who knows how to speak" spread in Kolwezi. Workers from the five camps either met daily at work or were frequently transferred from one camp into another. Several of my informants told me that they heard the "rumor" (*kavumo*) about *"baba* Placide" for the first time at work, where his teaching was discussed.

The next step, it seems, was an invitation from the local pastor to Tempels. Although this is now difficult to verify, I got the impression from my informants that in some cases the initiative came from the missionary, who may have thought that Tempels, with his "new method," could be of some help in his own catechetic work. From about 1955 Tempels toured the parishes in the miners' camps around Kolwezi. According to a weekly schedule of that period, he talked to large audiences in churches and community centers. I have no information about any activities outside Kolwezi. In any case, his public appearances were probably less important for the initial spread and consolidation of the Jamaa than the initiation into the new doctrine he gave to a large number of Africans who then started local groups in other places. Already at that time Tempels showed a strong tendency to "delegate" his charismatic authority to other missionaries and African laymen. As we shall see, this was perfectly justified by Jamaa doctrine. But it was also a preparation for his own retreat from the Congo and his leadership "from a distance," which became one of the characteristics of the Jamaa.

Let me summarize the important points:

1. A prerequisite of what we have called the "prophetic event" is to renounce everything that is "official," "theoretical," and "preconceived" and to abandon oneself to the risk of the entirely personal "encounter" with the African. It is obvious that Tempels had had experiences of this kind before he wrote "Catéchèse bantoue." But it is interesting, if not ironic, that he became a prophet, i.e., the actual leader of a movement, at a time when he occupied an important position in the church hierarchy.

2. Tempels had gathered his knowledge of Bantu philosophy as a missionary among the Baluba of the Lualaba region. With the publication of *Bantu Philosophy,* his proclaimed aim had been to help the African discover the basic values of his own tradition. But he became really successful only after he had left the tribal region and was confronted with "deracinated" people in an urban-industrial center, many of whom came from quite different traditional backgrounds.

3. In "Catéchèse bantoue" Tempels gives the impression that he has the "pagan" in mind when he speaks about the necessity of a personal encounter with the African. But the first group at Ruwe (and all later Jamaa groups) consisted of baptized and "practicing" Christians—people who were conscious of the problems caused by their religion, especially by the demands of Christian marriage.

THE DISTANT LEADER

Preparing the Retreat

In 1957 Tempels was transferred from Ruwe to Musonoi, a similar but larger and more modern settlement near Kolwezi. Here, as at Ruwe, his activities were divided between his duties as the pastor of a large parish and his work with the Jamaa. In Musonoi he witnessed Congolese independence (in 1960) and Katangese secession and lived through a great deal of the disturbances that followed, especially in 1961–62, when even the relatively sheltered settlements of the Union Minière became the scene of tribal fights and terror exercised by gangs of the *baJeunesse*.[6]

Nothing in the documents and information accessible to me indicates that Tempels' ideas underwent any radical transformation during this time of external turmoil. Nor does it appear that the demands on his authority caused by the spectacular numerical growth of the Jamaa made him change his conception of the "prophetic event." This is documented in a letter to a confrere, a pastor at the miners' camp at Kipushi, near Lubumbashi. This missionary had written to Tempels about the difficulties caused by his local group of the Jamaa. The answer is dated "Kolwezi, February 18, 1961." I quote a passage in which we find exactly the same way of thinking and almost the same formulations as in "Catéchèse bantoue," and the fact that now the Jamaa existed as a movement seems to have had no effect:

> It is somewhat unfortunate that here in Katanga, because of the transfers of workers, the pastors in different parishes have to deal with people who come from a place where they have been living the spirit of community, i.e., the Jamaa, and who now, in their new parish, continue to live according to this spirit. This might give the impression that the Jamaa is something preconstituted, a kind of organization or movement that has its own existence. But despite such inconvenience, the arrival of these people in a new parish could be an advantage for the pastor; through them it could become easier for him to get in touch with his people, a more intensive contact than he had had before. It is through these increasingly personal contacts that, gradually, the Jamaa *begins* between priest and believers; the Jamaa is born only at the moment of this contact. . . . This encounter between the priest and his people is something that has to begin in every parish.

"Encounter," with emphasis on the initial contact ("beginning" of the Jamaa) is as much as ever the pivot of Tempels' thinking in the early sixties. However, there are now more and more signs of defensiveness and of his reluctance to assume overt leadership of

6. Half-criminal, half-political gangs of adolescents, in this case probably linked to the *Balubakat*, the party of the Luba Katanga opposed to Tshombe (cf. Young 1965:302–4, 335, 590 f.). A very involved but sketchy account of these troubled times at Kolwezi may be found in the chapters on Tempels and the Jamaa in Philippa Schuyler's *Jungle Saints* (1963:175–211).

the movement. His pronouncements about the Jamaa sound increasingly bitter and radical, if not unrealistic. His message of "personal encounter" had had an impact beyond his expectations, and, all of a sudden, he realizes that again he is the center of discussion and a target for attacks from his fellow missionaries; many of them had changed their attitude from sympathy with a "new method" to fear for their crumbling authority as official religious leaders in a postcolonial situation.

Tempels had to defend himself on two fronts: (1) he had to face an increasing number of complaints about the "exclusiveness" of the Jamaa people and about their insubordination and (2) his colleagues also began to have doubts about the orthodoxy of Jamaa doctrine.

To both allegations he answers with arguments, familiar to us from "Catéchèse bantoue": The only thing that really counts is the "encounter" between the priest and his people. So much emphasis is laid on the "beginning," the initial contact of love, and so little importance is attributed to "organization," that Tempels can get carried away and maintain: "The Jamaa does not exist. The Jamaa must be *born* in the parish through encounter" (1962:28).

In much the same way he tries to handle the problem of a specific Jamaa doctrine: wherever people talk about their religious conceptions, they will end up by using a certain "language," consisting of "expressions," "modes of presentation," "images," and "parables" adapted to their mentality. But this, he declares, is not a "new doctrine"—it is nothing but "the eternal doctrine of the church" (*ibid.*, 84).

But not all of Tempels' confreres were critical. Others were enthusiastic about the new movement and asked for "programs, rules, and facts about the organizations." They invited him to help with the introduction of the Jamaa in their parishes. But he did not like these visits:

Many *bababa* and *bamama* [members of the Jamaa] would gather spontaneously in order to see me, etc., and such a demonstration could "prove" or leave the impression that the Jamaa is really something that belongs to the Reverend Father Tempels [*ibid.*, 29].

And in the same document he comes to a rather strange conclusion:

When you speak of the Jamaa, you had better talk less about Father Tempels. I say this for a simple reason: It is the essence of the church to be "Jamaa." Christ has thought, wanted, and ordered the church to be that way. Therefore, if you want to stay objective, you should not talk about me. *I did not invent nor did I start the Jamaa* [*ibid.*, 27; my italics].

If we accept Tempels' word, we are now left with a strange task: to analyze a charismatic movement that "does not exist," that was started by a founder who has "not invented" it, and that centers around a prophetic message that is "not a new doctrine."

The Second Exile

On Sunday, April 8, 1962, Musonoi saw a gathering of some 1,000–1,500 Jamaa people bidding farewell to "*baba* Placide," who was leaving the Congo. Officially he was returning to Belgium for his vacation. But, as it soon turned out, his departure would have become necessary for reasons of health. Tempels had to undergo a serious operation, the consequences of which forced him to stay permanently near a hospital. He has not left Belgium since.

There has been some discussion about the actual sequence of events. Tempels was accused of fleeing the responsibilities he had taken on by propagating the Jamaa. Indeed, it seems to be true that he made the decision to leave the Congo before he knew about his condition. But in the light of the facts presented in the preceding section, the question of the particular decision loses much of its importance. Tempels had been retreating for quite some time before leaving Africa.

One of his confreres, in a report on the farewell meeting at Musonoi, quotes him as saying, "Our Lord said: I came to bring fire on this earth. I want you to spread it among men. And I, too, shall go to spread it." This is an allusion to Luke 13:49—quoted in a rather free adaptation for his own purposes, as was typical of Tempels. It indicates that the departing prophet was certain of the success of his message. He was also prepared to continue his mission in Belgium.

Tempels' return to the Franciscan monastery in his home town was called a "second exile" because his self-imposed departure turned in fact into a confinement of sorts. Acting on denunciations from a group of French ultraright Catholics [7] (and others, probably), the ecclesiastical authorities forbade Tempels to publish, or to speak publicly, about his ideas. Later, through the intervention of his friend, Cardinal Cardijn, he was cleared, and the ban was lifted (in late 1965). But his local superiors did not act, claiming that they had not received an official order from Rome. Despite these restrictions, Tempels has had considerable influence on groups of Catholics in Europe who accepted his message of the "personal encounter."

More important for our purposes is the fact that the ban apparently never affected his correspondence with the Congo. Tempels had always been a prolific writer of letters. His correspondence must have grown considerably after his separation from the Jamaa. Every Jamaa leader of any importance whom I met during my field work claimed to be in contact with "*baba* Placide." Some may have said this in order to gain prestige, but for the majority the claim was based on facts. My information is not complete enough to allow any straightforward conclusions as to the importance of this correspondence for the further development of the Jamaa, but certainly it must not be underestimated.

Tempels himself is very conscious of his role as a distant leader. In an interview he pointed out to me that he was now in much more effective contact with Jamaa groups than he was during his stay at Ruwe and Musonoi, when much of his time was taken up by his pastoral duties.

7. These machinations were initiated by a French priest. In 1963 two young ladies visited Tempels in Hasselt and discussed Jamaa ideas with him. The records of these conversations were not kept confidential (as was agreed upon). They were included in a dossier for the Vatican and, later, in a violent attack, were published by the French ultrarightist monthly *Le monde et la vie* (No. 155; April, 1966). Most of the incriminations are aimed at the "sexual" aspects of the ideas of "encounter" and initiation into the movement (cf. Chapter 4).

The Belgian *Europe Magazine* (No. 1107; August, 1966)—a few degrees to the right of *Le monde et la vie* and more "popular" in its approach—writes under the heading, "The Virgin Mary in Your Bed": "This Franciscan should tell these absurdities to the Negroes of the Congo who are incapable of formulating spiritual conceptions without attaching them to their erotic obsessions; but it seems that he himself seriously believes in them." The direction of these attacks becomes visible when the writer, trembling with indignation, declares, "In fact, Father Tempels admits being a firm partisan of racial integration."

The Founder Enters the Myth

When the founder of a prophetic-charismatic movement disappears—because he dies, or is arrested, as was often the case in Africa and Melanesia—he "enters the myth." So frequent, almost universal, is this transformation that it has become a commonplace in the literature.

I shall now present evidence which will both corroborate and modify some of the familiar conceptions, especially one assumption implicit in almost all accounts: that "entering the myth" necessarily means "apotheosis"—elevation to supernatural rank and importance. Evidence that this is not necessarily so comes from a number of stories told about the beginnings of the Jamaa at Ruwe. The versions vary a great deal in detail, but all belong to an emerging myth—the myth of the *baba saba,* the seven fathers, to whom the Jamaa owes its origin. For several reasons I regard the discovery of this myth as one of the most interesting findings about the movement.

1. The diffusion of the myth is (still) very limited. All variants come from Kolwezi or Kolwezi-oriented groups. Informants in Lubumbashi had heard about it but did not accept it. It was unknown to the group in Kinshasa. I do not have any information about its occurrence in the Kasai province, although it would seem probable that (from the circumstances of its origin; cf. below) it was spread to this region by Jamaa members returning from Kolwezi to their native villages.

2. All variants deal with the same basic issue: a list of "founding fathers at Ruwe" (even though they do not agree on particular points, e.g., the names on the list).

3. All informants differed in their degree of acceptance of the myth; some offered it as the truth about the origin of the Jamaa, while others regarded it as an interesting anecdote.

Here, first, is a generalized version of the myth of the *baba saba:*

The Jamaa emanates from the thoughts of God. Before the beginning of time it existed with God.

In "1955" [8] a group of seven *bababa* and seven *bamama* (i.e., seven married couples) got together at Ruwe and began to unite their thoughts about the essence of their Christian faith and their

---

8. I.e., sometime in the fifties. The date is not historically accurate.

marriage. They came to an understanding and thus "rediscovered" the thought of the Jamaa, which had been lost among men. The seven fathers were:

Mathieu Binga (now at Musonoi)
Laurent Mujanshi (now at Musonoi)
Anastas Banza (now at Ruwe)
Sylvain Mutombo (now at Bukama)
Valentin Kaumba (now at Lubumbashi)
Joseph Tshibangu (now at Luluabourg)
René   ?   (now at Mwene Ditu)

At the same time there happened to be a priest at Ruwe who was not like other missionaries: *baba* Placide. He was received by the *bababa na bamama wa kwanza,* the fathers and mothers of the beginning; they exchanged their thoughts, their deepest feelings and aspirations, and were united in love. This was the beginning of the visible Jamaa.

Whenever I asked the question about the origin of the Jamaa, an informant would invariably start with an account of the "Jamaa with God"—its existence before time as the source and model of every "visible" Jamaa on earth. So important was this aspect that many refused to discuss the historical origin. In one recorded instruction it was put like this: "Many people will think that the Jamaa was started by a person from this world. This is not so. No person from this world started the Jamaa; nor did the Jamaa begin here in Kolwezi" (T 9).[9] Others would start their story with a distinction between the visible and the invisible Jamaa. But even those who acknowledged the fact that the movement was started by men were very vague when it came to details; clearly, historical facts were not important to them.

In its tendency away from historical detail toward standardization and stylized expression ("seven" fathers!), the story of the *baba saba* is a myth in the making. Except in one or two cases, every informant had his own list of the seven; some could give only three or four names, while others included names of important Jamaa leaders

9. For the context of this quotation see the document in Appendix V from which it is taken.

who were definitely not members of the first group but whom they regarded as heads of their lineages in the Jamaa. The question of lineage and descent in the Jamaa—perhaps the most important function of the myth—must be left for later discussion.[10]

Highly interesting were the reactions I got when I questioned Sylvain Mutombo and Laurent Mujanshi, who are both on the list of the *baba saba*.

S. Mutombo laughed when I mentioned the story. When I proposed a list of names (more or less the same as the one quoted above), he agreed that all those had belonged to the first group, but there had been others, too. Finally, he told me, now seriously, that the "seven" are those who stayed in the Jamaa, while others had gone other ways. It did not seem to bother him that, a few moments earlier, he had given me at least two names of people from the first group who had not left the Jamaa but who were not on the list I had proposed.

L. Mujanshi first reacted quite seriously: Yes, that is how it was. We were seven. Then his wife, overhearing the conversation, intervened: "He should stop telling such nonsense. Everyone knows that there were many more at Ruwe than just seven." Then both Laurent and his wife blamed another of the *baba saba*, Mathieu Binga, for inventing the story. He had made it up to please a delegation from the Kasai, led by Abbé G. Mukenge, who had come to inquire about the Jamaa.

We now come back to our initial problem—Tempels' reception into the myth. It will be clear from the information presented that the myth of the *baba saba* reserves to the founder of the Jamaa a much less important role than the historical facts would call for. Two reasons, probably not mutually exclusive, could be given: (1) the myth reflects Tempels' constant claim not to have "invented" the Jamaa; (2) its function is to re-Africanize the origins of the Jamaa by playing down, consciously or unconsciously, the importance of the European prophet.

10. One informant came up with seventy-seven instead of seven founding fathers (without attempting to give a list of names). I asked, "Why not seventy-six or seventy-eight?" She laughed and said, "The whole story is just a manner of speaking [*namna ya kusema*]; we tell it in order to please the big ones [*wakubwa*, i.e., the members of the first group who are recognized as leaders]."

Exit the prophet? This seems to be Tempels' fate as a "distant leader." But in evaluating evidence such as the myth of the *baba saba,* it should be kept in mind that only four or five years intervene between his departure from the Congo and the recording of the ethnographic material. It would be premature to draw any far-reaching conclusions.

2 ✿ THE FOLLOWERS

INTRODUCTION

If one tries to understand what moves a movement, the founder, prophet, and leader will be the most obvious point to start with. We are used to identifying the major organized religious traditions with Buddha and Confucius, with Moses, Jesus, and Mohammed. Most of us grew up under the influence of one of these traditions; we were taught to keep our eyes on those towering figures, to expect from them directions for our lives, to see the world through their teachings. It would be easy to demonstrate from the literature on prophetic-messianic movements that this point of view, so deeply rooted in our own culture, is implicit in most attempts at description and analysis. I, too, have argued that "the leader" is the most important key to these movements—*if* it is understood and kept in mind that his function is to formulate for a group of people a system of orientations.[1] Such a system of orientations may be the result of a creative effort; in this case it is all the more interesting to the analyst trying to explain change and the emergence of new orientations. But a prophet's message has a chance to be accepted by a group of followers only if he addresses himself to their aspirations, needs, and "dreams"[2] and if he talks in categories which are in some way familiar to his audience.

In our description of the Jamaa movement, we now turn to "the followers," not only in order to trace the social impact of Tempels' message but to reconstruct the frame of reference of the doctrine,

1. Cf. our remarks in the Introduction and in my paper on "Leaders and Leadership in Prophetic-Messianic Movements" (Fabian 1963).
2. As we shall show in Chapter 4, the charismatic message and the dream life of the followers are closely related, not only a priori (because of our theoretical assumptions), but also on account of ethnographic evidence, such as that presented by the *mawazo* doctrine in Jamaa thinking.

the problems and dilemmas it was intended to solve, the models on which it could draw, and the realities it had to define or redefine. The concrete context in which the Jamaa originated is the world of the urban-industrial centers of south Kantanga,[3] more precisely the camps (settlements) of the mining trust.

The typical member of the Jamaa in Katanga is an employee of the Union Minière.[4] It is to be expected that Jamaa doctrine addresses itself to this social environment, both reflecting and defining the realities of daily life in the copper mines. Before I discuss some of the details of this intricate relationship between reality and ideology, I should like to introduce the topic in a general way by a

3. This would be the place to include references to the vast literature on urbanization in central Africa, but I do not think that such a digression is warranted by the aims and the scope of our study. Limiting myself to the time and space relevant to our study (essentially the post–World War II development in the industrial centers of south Katanga), I shall merely point to the following authors quoted in the bibliography: Bertieaux (1953), Caprasse (1959), Chapelier (1956), Comhaire (1956), Debra (1949), de Briey (1952), Denis (1956, 1958), Dethier (1961a, 1961b), Doucy (1954), Doucy and Feldheim (1951, 1952, 1958), Forthomme (1951, 1957), Grévisse (1951, 1956, 1958), Minon (1960), Mottoulle (1946), Vannes (1959). The majority of these authors were associated with the Centre d'Etude des Problèmes Sociaux Indigènes at Elisabethville/Lubumbashi, which published monographs as well as a periodical, Problèmes sociaux congolais, most often cited as Bulletin CEPSI. An excellent bibliography concerning urbanization in Africa (with special emphasis on the holdings of Belgian libraries) was compiled by Verhaegen (1962). Independence in 1960 has resulted in an almost complete interruption of urban studies by Belgian scholars (many of whom had positions in the colonial administration), but there are new initiatives, especially at Lovanium University at Kinshasa. Congolese scholars are contributing to these studies in increasing numbers. As an example, I should like to point out a paper by Mwepe Kyabutha (1967) dealing specifically with Katanga. It is a fairly general contribution, but to us it is of special interest because the author shows a tendency to blame industry and urbanization for the disintegration of the traditional order in a way that reminds one of the writings of "concerned colonials" a generation ago. Finally, I should mention the sections dealing with the Congo in the UNESCO volume edited by Forde (1956).

4. Here and throughout this study we shall use this short form of the full name, "Union Minière du Haut Katanga." For the history and ramifications of the company see the publications "Union Minière du Haut Katanga" (n.d.) and D'Ydewalle (1960), both of which glorify their subject. A critical assessment may be found in Joye and Lewin (1961) and Gérard-Libois (1966). When J. Mobutu nationalized the Union Minière in 1967, the name was changed to "Gecomin," but almost everyone went on using the old label, which, as "Union Miniele" (with such variations as "Minion Miniele"), had become part of the Swahili vocabulary.

brief report of a striking conversation with one of my informants at Musonoi.

Adolphe Lubala, in his late fifties and father of twelve children, is the type of the ideal employee. He is "stable," quiet, and competent; his disciplinary dossier is excellent; his professional rating (cf. below) is very good. One day, in the course of a long conversation about his work and about the relations between whites and Congolese, he came up with a surprising statement: the Union Minière is really like the Jamaa. People of many *kabila* (tribes, language groups, races) are together for a common purpose, as is the case with Jamaa groups. And it is *mapendo* (love) that keeps them together. In any case, he told me, this is what unites me with "my white man" (*muzungu yangu*).[5] If a white man had an accident in the mine, I would carry him in my arms and not be afraid of him because he is a white man.

I have heard many statements of this kind, sometimes less explicit but pointing in the same direction: Jamaa doctrine, modeled after the realities in urban-industrial Katanga, in turn becomes a means for understanding and accepting those realities—a classical case for the double function of cultural "blueprints" as *models of* and *models for*.[6]

THE UNION MINIERE CAMP AS THE ORIGINAL ENVIRONMENT OF THE JAMAA

The Camp: Ecology and Population

The following considerations will be restricted to the urban-industrial complex of Kolwezi, the "Groupe Ouest" in Union Minière

---

5. The possessive expression *muzungu yangu* (*yetu*), my (our) white man, is widely used in the urban centers of Katanga. The apparent idea behind this formula seems to confirm the claim of many colonials that "paternalism" is always a double-sided relationship. Undoubtedly *muzungu yangu* expresses reciprocity, if not "possession," as *perceived* by the Congolese employee, i.e., perceived in terms of his culturally determined conceptions of relationship and alliance. But if one looks at the actual balance of goods and services exchanged, one need not invoke Marx in order to see that the "real" relations are quite different. This "real" constellation was overlooked, for example, by Leblanc in her cultural-psychological explanation of Congolese "parasitism" (1960:25 f.).

6. This contrast was applied to symbol systems by Geertz (1966:7 f.).

administrative language.[7] Prospecting had reached the spectacular deposits of copper and other minerals early in this century; first attempts to set up a furnace date back to 1908. But as a city, Kolwezi was founded only in 1938, and it was developed to its present form and importance in the years after World War II.

The urban complex, the total population of which was estimated at the time of my field work at 120,000–130,000, consists of a cluster of four different kinds of settlements:

1. A modern "core city," containing (*a*) residential quarters for the white and upper-class Congolese population (the former being predominantly personnel of the Union Minière and affiliated companies, the latter mostly employed by the government services, local administration, and other Congolese agencies, plus a few independent businessmen and high-ranking Congolese employees of the Union Minière); (*b*) industrial (i.e., non–Union Minière) and commercial sections (the latter predominantly under the control of Greek, Portuguese, and Italian merchants); (*c*) hospitals, schools, churches, and recreational facilities; and (*d*) a barracks-like settlement, housing approximately 1,000 members of the police and their families.

2. The former "C.E.C." (*Centre Extra-Coutumier*), the official, i.e., planned and administered, Congolese city (privately owned lots and houses; simple but sufficient municipal services: electricity, water, sewage, telephone, main streets tarred and lighted; small stores and bars; elementary and trade schools; churches).

3. A large squatters' town, called "Caroline" (officially nonexistent; no services).

4. Five miners' settlements (camps) of the Union Minière: [8] Kolwezi, Musonoi, Luilu, Ruwe, Kapata (fenced, but usually not guarded; standard-type company-owned housing; all services except private telephone; a church, elementary schools, social and medical centers, stores, recreational facilities).

The area occupied by this cluster of settlements is considerable, and intracity means of public transportation are notoriously poor. Most workers live within walking distance (up to three miles) of

---

7. Concerning the urban geography of this area see Chapelier 1956.

8. For the sake of simplicity I list only the settlements for the employees of the Union Minière proper. The affiliated company, Metalkat (copper-refining plants), runs a similar camp in the Kolwezi area which appears occasionally in our documents but with which I had very little contact.

their place of work, but many students attending school in the core city have to spend up to three hours walking.

Kolwezi is situated on the Katanga railroad connecting Angola with Zambia. A tarred highway leads from Kolwezi to Lubumbashi and then south to the Zambian border. Roads to the west (the Dilolo-Angolan border) and to the north (Kamina, Bukama) are viable for trucks and jeeps. An airport is served regularly by Air Congo. Travel and communication between Kolwezi and other industrial centers of south Katanga (Jadotville and Lubumbashi), as well as with the immediate hinterland and the Kasai province, are surprisingly frequent. Industrial workers and other members of the new urban population tend to maintain their links with their native villages through visits and mail.

Musonoi became the most important base for my field work. It is with this "camp" in mind that I shall try to fill in the ecological background for the settlements of the Union Minière.[9]

All camps, except for the one known as "cité Kolwezi," which is partly surrounded by the core city, lie at some distance from the center (two to eight miles). Streets, houses, and communal buildings are planned in regular, standard-type patterns. But jacarandas and tulip trees lining the main roads, small parklike sections, and euphorbia hedges separating the individual *lupango* (lots) allocated to each private house make the camps look more like an African version of an American suburb than the barracks which they essentially are.

The center of the camp is formed by a cluster of communal buildings: the Roman Catholic church (usually with a rectory and a community center); stores run by the company (*cantines*); a stadium; a social center (bar, dancing, auditorium); and, after 1960, a police office. In Musonoi, the offices of the camp administration (*chef de camp*), the market, a second church, a *foyer social* (center for adult education), and the medical center lie at some distance from the present center (which was built when the camp was expanded). Two large elementary schools serving Musonoi are situated at the southern and western peripheries.

The residential sections of a camp are arranged as large blocks,

9. Some statistical information concerning the population of the Kolwezi complex (composition in terms of sex, age, ethnic origin, stability, etc.) is given in Appendix I.

usually distinguished by the type of houses. At Musonoi—which ranks between Ruwe, the oldest, and Kapata, the most modern of the camps—houses are solid one-story brick structures covered with corrugated iron. The floors are of cement, and metal window frames and doors are used as a protection against termites. All houses are connected to the electricity and water networks, but no provisions are made for heating. At an altitude of about 4,500 feet this can lead to considerable inconvenience, especially during the dry season (May–October). In size and comfort, houses vary between rather gloomy-looking two-room places and sizable homes with large windows and porches. Homes are allocated by the camp administration according to a number of criteria: (*a*) size of the worker's family; (*b*) his *ancienneté,* i.e., years of service; (*c*) his professional rating; and (*d*) his ability to adopt a quasi-Western style of life ("cleanliness," adequate furniture, etc.). Thus, to a certain extent, the morphological divisions of a camp express social status. Indeed, such differences are recognized, and workers will try to improve their situation by moving to a larger and better house. According to my observations, the awareness of these differences does not reach a level which would be sufficient to influence patterns of social interaction. But there were indications that physical distance, or closeness, created vague feelings of solidarity. People living close to the main parish of Musonoi would refer to those living in the eastern section of the camp as people from a different neighborhood (a fact which had some influence on the development of the local Jamaa group; cf. below).

A very important point is that the camp administration hardly ever considers tribal affiliation in allocating homes. The worker who joins the Union Minière has to put up with the neighbors he meets. He may or may not choose to be on friendly terms with them, but open conflict would result in considerable difficulties for him and his family. Most close interfamily contacts are probably still based on kinship or tribal links, but membership in a working team, an organization, or a movement (like the Jamaa) induces many to cross the boundaries of interaction defined by tradition.

The occasional outside observer of the camp would be impressed by the apparent lack of an atmosphere of confinement. At any time of day the camp is bustling with activity: men riding their bicycles or walking in small groups, coming from or going to work; women carrying heavy loads on their heads; children playing or returning from school; all of them accompanied by, or chasing, dogs, chickens, and goats. Visits between camps, and between camps and city, are not limited (with some exceptions, which will be discussed later). Almost every night, but invariably on Sundays and holidays, in some corner of the camp there will be a *kilio* (funeral rite), a traditional or semitraditional initiation, a wedding, a prayer meeting of some religious group. People sing and clap their hands; the drums are as powerful as in the village back in the bush, even competing with the hi-fi system of the "bar."

The Camp: Realization of Paternalism

Ever since Hodgkin used the label, "Platonism" has been a tempting formula for characterizing Belgian colonial policy. Especially now that some time has elapsed since the end of colonial rule in 1960, an observer not familiar with the cultural background from which ideas, programs, and justifications for domination were drawn may be willing to agree with Hodgkin's verdict. Indeed, Belgian colonial policy shared with Plato a vision of the totalitarian unification of human ideals and utilitarian aims, the rigid horizontal stratification of society, and the pyramid-like distribution of access to goods and power. But it always lacked its theoretical, utopian aloofness. Hodgkin comes closer to reality when he describes the ingredients of "paternalism" as

> the Catholic conception of society as a hierarchy, in which the ruling element is responsible for providing the conditions for a "good life" for the ruled; the large corporations' ideas of workers' welfare as a means to good industrial relations and maximum output; and the colonial Government's view—that it is desirable and politic to concentrate upon the effort to increase the material prosperity of the mass, and to equip them, through education, to play a useful, if subordinate, part in a modern society, before any moves are made to train an African élite or grant political rights [1956:51].

Inasmuch as these aims were reached under Belgian colonial rule, this was not the realization of a utopian dream; it was the success of very practical, down-to-earth arrangements between the European power groups fighting for their own, by no means identical, interests. The constant struggle between those power groups (the missions, private enterprise, government-linked trusts, political parties), the never-ending discussions about the aims of colonial policy, and the deep political and ideological divisions even between members of the same colonial administration tend to be underestimated in recent writings.[10]

The worker of the Union Minière quoted at the outset of this chapter told us that his company was "like the Jamaa." In more theoretical terms, this means that the system of orientations that makes up Jamaa ideology corresponds to the world of the Union Minière as it is experienced by its workers. But "the world of the Union Minière" of which our informant is a part is not the reality of the Union Minière as an industrial and commercial trust with its complicated national and international ramifications; it is rather "the white man" whom he encounters at work and in the camp. His interaction with the white man is restricted to the limits of certain well-defined roles. In this section, I shall describe the rules for the white man's behavior toward Congolese workers by drawing on a manual for administrators of camps (*chefs de camp*). The fact that it was issued in 1940 does not diminish its value as a source for the ideology that guided Union Minière officials in 1966–67. From many conversations with representatives of the native labor management and the technical personnel, I was convinced that, except in minor details of style and language, nothing had changed. Most *chefs de camp* were still Belgians; only after the crisis in spring, 1967, was this part of the administration Africanized.

Despite all its humanitarian overtones, the manual leaves no doubt that the principles of action it defines are unabashedly utilitarian and profit-oriented. The argument runs as follows:

All major industrial operations of the Union Minière began in the traditionally underpopulated areas of south Katanga, whose inhabitants suffered from chronic malnutrition and were thought to be unfit for industrial labor (Mottoulle 1946:8 f.). This made it necessary to recruit workers from distant regions. Such recruitment, usually carried out by specialized agencies, was very costly for the

10. This is what I would criticize in Onwumelu's otherwise interesting and useful study, "Congo Paternalism." In his conclusion, he states, for example, that, "undisturbed by international pressure and Congolese opinion, the Belgians pursued their concept of paternalism" (1966:362). It is understandable that African writers try to make their case against colonialism as strong as possible. But, in the field of scientific understanding, they will not reach their goal if they simplify the issues.

employer, since it was subject to considerable losses (desertion, death during transport). The best way to avoid the expenses, risks, and uncertainties inherent in the recruitment system was to get the workers to settle down in the industrial regions. Such a policy of *stabilization* "consists of all normal means for making the black worker like his work and stay attached to it as long as possible" (*ibid.*, 11).

Such stabilization was supposed to have favorable results for "the worker himself, for his family, his original native community, and for the entire colony," but above all it was to provide the company with a labor force *"à haut rendement"* (*ibid.*). We shall see presently what those "normal" means of stabilization were and what sort of attachment the worker was expected to develop.

The manual then goes on to treat the roles which the different representatives of the management (the local director, the doctor, and the *chef de camp*) were to play in this project. It is the task of the *chef de camp:*

— To watch over the physical and moral well-being of the blacks confided to him;
— To keep up among these people a good spirit and a healthy discipline in order to ensure better performance at work;
— To make an effort in keeping as long as possible in the service of the society an indigenous labor force which is hard-working, disciplined, and capable of producing superior results for the industry;
— To watch over the costs for this labor force [*ibid.*, 14 f.].

I should like to stress the success of this program for "stabilization." In 1966 an official of the Union Minière declared to me that its aims had been reached to the complete satisfaction of the company. Children of workers and migrants attracted by the urban-industrial centers constituted a more than sufficient reservoir, even though decreasing demands due to automation were counteracted by programs of expansion.

The manual then names four "normal means" of implementation:

1. No "abnormal pressure" (*ibid.*, 17) should be exercised upon recruitment. In insisting on the principle of liberty in accepting the contract, the company wishes, above all, to maintain *"le bon moral"* of its native labor force (*ibid.*).

2. The duration of the contract should be at least three years so

that the links between the workers and their traditional environment can grow weaker, while at the same time their adaptation to the new world and their performance are likely to increase (cf. *ibid.*, 17 f.).

3. As many workers as possible should be married; at the same time, concubinage and polygamy should be discouraged, "but without force" (*ibid.*, 19).

4. The fourth point, called "satisfaction of the physical, moral, and social needs with respect to a healthy and moral life" (*ibid.*, 21), contains a long list of the *chef de camp*'s duties and prerogatives: maintaining a personal file for each worker, administration and allocation of housing, maintenance of the settlements, food provisions, payment of wages, control of privileges, control over working hours, "palavers" and complaints, disciplinary actions, social work, schools—a "total" program, indeed.

No secret is made of the official image of the native worker. The policy of stabilization, with its emphasis on contracts of long duration, is

> a guarantee for the employer against the natural instability of the native character [*ibid.*, 18].

> The colonizer must never forget that the Negroes have the souls of children, souls which can be molded by educational methods; they look, listen, feel, and imitate [*ibid.*, 5].

One point deserves our special attention. The manual states:

> Education is confided to black elementary school teachers [*instituteurs*], supervised by the Reverend Fathers [*ibid.*, 33].

By delegating education to the "Reverend Fathers," the Union Minière was following the example of the larger colonial society which gave (at least until quite late in the colonial era) the educational monopoly to the missions. But the Union Minière did not bother with the scruples of the colonial administration, which had to treat Catholic and Protestant missions on an equal basis. The fact that the manual allows parents to send their children to schools of other denominations, "because the principle of religious freedoms must be kept intact" (*ibid.*, 32), is contradicted by Union Minière policy. In 1966–67, Catholic churches were still the only ones allowed inside the camps; the buildings were constructed by the company, and the missionaries were on its payroll.

An interesting point is touched upon at the very end of our document, where the terms of collaboration between *chefs de camp* and missionaries are defined (*ibid.,* 38 f.); again, the guiding aim and principle is

> the necessity to maintain the discipline we have succeeded in establishing among our black personnel, a discipline which is the foundation for its normal evolution and its profitable performance [*ibid.,* 39].

Clearly this is a warning for all missionaries who may disagree with the policies of the Union Minière. I know of at least one case where such disagreement has led to the removal of a pastor from a camp.

Let me emphasize again that in 1966–67 the principles of the manual were carried out almost to the letter. Their implementation had led to a spectacular success of this "policy of stabilization" as far as the *internal* operation of the system was concerned. The fact that, seven years after independence, historical and political circumstances had made Union Minière social policy an anachronism had only slight effects on its efficiency and on the outlook of its practitioners. Indeed, I should not be surprised if the system went on functioning even after complete Africanization of the administrative personnel. Its power is based to a great extent on the fact that the moving principles are *not* moral and humanitarian (even though the language may suggest this) but strictly technical and commercial: maximum output at minimum cost.

We may now summarize the major assumptions and principles upon which Union Minière social policy hinges:

1. Stressing the "childlike" nature of the native reinforces in the white man the basic attitude of benevolent paternalism. This all-pervading norm of role behavior is an excellent device to hide from the Congolese as well as most of the white employees the real nature of the relationship: unimpeded manipulation of a cheap labor force.

2. Long absence from the native village, emphasis (in housing, wages, etc.) on a nuclear family, more or less forced exposure to a school system run by the missionaries, a shrewd system of rewards and punishment (e.g., in professional ranking; cf. Appendix I)—all this is intended to induce in the Congolese a long-lasting identification with the camp (or the Union Minière) as a total universe.

3. The terms of collaboration with what is essentially an outside agent—the Catholic mission—are dictated by the Union Minière; the aim of education is not intellectual development and eventual opening-up of the closed system of the camp but—as stated explicitly in the manual—"to give the sons of our workers an education which will allow them to become good workers later on" (*ibid.*, 45).

The Camp: Ambivalent Reality for the Colonized

Union Minière social policy has been surprisingly successful. On the whole, it has operated without the use of physical force. This could be taken to indicate that, to a great extent, the system did meet the expectations of the workers. As the manual states, a worker who renews his contract and stays in the camp proves that he is "happy" (*ibid.*, 12). But if this really were the case, one would hardly expect to find charismatic movements, ethnic organizations, and increasing labor union activities in the perfect society of the workers' settlements.

The data available to me do not allow me to present a complete and adequate assessment of the attitudes Congolese workers take toward the camp. Instead, I shall try to illustrate for a number of situations what appeared to me to be a common characteristic: a view of the camp as an ambivalent reality. The social and economic advantages over the life in the village are recognized, but this new experience is not integrated into the larger system of beliefs and ideas about the meaning of the cosmos, the essence of human relationships, and the desired goals of human fulfillment.

The "policy of stabilization" in the permanent, family-centered settlements of the Union Minière was conceived in order to replace long-distance "recruitment" of workers. Caravans of recruits in chains, or linked together by wooden planks, could be seen arriving in Katanga up to the late twenties. But decades of attempts to change the image and style of labor recruitment were not sufficient to assuage feelings of confinement and estrangement shared by a majority among the inhabitants of the camps.

The same informant who compared the Union Minière with the Jamaa was very much aware of the countless restrictions on his life in the camp. He had to put up with a host of vague but nevertheless effective unwritten rules. In one conversation he summed up his feelings in the following way: "The camp is like a prison;

not a prison that you can see with your eyes; it is a prison of the soul." He complained that the whites, some of whom were very friendly at work, would never come to the camp just for a visit. Rules against fraternization between superiors and subjects are quite common in European administrations and companies. But in the European context they are not likely to create the feelings of disappointment and frustration which are the result among Congolese workers. After all, the Union Minière has trained its white personnel to maintain extremely personal and "humane" relations at work. Attachment to the white master is favored as an important condition of good performance. But this is where "paternalism" ends. Any communication between the races beyond those limits could upset the delicate equilibrium of the system.

Barely hidden behind the external appearance of vitality and activity in a camp is an all-pervading mood of *tristesse,* as one informant put it—a mixture of dissatisfaction, disappointment, and lack of hope, reinforced but not primarily caused by the difficulties of the postindependence period. Usually once a month, when wages are paid, a tangible change occurs in the attitudes of passive acceptance and stolid routine. One or two days of unrestrained consumption produce a state of euphoria mixed with aggressiveness, especially against the white man in the camp, who obviously has no need to participate in this desperate attempt to have some *furaha* (joy),[11] since he can rely on a constant and never-failing supply of money. It must be realized that the wages (frozen by the government in an attempt to halt inflation) are kept in the not easily definable range just above the minimum necessary for survival but below the minimum that would be sufficient to satisfy the expectations of people who are caught in a process of modernization, have access to information about the world outside, and can compare their standard of living with that of their white masters.[12] One attempt

11. Joy, *furaha,* is a current term in the language of the camp and of the Jamaa (for its use in Jamaa doctrine see the vocabulary, no. 15, in Chapter 3). Louis Ramasani, a Jamaa leader in Kinshasa, contrasted the atmosphere in the cities of Katanga to the one in the capital by pointing out that the people in Katanga were concerned with *kazi,* work, while those in Kinshasa were concerned with *furaha,* joy, distraction. (This, by the way, was for him an explanation of why the Jamaa had so little success in Kinshasa.)

12. To put it in more concrete terms: in 1966–67 a worker's average monthly income in Congolese money would have bought two bottles of his superior's favorite Scotch.

to escape at least temporarily from this situation is the custom of *dikilimba*,[13] known almost everywhere in urban Africa: several families pool their income, and each month one of the members of such an association will have a sufficient supply of money while the others try to get along until their turn comes. Because these arrangements seldom work and are the cause of endless palavers, the camp administration has prohibited the custom.

Occasionally, diffuse feelings of anxiety and aggression may break out in a panic. Such a case was reported by the missionary at Musonoi. A woman died—probably from a heart attack—in the market place just after she had drunk from the water pipe. Immediately several men ran through the camp telling everyone not to use the water from the central system since it was poisoned by the whites. Soon after that, a crowd of Catholic women gathered at the rectory asking the missionary for water; he, as their *nduku* (brother), would not try to poison them. It did not occur to them that his supply came from the same system. When the situation threatened to get out of hand, the missionary called on the *chef de camp*. Several of those who had spread the rumor were arrested and punished.

But the camp's many subtle boundaries that convey a sense of imprisonment to its inhabitants are surprisingly often experienced as positive. Paternalism has made life in a camp on the whole more secure than existence back in the village, especially after the virtual disintegration of the medical and educational systems set up by the colonial government. More than 50 per cent of the workers living at Musonoi had joined the Union Minière before independence in 1960 (cf. Appendix I); the average duration of the period spent under contract among workers of the Kolwezi area was 8.99 years. Such prolonged separation from the village society has had its effects on the outlook of many workers.[14]

Most likely to cause objections from outsiders are certain rules which seem to restrict the freedom of assembly. For any large festive gathering in a private home (such as weddings, funerals,

13. Cf. Ghilain 1968.
14. Individualization of behavior, increasing importance of the nuclear family, and involvement in religious, social, or political associations have been described in the vast literature on urbanization-industrialization in central Africa. Cf. above, Chapter 1, note 2, esp. Forthomme (1957), Dethier (1961a,b), and Mwepe Kyabutha (1967).

etc.) the host needs a permit from the *chef de camp*. In order to get the permit, he must submit a list of the guests he expects. On several occasions my informants insisted on the advantages of this seemingly repressive system. For them it worked as an effective and necessary means of protection against unwanted visitors and the usual crowd of parasites in a situation where resources are limited and the rights and duties of hospitality are no longer guaranteed by the sanctions of traditional society.

Less easy to assess, since it is not on the level of "everyday" action, is the ambivalent reality of the camp in the context of magic-religious beliefs. Let me introduce the problem by citing a case. In 1960 or 1961 one of my informants overheard a Congolese schoolteacher talking about the devotion and the sense of awe one should experience upon entering a church. As an example he re-called an experience he had had as a child. His father, a worker living in a camp, had taken his wife and children back to his native village (somewhere near Kapanga, Lunda territory). The day after their arrival, the family was led by the grandfather to a place outside the village where a tree symbolized the presence of *shaka-panga* (the creator).[15] There he took a branch, dipped it into a container of ritual water, and sprinkled the family while asking *shakapanga* to cleanse his children from all impurities they had absorbed while living in the camp together with people from strange tribes.

This story is interesting, not only for its content (the camp as a profane place), but also because of the context in which it was told. The teacher, describing the camp as a dangerous and impure world in contrast to the village, at the same time interpreted a religious attitude expected in the camp (entering the church) in terms of an experience he had had when he was exposed to tra-ditional religion.

Distance from the village means distance from the focus of integration of the traditional system of religious and metaphysical beliefs; more concretely in the African context, it means distance from the place where the life-giving ancestors dwell and where they may be venerated properly. It should not be surprising that elements usually integrated in the traditional system, but less personalized and localized than ancestor and spirit worship, gain

15. Cf. van Avermaet and Mbuya (1954:598 f.).

importance in the camp. The whole gamut of what is usually referred to as "magic" and "sorcery" is common practice in the camps. In fact, settlements of the Union Minière have a special reputation for these things, in much the same way that marginal and minority groups have often been respected and feared in traditional contexts.[16] Most workers resort to some *lawa* (medicine) in order to protect themselves against evil influences at work. Many other examples could be cited. What seems to me most important in this development is the fact that, as a belief system, "magic" is shared, and operates, beyond tribal boundaries. There can be no doubt that the universalist outlook in Jamaa doctrine has profited from this evolution in the urban-industrial centers.

Extremely ambivalent is the situation in the camp for (Catholic) Christians. Most of them were baptized in their native villages, where the mission represented one of the dominant aspects of the colonial situation. Generally, missionaries were thought to be useful as educators and occasionally as protectors against both the government and the traditional authorities, but on the whole their influence was hardly strong enough to challenge the integration of the cultural and social systems they tried to influence. In a camp the situation is different. The physical arrangement alone—the Catholic church is the center of the camp—suggests that the *mon père* is but another representative of the Union Minière, and this is not too far from the truth, if we recall the directions of the manual defining the role of the missionaries. A Congolese worker who identifies himself with the *mon père* by practicing his religion will be caught in a dilemma. As a member of the church he shares one of the most important attributes of the white man; but, on the other hand, he will be criticized for his collaboration with the colonizers. His situation is often further complicated when his white superior at work tells him not to believe in the nonsense the missionaries preach.[17]

16. A classical example would be the image of the gypsies in European folk culture. In the Lunda-Luba region, according to my own information, two tribes at the northern and southern peripheries are reputed for their strong magic: Tshokwe and BaSonge (BaKabinda).

17. All this applies a fortiori to members of the Jamaa. Elsewhere I have analyzed a concrete situation of conflict in which a woman member of the group at Musonoi faces her husband's pagan and noninvolved Christian relatives (Fabian 1967).

Tempels and the Camp

In Chapter 1, I pointed out that Tempels, although he had spent most of his early years as a missionary in a traditional, village-centered environment, became a successful prophet only in the camp. What was his attitude toward the social policies of the Union Minière? At first, it is somewhat surprising to realize that he shared and accepted this ideology to a great extent. But then this confirms the hypothesis which explains his success as a "rebel" and a prophet. He was able to provide new orientation for his followers because his message reflected the new environment in which they had to live.

In *Bantu Philosophy,* a book "addressed to colonials of good will" (1959:119), he states the aims of colonization and of his own contribution: to set out from "the true, the good, and the stable in native custom" (*ibid.,* 18) and help the natives build their own "stable and noble" civilization (*ibid.,* 113), a civilization which would be founded on a "healthy and stable basis": Bantu wisdom (*ibid.,* 114).

"Stable," "healthy"—it will be recalled that the manual of the Union Minière employs a very similar vocabulary. In fact, Tempels seems to endorse the social policies of the Union Minière in a paper titled "Justice sociale," written shortly after *Bantu Philosophy,* in which he defines the following means of an "illuminated social policy" (1945:74): (*a*) "stability of work," (*b*) "a milieu in which the worker can live and settle down," (*c*) better housing "adapted to his family situation," (*d*) "arranging the camp like an indigenous village, no longer like temporary quarters," (*e*) additional education in evening and Sunday courses, (*f*) social work, and (*g*) a clubhouse for the workers (*ibid.,* 73). Again, in much the same way as the manual, he stresses the importance of a family-oriented policy. One should recruit married workers because the young people growing up in the camps will constitute the best supply of labor. "Therefore, a family-centered policy must resolutely be pursued" (*ibid.,* 74).

There is certainly some truth in the allegation that Tempels contributed through his writings to Belgian paternalist ideology. But our study tries to stay away from such generalizations. Analyzing one specific result of Tempels' activities, the Jamaa, should contribute to a better knowledge of the processes of change in the colony through distinction and separation of factors, not by lumping them together in order to make colonialism appear more unified and therefore more vicious.[18] One distinction to be made is certainly that Tempels talked about social justice, and *not* about output and profit, as does the Union Minière manual. Only then can it become an interesting problem to look for the mutual interdependence of those two ideologies.

THE JAMAA AT MUSONOI

Origin of the Group

Beginnings of the Jamaa at Musonoi: [19] An account by Laurent Mujanshi, member of the first group at Ruwe and founder of the group at Musonoi.

> When I left Ruwe I came here to Musonoi, in September, 1957. I went to work; there I was given the work of a mechanic, which

18. Cf. our remarks in note 9, above. Onwumelo deals with Tempels and traces his impact on Belgian colonial ideology (cf. his bibliographical notes). In his critique of *Bantu Philosophy* he overlooks, like everybody else, the specific character of this book as the first formulation of what later became the message of the Jamaa (cf. Onwumelo 1966:105–8). I refer again to my critique of Boulaga's (1968) critique (Fabian 1970b).

19. The Jamaa at Musonoi was chosen as a permanent base for field work and will now serve as a paradigmatic case in my description of the movement, for the following reasons:

1. Since the breakup of the "first group" at Ruwe, the Jamaa at Musonoi, led by Tempels himself during his last years in the Congo, is historically closest to the original Jamaa.

2. The Jamaa at Musonoi, unlike many other groups in the urban centers of south Katanga, operates in the original environment of the movement: the camps of the Union Minière.

3. At the time of my field work, this group was about ten years old. It was no longer in the "virulent" stage of charismatic enthusiasm, but it was still a vigorous center of the movement. It also represented all major phenomena of the later stages, such as struggle for leadership and succession, factions and "deviations," standardization of doctrine—phenomena of incipient "routinization of charisma," in Weberian terms. As such, Musonoi presented ideal conditions for scientific observation.

4. The local pastor, who had been working with Tempels for many years and became a member and leader of the movement, was willing to introduce me to the Jamaa. Within certain limits which will be discussed later, he was an excellent informant and guide.

was what I wanted. Once they had appointed me mechanic, they sent me to the other mechanics so that they could show me the way the rails run in the mine. Because if you don't know the rails, you'll cut the wires of the overhead system.

They entrusted me to a *baba* named Maweja Theodore. We started to go around while he explained the rails to me: he is a mechanic— I am a mechanic. He had volunteered to show me around. So we went down into the mine, up and down all the time. After a while I started to talk to him: *"Baba,* I have something in my heart [which I have to tell you]." Meanwhile Theodore had met Mwangayi Daniel. He said: "He has something in his heart, what is it?" I told him: "I have something concerning God, these are the things in my heart. If you want, I can tell you about them."

Truly, he stopped and asked: "What are those things?" I told him: "Look, I am separated from you because I belong to a different tribe. In heaven, people are united. The saints are united with God. The angels are united with God. But we Christians on earth are not united with God; nor are we united among ourselves. There is division among us. But if you want to realize what it means to be *baba,* what it means to be man, then first learn the instructions of the Jamaa."

He listened and asked: "What is that, the Jamaa? First tell me something about the Jamaa so that I understand." So I began: "The beginning with God; how God began to create heaven, earth, angels; how he sent man on earth; he created man on earth and he lived on earth. And finally, God sent his son on earth, in the arms of the Virgin Mary, so that he could save us from satan's slavery." This is how I went on with my talk to Maweja Theodore, there on Dump 114.

Then we left Dump 114 and descended into the mine of Musonoi. There we met Kapongo Ignace and *baba* Mwangayi Daniel. Immediately, Maweja Theodore called them: "Ignace, come and listen to this *baba.* Together with Daniel we were on that dump, and he really told us something. Come and listen to what this *baba* has to say." And *baba* Kapongo Ignace stopped and stayed there.

So I started to talk about the beginning, between God and man. I began to tell how God created man, how he sent man on earth. . . . And *baba* Ignace, too, felt how his heart changed, [and he realized] that this was the truth. *"Baba"* [he said], "this is something of value [*kizima;* lit., alive, complete]; go back to the dump in their engine" (he was a foreman of the engineers). So we drove up and down again, and then it was time to leave our work at the Union Minière. Then we arrived in my house. I saw Ignace Kapongo, Maweja Theodore, and Mwangayi Daniel. Each called people from his own tribe, but [it would be better to say] they called everyone. All the different tribes came together in one place. Well, I was a stranger; I had just come from Ruwe, and I did not even have a chair to sit on. They all tried to get into the house, the small house I lived in. In this small house I started the instructions about Lord Jesus, the Virgin Mary, and God the Father. People from all over the world listened and followed these instructions. But the *bababa* at Ruwe with whom we began [the Jamaa] had not yet started to go out and teach, not one among them [T 51].[20]

Laurent Mujanshi's story is a valuable document; with its regard for minute and seemingly unimportant detail, it carries the mark of authenticity. On the whole, it can be accepted as an accurate account of the origins of the Jamaa at Musonoi, even though it will be subject to a few modifications. During my field work I had the exceptional opportunity to meet and interrogate the first three "disciples" of Laurent:

1. Theodore Maweja, who had returned to his native village near the mission of Lukalaba/Bakwanga in the south Kasai, but who came to Musonoi to visit his "father" Laurent and his own "children" (i.e., those he had initiated into the Jamaa).

2. Daniel Mwangayi, who is now training locomotive engineers in the mine of Musonoi. He is *personnel de cadre,* i.e., a member of the highest rank of Congolese employees, equal (in many privileges, housing, etc.) to European personnel. He lives in the "white" core city of Kolwezi.

3. Ignace Kapongo, who has about the same function as Daniel, but on a lower rank. He lives in the camp of Musonoi and is a prominent member of the group.

With D. Mwangayi and I. Kapongo I was able to check the story of Laurent Mujanshi; Ignace was present when it was recorded. The results of our discussions are quite interesting.

Laurent's claim to have been the first one to spread the Jamaa outside Ruwe and to have instructed a sizable group of followers at Musonoi seems to be justified. To his authority as a founder he owes his present prominence as a leader. But knowledge of and interest in the Jamaa had spread from Ruwe to Musonoi and the other camps before he talked to Maweja Theodore on "Dump 114." Transfer of workers from one camp to another became a major factor in the spread of the movement. I. Kapongo hinted at the

20. Recorded February 2, 1967, at Musonoi.

possibility that Tempels may have had a hand in Laurent's transfer from Ruwe to Musonoi. He and his friends had heard about the Jamaa and had listened to *"baba* Placide." When they approached him and expressed their desire to hear more about the new doctrine, he told them that they had to find a *baba* and a *mama* among the members of the first group who would tell them more about the Jamaa (this, as we shall see later, suggests that formal initiation was already developed). At that time, several people who had been in contact with the Jamaa at Ruwe had already moved to Musonoi. But, according to Ignace, they refused to introduce new members to the Jamaa because they thought it was too much work.

Daniel Mwangayi also had heard about the Jamaa before he met Laurent Mujanshi. In 1956 he was living in the camp of Kolwezi. Through the local pastor he had met Tempels and had attended several of his catechetical meetings. Apparently, those meetings were interrupted when Tempels stayed for some time at the construction site of the Marinel Dam and hydroelectric plant (about forty miles north of Kolwezi). Meanwhile, Daniel Mwangayi met Laurent. Again, his account differs somewhat from the versions told by Laurent and Ignace. For instance, the first encounter between Laurent and Theodore Maweja appears in a different light. The latter was trying to find some *miti* (a piece of wood, but also used for "magic medicine") for his child: "When they got into a conversation, Laurent told him, 'I know the things of God.'" Maweja Theodore must have been rather annoyed with Laurent, because he answered: "They don't mean anything, the things of God you know" (T 68). Daniel Mwangayi intervened at that moment. It was only after Theodore and Laurent had talked for a second time that Daniel approached Laurent:

> We were doing the night shift. But I did not give an engine to Laurent. I was the supervisor for the entire mine, and I did not give him any work. Then I called Laurent and made him sit down. We stayed together, and I began to ask him. He started to talk about the same things I had heard from *mon père* [Placide], the *père* who lived at Ruwe. And I said: "So this is it." He said: "Yes." Well, I thought, you have been living at Ruwe for a long time, perhaps you learned a lot about it; I tried to follow his teaching because I was burning inside from desire to know a way to follow God. . . . When I arrived at Musonoi, we started those things with *baba* Laurent: I, Maweja, and *baba* Ignace, the three of us. We had long conversations. After

two or three days I said: "All right, it will be good to inform many people; there are many Christians who love the things of God." But *baba* Laurent got scared. I said, "The *changa-changa* [*chef de camp*] knows me. If I do something, he will know that there is not going to be any trouble" [*ibid.*].

Daniel then says that he went around the camp to find a place that could accommodate the many people who soon were listening to Laurent's instructions. Finally he found such a place in the social center (*foyer social*). He confirms Laurent's claim to have been the first to preach Jamaa doctrine while all the others were still afraid to speak up. But, in his account, he himself comes out as the protector and sponsor of Laurent—as the one who made his mission possible.

These reports on the beginnings of the Jamaa at Musonoi reflect the general pattern in the propagation of the movement suggested in the preceding chapter:

1. Initial interest in the Jamaa is created by Tempels' peripatetic teaching of a "new" catechism; in most cases it is deepened by personal contact at work with members of the first group.

2. If approached directly, Tempels always refers to members of his first group and, perhaps, tries to "plant" some of his followers in Kolwezi and in the camps nearby. Then a group gathers around one or several members of the original group.

3. A consolidation of a local group is reached when the new leader, often through Tempels' intervention, wins the approval of the local pastor. Then the Jamaa will be given access to official meeting places (official in the sense that they are set up by the Union Minière or the mission). The movement begins to operate as one of many pious societies or *mouvements* (e.g., *Mouvement familial, Mouvement de jeunesse*).

The further early development at Musonoi (1957–60) which, later on, gave this group its extraordinary prestige in the movement is marked by the fact that Tempels himself became the local pastor. At about the same time another of the *baba saba* (the seven founding fathers) was transferred from Ruwe to Musonoi and began instructions in the doctrine: Mathieu Binga. In 1966–67 it was my impression that he was a more respected leader than Mujanshi Laurent, even though Ignace Kapongo assured me that he had started much later than *baba* Laurent and then only because the latter could not keep up with his many obligations at Musonoi and other camps. According to Ignace, a *mama*, Charlotte Nsuka, also a member of the first group, was very influential at that time.

Accounts by people like Laurent Mujanshi, Daniel Mwangayi, and Ignace Kapongo, who, as the very earliest founders or members, are *ipso facto* leading figures in the group at Musonoi, are confirmed—if not repeated—by people from the rank and file. I should like to illustrate this by the reminiscences of Pierre Mwamba. He and his wife, Therese Kapanga, are now rather prominent members of the group, but they joined the Jamaa at Musonoi in a very typical way:

My very first contact with the Jamaa was when I saw *baba* Placide Tempels. They [i.e., the people of the Jamaa] used to meet in what is now the second church. They said: "Pierre, this is what we are, this is what the Jamaa is about." But I was not impressed. [I thought,] "I'll find out when he [Tempels] comes."

One day I worked together with *baba* Benoit. We started a conversation, and he told me things that sounded like the instructions by *baba* Placide or *baba* Laurent. "They have a very good doctrine," he told me. "Whoever listens to it will be filled with joy." So he started to speak to me, and we discussed what it means to be Christian. We questioned each other, and I began to feel tremendous joy in my soul: from that moment on, my soul caught fire [T 31].

Pierre and his wife then joined those who were following Laurent's instructions at the social center. Both assured me that at that time many more people were involved with the Jamaa than nowadays because many had been fired or transferred since; others left when the "difficulties" in Katanga started (1960–63).

At the end of Chapter 1, I mentioned the difficulties one encounters when Jamaa people are questioned about the origin of the "visible" Jamaa. What matters to them is the "rediscovery" of the eternal Jamaa that was lost among men. This explains why, even among my informants at Musonoi, I found so much reluctance to go into historical detail. Still, there is no reason to doubt the validity of the accounts quoted. All of them confirm a number of characteristics typical of the emergence and propagation of the movement:

1. At the beginning is what we have called the "prophetic event"

—Tempels or one of his first followers has an "encounter" with a candidate.

2. The important issue in this first contact is *mafundisho*, a doctrine that will give better understanding of oneself and of the world as it is experienced in the immediate environment of the mines and the camps. There is no trace of millenarian, nativistic, or separatist overtones.

3. There is nothing that would connect the constitution of the Jamaa group at Musonoi with a *specific* impulse from the social or cultural environment.

4. Nothing in the information on the earliest stage of the group at Musonoi allows us to think of the recruits as marginal, frustrated, and deprived people, at least not in comparison with the population of the camps in general.

5. On the contrary, the movement seems to have been completely integrated into the specific environment of the Union Minière settlements. Since it was regarded as a church affair and did not interfere with the rules of discipline and order in the camps, the administration did not take any interest in the new movement, while others, e.g., the Kitawala and the Bapostolo, were being watched quite closely.

6. The only visible pattern of organization in the Jamaa at Musonoi during the early time of its development is alliance to a "teacher" who gives instructions in Jamaa doctrine.

Members and Activities

CHARISMA AND COUNTING

In August, 1966, after almost eight months of intensive and extremely fruitful work on the language and doctrine of the Jamaa, I was struck by a kind of panic, probably common to anthropologists who work under similar conditions and with similar aims. Although I had acquired a very intimate knowledge of the group at Musonoi (and had had more than superficial contact with other groups), it suddenly occurred to me that I would not be able to reinforce my insights with "hard," quantitative data. Immediately I sat down and prepared a census questionnaire. Before this questionnaire got to its final form, it went through many discussions with Father B., the local pastor and a very influential leader of the Jamaa. Together with him I tried to anticipate all possible difficulties which were likely to arise when one tried to "measure" charisma. Finally, we agreed on the following procedure: the questionnaire would not be distributed, nor would the action be announced to the group; instead, he, and occasionally I, would interrogate members of the Jamaa in the office of the parish, in much the same way that the routine work of the ecclesiastical bureaucracy is performed. Clearly, this was going to be a long-term project.

We had started to fill out the forms (and had completed about fifteen) when Laurent Mujanshi rushed into the office, shouting in uncontrollable rage that he did not want his name to be taken down. I was not present when this happened, but I take it that Laurent represented the views, or rather the fears, of many. The main factor in this violent reaction was, I assume, a very deeply rooted re- luctance to give one's name away. This is certainly based on tra- ditional beliefs concerning the essence of the name. But it is also very strongly conditioned by experiences with the colonial regime, which exercised power through "inscription."

Father B. tried to save the situation by explaining the aims of the survey, to no avail. He himself then became rather insecure, pointing out that Tempels would never have gone along with such a thing. A further attempt to work with the questionnaire, in the parish of the C.E.C. at Kolwezi, ended in a similarly disastrous way when the pastor discovered that copies had been taken from his office and were being circulated as evidence of his dubious intentions vis-à-vis the Jamaa.

Exact figures on membership in a Jamaa group, then, are not available,[21] not only because subconscious fears of bureaucratic procedures and conscious objections against "measuring" charisma prevent an adequate census but also because the concept "member" lacks precision. People who are not, or not yet, initiated in the technical sense participate in the activities of the group; others who are full members and are perhaps quite influential may rarely attend meetings. There is also a considerable number of "drop- outs"—members who have lost interest and no longer participate in any of the activities but would still claim to be Jamaa if questioned.

21. Estimates are based on extended contact, inferences from attendance at meetings, etc.

Taking into account all these possible sources of error, I estimate the number of couples who made up the active core of the group at Musonoi at about one hundred.

FACTORS DETERMINING MEMBERSHIP

Members of the Jamaa are Roman Catholic and are married. Except for these two basic requirements—connection with the Catholic church and a relatively stable (and monogamous) marriage situation—I was unable to detect any other cultural or social factors selecting for membership in the movement.

As to its ethnic composition, the group seems to reflect more or less the ratios in the total population of Musonoi (see Appendix I). I do not recall meeting any Dembo or Sanga (i.e., people from the immediate surroundings of Kolwezi) in the group at Musonoi; the only foreign members came from Ruanda. It is a widespread idea in Katanga that the Jamaa is dominated by people from the Kasai. For this I have no evidence. Laurent Mujanshi and Mathieu Binga, the two most influential leaders in 1966–67, are Ba-kete, people from the Kasai in terms of popular classification but hardly representative of the type "Luba-Kasai," considered to be the most ambitious, competent, and also difficult ethnic group in the urban-industrial centers of Katanga.

As to social and economic status, it seems that most Jamaa people at Musonoi belong to the middle and upper ranks of the professional rating applied by the Union Minière. The average rating in a small but not selected sample of 18 workers from the Musonoi group was close to *cote* 12 (this would put them into the 25 per cent slot; see Appendix I). But, if this is true, its implications should not be overrated. Inquiry among European supervisors showed that workers belonging to the Jamaa were generally considered to be quiet, reliable, and conscientious but otherwise very inconspicuous.[22]

As far as I can see, the only striking fact about membership in the group at Musonoi is that not a single *moniteur* (teacher at the Union Minière–run elementary schools) belongs to the movement.

---

22. A representative of the labor management at the Union Minière did me the favor of looking up fifteen personal dossiers of somewhat prominent Jamaa members at Musonoi. Only one had a bad disciplinary record, two had had difficulties but had improved, and the others were considered excellent workers.

This is in sharp contrast to many rural groups, where teachers tend to be the core of the Jamaa.[23]

I shall deal with the procedures of recruitment in Part II, in the discussion of initiation. I might just add here that, during the period of observation, membership remained fairly stable; losses due to transfer or return to the village were compensated for by new candidates. In neither direction was the movement important enough to cause major changes in the composition of the group.

The Jamaa group at Musonoi, then, appears to be very well integrated into the particular social and cultural environment of the camp. Nothing indicates that the group owes its cohesion to some antagonism or opposition to specific groups or issues. Nor does it seem, on this level of analysis, that the positive incentives are extraordinarily strong. A Jamaa member may find a certain degree of economic and social security in his group; mutual assistance is one of the proclaimed aims of the movement. But two things must be kept in mind: (*a*) There is very little at stake. Mutual help and assistance are not really organized by the group and therefore stay within very narrow limits. No one is in a position to give away very much; no one has enough prestige or actual power in the Union Minière to be important in questions of promotion and privileges. (*b*) Such mutual help follows exactly the pattern set by customary assistance within a group of "relatives" (in terms of extended family, clan, tribe, etc.). There is a tendency in the Jamaa to replace "relatives by blood" with "relatives by spirit," and this actually creates a host of conflicts and complications; but no Jamaa member has cut all ties with his kinsmen in the camp.

23. Until independence in 1960, elementary schoolteachers constituted the upper rank of the *evolués* (others, such as the native clergy and a few better-trained medical and social assistants, were never numerous enough to appear as a "class"). In Musonoi, during the time of my field work, they gave the impression of having been overtaken by the course of events. Trying to preserve their (no longer uncontested) elite status, they showed strong aggressive tendencies, not only against administration and mission but also against the sort of change advocated by the Jamaa. Above all, this became visible in their "traditionalist" attitudes toward marriage and the position of their wives. Much more than even the traditional definition of roles would allow, they acted as family despots, excluded their wives from their social life, congregated in exclusive groups, etc. This regressive tendency, especially concerning the position of women in society, is also noticeable in some of the responses of high-school students at Kolwezi (see Appendix II). The prominence of teachers in rural Jamaa groups reflects the fact that there the elite status is not being challenged.

A very important aspect of interaction within Jamaa groups is the establishment of personal (often intertribal) links of friendship. Again, this is perhaps somewhat more frequent in the Jamaa; it is certainly a very prominent issue, because it is taken to be a "proof" for certain principles of doctrine. But I doubt that it would be possible to demonstrate statistically that this is more important in the group than in the general society of the camp.

What happens if a member of the group leaves the camp but does not return to the village? One such case is Daniel Mwangayi, a member of the original group at Musonoi. While he was still living in the camp, he started building his own house on a lot in the C.E.C. of Kolwezi. He had done this without permission from the Union Minière, and this could have cost him his job. But apparently his initiative was somehow appreciated; he was promoted to the *personnel de cadre* and given a house in the core city. He no longer participates in any group activities (there is no Jamaa in his present parish), but he stays in close contact with his friends at Musonoi, Laurent Mujanshi and Ignace Kapongo. I asked him whether he did not think that his professional success and his physical and social distance from the Jamaa in the camp had changed his outlook. His answer was (very typically, as we shall see later) that the Jamaa is an attitude, not a matter of organized activities. When questioned about the doctrine, his responses and his way of presenting a *mafundisho* (standardized instruction) would be in no way different from those of "active" members at Musonoi.

ACTIVITIES: A MOVEMENT WITHOUT RITUAL?

If the movement is so well integrated into the social and cultural context of the camp, what leads people to associate certain families with the label "Jamaa"? Above all, it is the common, and to a certain degree public, activities of the group. "Activities" are defined as any actions which can be distinguished from other actions by the fact that they (*a*) are carried out as the enactment of Jamaa doctrine and (*b*) involve the entire group or a segment which, under certain circumstances, may represent the entire group.

Some observers (and defenders) of the Jamaa have noted the absence of elaborate ritual and ceremonial otherwise typical of such movements (e.g., Kibangism and Bapostolo). I must confess that, during several months, I looked for support of this view and was very much impressed by lack of ritual as a distinctive characteristic of the Jamaa—until I came to realize something which is so obvious that it can indeed escape attention. The Jamaa has, on the whole, not severed its links with the Catholic mission. Jamaa members fully participate in the elaborate ritual activities of the church. Indeed, very regular, if not daily, use of the sacraments (communion, confession) is one of the few explicit rules directly guiding behavior. The ecclesiastical calendar, prescribing different liturgical and paraliturgical activities for different times, marks the seasons of the year more effectively for Jamaa people than for "ordinary" Christians. Jamaa people are very much aware of the importance of all this. In the conversation with Daniel Mwangayi reported earlier, I stated that he did not participate in any of the activities of a local group, but in the light of what has just now been said about the role of official liturgy, Daniel's answer must be accepted and lead to a modification of this point of view:

> Whether I live together with members of the Jamaa, or whether I live alone—I cannot give up connection with a priest, I cannot stop going to mass and confession. Because this is what I started with in the Jamaa [T 69].

ACTIVITIES: THE MEETING

The Jamaa, then, if it is less exotic in the eyes of a non-African observer, is hardly less ritualistic than other charismatic-prophetic movements.

Practically the only common activity specific to the Jamaa is the meeting of the group, most often referred to by the French term *réunion* (the Swahili word *maungano* is hardly ever used). But the term *réunion* covers a very wide range of gatherings on different occasions, with different participation and following different patterns. There are almost no explicit rules concerning the meetings, but all of them conform in some way to the pattern set by the weekly *mafundisho*.

1. The *mafundisho* meeting. At Musonoi this took place every Thursday (unless it conflicted with some holiday) at 5:00 P.M., when people came back from the day shift. The location was the assembly room of the main parish, a hangar seating 350–400 people on low wooden benches. Attendance varied from thirty to more than a hundred people; usually there were sixty to seventy,

not counting babies and toddlers. In Musonoi, men and women would sit separately, facing each other. Speakers usually talked from a bench between the two groups but might also choose any other location. In fifteen regular weekly *mafundisho* I attended at Musonoi, only once did a female member speak, and then only very briefly.

A typical *mafundisho* meeting has the following form:

a) It starts with an introductory prayer recited by a member (there is no appointed prayer leader; usually this function is performed by someone who intends to give the *mafundisho*). This may be followed by a Jamaa hymn, by a short interval of silent meditation, or immediately by

b) The *mafundisho* proper, i.e., an instruction in standardized Jamaa doctrine (cf. Appendix III). One speaker usually takes ten to thirty minutes; there may be up to four speakers if they do not together exceed sixty to ninety minutes. Content, form, and function of the *mafundisho* will be discussed at length in the chapter on doctrine.

c) Announcements on "current affairs" are made and discussed after the *mafundisho;* occasionally they precede the instructions.

d) The session is occasionally concluded by a hymn, but there is always a final prayer; and the priest, if he attends, pronounces a blessing.

e) Very important, although not an official part of the meeting, is the informal gathering which precedes and follows it; however, this is hardly exclusive to the Jamaa.

2. Another weekly meeting (on Fridays) is also called a *mafundisho*. The instruction is given exclusively by the pastor. The circumstances at Musonoi did not allow my regular participation in this meeting. It appears, from the information I have, that this was a continuation of Tempels' "catechetic" sessions.

3. Other meetings take place at irregular intervals. The location is not the official assembly room but a private house of a member, and this usually excludes a gathering of the entire group. These nonscheduled meetings are held at night (during the week) or in the afternoon (on holidays). Many of them are just a continuation of the official *mafundisho;* apparently they were much more frequent in the earlier, more enthusiastic years. A visitor from another group may occasion a meeting; so may a recording session with the anthropologist. In fact, this became quite a problem during my

field work. Whenever I called on an informant who was willing to talk to me alone, I had to ask my more private questions very quickly, because there would soon be a small gathering. I do not believe that this had much to do with curiosity; after more than a year of almost daily contact, even an anthropologist is no longer a curiosity. Rather, it expresses a basic Jamaa doctrine that any actualization of the doctrine, whether recitation of *mafundisho,* discussion, prayer, or singing, calls for congregation—actualization of the group—and vice versa.

4. The second part of the principle just formulated applies to meetings of the group, or a subgroup, on occasions not specific to the Jamaa, such as a wedding, a baptism or first communion, a *kilio* (a general term for rites connected with death, burial, mourning),[24] illness, or some other situation of joy or crisis. As to external form, both types 3 and 4 follow the pattern set by the regular *mafundisho:* there will be instructions in the doctrine; depending on the occasion (e.g., in a case of illness), there may be more prayer, and especially more singing, than in the weekly meeting. Often the session is interrupted or followed by a meal, to which the participants make their contributions.

5. In Kolwezi, where the Jamaa is represented in all parishes except in the core city, intergroup meetings are quite common. The first type is probably unique in the movement. Every other Sunday, members from all groups in the area gather for the so-called *pulan* (from French *plan*). This goes back to 1961, when members of the Kolwezi groups decided to formulate and write their *mafundisho* in order to unify teaching. The result was a brochure (53 type-written pages), *Mafundisho ya Jamaa katolika* (Teaching of the Catholic Jamaa). But the *pulan* meeting continued and has since taken on a different function. The location has always been the assembly room at Musonoi. Typically, the *pulan* proceeds as follows:

a) Introductory prayer, followed by a call to all groups to present their candidates for the first and second degrees of initiation. If candidates are present, they rise, so that everyone can see them, and then leave the meeting.

---

24. For terminology and mourning customs in Luba culture see van Avermaet and Mbuya (1954:64) and Theuws (1960; 1962:165 f.). In a more restricted sense, the celebration of *kilio* corresponds to the Luba *kusubuka,* ending the mourning period.

b) Announcements and "current affairs"; discussion of problems regarding all groups of the area.

c) A *mafundisho* by one or several speakers, geared, according to my observations, to the preceding discussion.

d) Final prayer and blessings.

Evidently, participation in the *pulan* is limited to the fully initiated. At one occasion, only members of the group at Musonoi were present; in all other cases the groups of Ruwe, Kolwezi, Kapata, Luilu, and Metalkat had sent members. Attendance ranged between 100 and 150 persons.

6. Most important among other intergroup meetings is an Easter rally of all groups in the area. The custom goes back to the first years of the movement. Other major centers (Lubumbashi, Jadotville) now have their own Easter meetings. I attended this *réunion ya Pâques* on April 10, 1966. Groups from all parishes in the area gathered in the large courtyard of the *foyer social* in the camp of Kolwezi. Some visitors had come from as far away as Kasai province. But most informants commented that attendance was no longer what it used to be. Groups from all over Katanga used to come to the meeting. According to my own (conservative) count, 650–700 persons had gathered when the "program" started at 11:00 A.M. with a short welcome by the leader of the group at Camp Kolwezi. This was followed by almost an hour of singing, interrupted by short prayers (an abbreviated form of the Rosary). Singing was led by a small group of men who had the words for hymns specially composed for this occasion. The second part of the meeting started around noon with the *mafundisho*. Speakers were the local pastor (a member of the Jamaa), Monica Kabole (a prominent member of the group at the C.E.C. of Kolwezi), Laurent Mujanshi, and Mathieu Binga (both from Musonoi). All of them developed their speeches from the occasion of the day, the celebration of Easter, by linking it in some way or other to standard topics and formulae of Jamaa doctrine. After the *mafundisho*, the local groups gathered in separate circles or clusters. There was a little food and something to drink, but everyone complained that it was a few days before payday and that no one had much left for making a contribution. Most of the groups left around 2:30 P.M.

7. Other intergroup meetings may be called on occasions similar to those listed in type 4, but they are much less frequent. I par-

ticipated in only one intergroup *kilio* at Kapata and in the celebration following the ordination of a Congolese priest, son of a prominent Jamaa family, at Musonoi and Kapata. In the latter, the "official" part was taken up by the liturgy; then followed a social gathering, a common meal, some singing, and brief announcements but no *mafundisho*. The *kilio* at Kapata followed the pattern of the Easter meeting.

The only other group activities I observed at Musonoi were collections of money for various purposes, such as a contribution to a common celebration, assistance for members in need, expenses caused by visitors, etc. Most of these collections took place during or after the weekly *mafundisho* meeting. There is no appointed treasurer; usually the amounts were not very significant. The group has no permanent common funds.

Often mentioned by outside observers is the assistance the group will try to give the local pastor. Women clean and decorate the church; men often take responsibility for order and calm during Sunday masses (quite a task, if one tries to control 600–700 children). This assistance, which reflects a latent Jamaa attitude that its members are the elite of the parish, is conspicuous (and often annoying) to others, but it is hardly a very important function in a fully developed Jamaa.

In contrast to other religious groups in the camp, Jamaa people do not wear any insignia of their membership in the movement. Often I heard people say that one can recognize Jamaa people from their dignified way of walking through the camp; it did not strike me as particularly "Jamaa." Laurent Mujanshi and a few other members of the group at Musonoi would wear a rather large cross or medal as a pendant; many carry their rosaries visibly during the meetings; but all this is a far cry from the elaborate "biblical" attire of the Bapostolo and related movements.

In summary, observable group activities in the Jamaa center around the weekly *mafundisho* (instruction in the doctrine), which constitutes the model for all other gatherings on group or intergroup bases. There are only traces of economic functions (occasional collections); nothing indicates that the group may represent its members for political or social purposes. As has been said before, the camp administration regards Jamaa activities as strictly a church matter.

Unity and Diversity:
Patterns of Internal Organization

The Jamaa at Musonoi has no written or otherwise explicitly formulated constitution and no rules, functions, files, or records. An occasional observer who cannot spend enough time with the group to recognize the regular repetition of certain patterns of behavior, the establishment and functioning of leadership, the obvious identification with a limited and stable number of people based on a specific doctrine, may indeed be tempted to accept Tempels' definition of the Jamaa: that it is not a group, not a movement or organization, but simply an "encounter" between the priest and his parishioners. The preceding section certainly casts some doubts on this favorite axiom of Tempels'. Observations regarding membership and activities have served to define the outer limits of a Jamaa group, at least to a certain degree. But even during an extended period of (external) observation one finds very little that might reveal the internal structuring of the group. Actually, I can think of only three externally observable phenomena that mark distinctions within the group. On various occasions, opposition, or at least contrast, will become visible between (1) the local pastor and the group, (2) prominent members and "rank and file," and (3) the fully initiated and the lower ranks and candidates. I shall now examine each of these as indicators of structural differentiation in the group at Musonoi.

THE MISSIONARY AND THE GROUP

Tempels always insisted that a Jamaa group be "united" with the priest. The situation at Musonoi is somewhat atypical (but not unique) in that the local pastor "grew up" with both the founder and the movement and became a fully initiated member and a prominent leader. Jamaa teaching defines his position as a "father," the source of life (through the sacraments), but it does not reserve for him a position of doctrinal and disciplinary authority. On the other hand he is *ipso facto,* as a member of the hierarchy, the officially appointed leader of the parish. As such he constantly faces the dilemma of integrating the Jamaa into the church and serving as a central figure in a movement that differs in orientation and organization from this official church. The situation may be aggravated if the priest in question, like the pastor at Musonoi, does not just "act" either role in order to meet the expectations of his environment but identifies himself with Tempels' ideas—he, too, is a follower—and at the same time is separated from his Jamaa group by his own education, cultural heritage, and social and economic dependence on the church. Some of the problems he faces *qua* member of the clergy will be dealt with in another context. Here, I should simply like to suggest that the opposition of priest *vs.* group, with its two aspects of identity and separation, marks one of the basic structural divisions in a Jamaa group.

SPEAKER AND AUDIENCE

As a second point of departure in the search for internal structures in a Jamaa group I mentioned that, in the *mafundisho* meeting (and, consequently, in most other meetings), some members assume a more prominent role than others. Again, not very much is visible: a small group of members act as "speakers" of the instructions in the doctrine. All of them assume that role in a matter-of-fact way; nothing in their or the audience's behavior indicates that they act in a special or "higher" function. An occasional observer could easily get the impression that a *mafundisho* may be given spontaneously by any member of the congregation. But during the period of observation at Musonoi, those who talked at meetings (with one or two exceptions) included only seven persons: (1) Laurent Mujanshi, (2) Mathieu Binga, (3) Ignace Kapongo, (4) Leonard Mbay, (5) Pierre Mwamba, (6) Anaclet Tshikala, and (7) Paul Ngama. (1) and (2) were members of the first Jamaa group at Ruwe and founders of the group at Musonoi; (3) is a member of the very earliest group; (4) is linked to (1) and (3); (5) is prominent because of his close relation, through initiation, with the pastor; (6) and (7) represented the "young generation." In terms of alliance with each other, one could distinguish contrasting groups: (*a*) Laurent Mujanshi and Ignace Kapongo, (*b*) Mathieu Binga, Anaclet Tshikala, and Paul Ngama, and (*c*), as a third, "independent," group, Leonard Mbay and Pierre Mwamba. The major dividing lines run between (*a*) and (*b*), each commanding a large number of followers in the local group, and between what we might call the "group of speakers" (*a, b, c*) and the "audience" (see Fig. 1).

The division between audience and speakers is a fairly obvious one; it is easy to identify in the *mafundisho* meetings, provided the period of observation is long enough. But the line that divides, very roughly, the followers of L. Mujanshi and those of M. Binga is much more difficult to draw. It may occasionally become visible in the *mafundisho*. If more than one speaker talks in a meeting, both groups (*a*) and (*b*) will be represented (usually L. Mujanshi and M. Binga; later L. Mujanshi and A. Tshikala). Opposition is expressed in frequent references to each other within (*a*) or (*b*).

Groups of Speakers	(*a*) L. Mujanshi I. Kapongo	(*b*) M. Binga A. Tshikala P. Ngama
	(*c*) L. Mbay aud P. Mwamba	

FIG. 1—Jamaa Leaders at Musonoi

And on very rare occasions it may come to an open clash between groups on doctrinal or organizational issues. But it still would be impossible to understand the basis for these oppositions if the few symptoms just mentioned were the only information to go on. Alliance in the Jamaa is based on generation/filiation, a concept we shall discuss thoroughly as a key principle of Jamaa doctrine. The relationship between the one who administers and the one who receives initiation is viewed as one between parent and child. L. Mujanshi and M. Binga, who have initiated large numbers into the movement, are prominent because they are regarded as heads of lineages. How this works and what it implies for any given member of the group cannot be observed in the group unless one is led by a structural map of generation/filiation, based on certain principles of the doctrine *plus* information about actual relationships through initiation, which is very hard to get.[25]

MEMBERS AND CANDIDATES

The third indicator for internal structure of the group is even more elusive. Matters of initiation are "secret" in a sense which will

25. I might just add that the spatial opposition between men and women at the *mafundisho* meeting in Musonoi and the fact that the leadership group does not include any female members do not express a structural division typical of the Jamaa. Musonoi is about the only place where this arrangement prevails; it may derive from some purely local situation.

be discussed later. Consequently, there are hardly any visible patterns of behavior, association, activities, etc., specific to the rank that a member has attained. The only time that anything about initiation becomes visible is the presentation of candidates in the *pulan* meeting. But this meeting is not really a matter of the local group, so at this point it remains unclear whether, and to what extent, initiation contributes to the internal structuring of a group.

It is hard to believe that a group the size of the Jamaa at Musonoi could, over a period of ten years, remain as amorphous and structurally undifferentiated as observation of external indicators would suggest. For a deeper understanding of those few clues, I had to refer again and again to later discussions of relevant elements of the doctrine. This may be tiresome, but it is unavoidable, and it frequently reflects quite accurately the progress of understanding in the field. No matter how one approaches the group, it always seems to offer the same perspective: leaders and followers united in love and in their acceptance of Tempels' message. The few external signs of internal differentiation all point to the same source: the concepts of generation/filiation, defined in the doctrine and ritualized in initiation.

Tensions and Trends

As it appears so far, the Jamaa of Musonoi seems to have preserved the simplicity of a flock of disciples. But this impression changes quite radically as soon as attention shifts from structural arrangements to historical events. The Jamaa at Musonoi did not survive its first decade as the true and simple "union in love" Tempels had preached and founded. It has been affected by the advent of independence in the Congo; it continues to be affected by changes in its environment, the camps of the Union Minière; and it has had to face divergence and dissent from within.

SCHISM AND COMPETITION

The first fact that should be mentioned is the separation of a comparatively small group of Jamaa people (ten to twenty couples) from the local pastor and the official church. The roots of this schism probably go back to the beginnings of the Jamaa at Musonoi. The alleged leader of this group used to be one of the most successful teachers of Jamaa doctrine and introduced a considerable number of people to the movement. Tempels described him to me as honest but emotionally unstable and prone to "exaggeration." In early 1966, at the time of my arrival, the conflict between the dissident group and the pastor had reached its peak. Then, mainly through the efforts of I. Kapongo, there was a reconciliation of sorts, until, after my departure, the local pastor and another important Jamaa leader of the clergy decided to expel the leader publicly. During his "orthodox" period he attended meetings but never spoke in a *mafundisho*. I got acquainted with him without getting close enough to ask him about the schism. Among my documents there is a recording of his conversion and his ideas about the Jamaa. Nothing indicates that he propagated a different doctrine, although this may be representative of the general impenetrability of his group. The charges brought by "orthodox" Jamaa people against the dissenters (above all: exchange of women as proof of perfect union in love) are not easy to verify. In any case, they will have to be discussed in a broader context.[26] In my own observation I was struck by two facts:

1. For one year, at least, the dissenting group did not participate in the liturgy of the church (communion, confession). Given the importance attached to this matter by orthodox Jamaa groups, one is led to assume that the dissident group has found a substitute for the official liturgy. The alternative explanation, that it represents a movement without ritual, is very unlikely.

2. While there was open conflict between the dissenting group and the pastor and the church, communication between "orthodox" and "heterodox" groups was never severed. Nor was the conflict ever phrased in doctrinal terms. The charges always centered on "secret" and "immoral" practices. As a matter of fact, it may be wrong to speak of two neatly separated "groups." Coexistence of orthodox and heterodox Jamaa is by no means restricted to Musonoi. In Katanga it is so common that one should, perhaps, think of it as a normal situation and then rethink the implications of dissent and schism. In Musonoi, at least, there was never actual *separation* (except from the point of view of the church), and nothing indicates that an *opposition* existed which was disruptive to the movement. What makes this extraordinary constellation

26. See the section on heterodox groups in Chapter 4.

possible? I shall, at the end of this section, argue that it is the kinship ideology of the Jamaa.

Earlier we identified a line dividing the "speakers" of the ortho-dox group as an indicator of internal structural differentiation. For easier reference I should like to list again the persons involved (omitting the two "independent" speakers):

(a) L. Mujanshi	(b) M. Binga
I. Kapongo	A. Tshikala
	P. Ngama

In a historical perspective, i.e., viewing opposition in terms of concrete events rather than abstract categories, the constitution of the group can now be seen as a dynamic process.

First, an interesting observation: The contrast between (a) and (b) corresponds exactly to the spatial division of the camp into a western and an eastern section and to the organizational boundaries between the main and auxiliary parishes. The leader of the dis-senting group, if we may keep this label, lives in the western section and is most closely allied with group (a), L. Mujanshi and I. Kapongo. On several occasions there has been open conflict between the pastor and L. Mujanshi (cf. the incident with the census), whereas M. Binga has never shown any opposition (he was one of the few who filled out the questionnaire). P. Ngama in the Binga group acted sometimes as Father B.'s spokesman and troubleshooter, which added to the prestige of group (b). It should be mentioned that M. Binga was by far the better and more profound speaker. On the other hand, L. Mujanshi had founded the group at Musonoi, and this seemed to compensate for his shortcomings. In any case, during the years after Tempels' departure, authority and prestige of the competing leaders had led either to open dissent or to something that looked like a delicate equilibrium but may just as well have been a stalemate. The situation changed when M. Binga decided to leave the camp and return to his native village in southern Kasai. Rumor had it that he was leaving because he could not win against Laurent Mujanshi. But his age and family situation would have explained his decision, too. This was in June, 1966. From then on it was quite clear that the remaining members of group (b) were not prepared to acknowledge L. Mujanshi's "victory." In Sep-tember, A. Tshikala publicly claimed succession to M. Binga, whom, at the same time, he declared to have been the leader at Musonoi. A month later, in a *pulan* meeting, it came to such a violent clash between L. Mujanshi and A. Tshikala that Father B. had to break up the meeting. For several days L. Mujanshi virtually besieged Father B.'s office to get his support. A. Tshikala had his difficulties, too. He was vociferous and not really well liked by anyone. His image improved when he won the support of the respected P. Ngama. This, in a way, brought him approval from the pastor. The struggle went on during the final months of my field work, and A. Tshikala succeeded in defending the position of group (*b*). The further development is difficult to predict because, with Tshikala's outright claim to succession, a new factor has entered the scene: opposition between (*a*) and (*b*) is no longer between competing but essentially equal members of the original group; it is now a conflict between the founders and a new generation of leaders. In a *mafundisho* meeting in August, 1966, A. Tshikala expressed his feelings openly when he told the audience: "Some people talk constantly of the beginnings and of *baba* Placide, who himself introduced them to the Jamaa. But none of this means anything if they do not live according to the spirit of the Jamaa." Both A. Tshikala and P. Ngama had a favorite theme in their *mafundisho:* renewal of the spirit, not the forms.

TENSIONS AND THE FOUNDATIONS OF AUTHORITY

A look at two historical events which affected the Jamaa at Musonoi has brought additional evidence for the fact that the group is not exactly a "simple" flock of Tempels' followers. Leading members and their struggle for dominance are impossible to overlook. But we talk about leaders, about authority and domination, even though it would be extremely difficult to answer the obvious question: authority over, domination of, what? Nothing allows us to believe that Jamaa leaders have more access to economic wealth or political influence than other members. Nothing in Jamaa doctrine seems to provide them with special or supernatural faculties or functions.[27] Their position is, as I have pointed out, based on patterns of alliance. But this only pushes the question further back, since it

27. Later we shall have to qualify this statement; cf. our remarks on the importance of "teaching" and interpretation of dreams as vehicles of charismatic authority in the section "Teaching and Authority" in Chapter 4 and in Fabian 1966.

must then be asked what the basis for such an alliance is. As we shall see later, authority is defined in terms of *kizazi,* a network of (spiritual) generation/filiation. The leaders are seen as heads of "lineages." But this in itself does not explain the developments and events presented in this section.

Why should position in a lineage result in conflict and competition? Once, in a long conversation about the tensions and difficulties in Jamaa groups, I. Kapongo surprised me by his pessimistic attitude: *potopot ni fasi yote*—confusion and disorder are everywhere. By this he meant schism within groups and competition for power among leaders. And the reason for this is plain, he told me: *wantu wa Jamaa wanabengana*—Jamaa people do not act according to the rules which govern their relationships. This clumsy translation needs an explanation: *ku-benga* is a current verb in Katanga Swahili, but it is not listed in the Oxford *Standard Swahili Dictionary* (Johnson 1963), or in the classical dictionary by Sacleux (1939, 1941). It must have entered the language of the camp via Kiluba or one of the related languages. Van Avermaet's and Mbuya's *Dictionnaire Kiluba-Français* gives the following principal connotations: to lack respect, to be arrogant, to interact on equal terms with someone who does not occupy the same social rank as oneself (cf. 1954:62). It would seem rather strange that the noun *ki-bengo,* offense against the proper distance, could be regarded as a major source of evil in a group which professes to be united in love in order to overcome all the barriers that separate people. The explanation is simple if one remembers that *kizazi*—a network of (spiritual) kinship—is the organizational matrix of a Jamaa group. *Ki-bengo* in the Jamaa context, as much as in traditional kinship-based society, means lack of respect for the rules of such a system, transgression of the boundaries it sets, and deviation from the roles it defines.[28]

28. I should like to note, however, that, in the "secular" language of the camp, *kibengo* or the verb *kubengana* may have a positive connotation, describing the relationship between friends. For example, a relationship of *ku-bengana* is said to obtain between two *dis.* The term *dis* is one of the many linguistic curiosities in Katanga Swahili. Apparently the Congolese observed that French-speaking whites frequently introduced statements, questions, or demands (especially in informal situations, from friend to friend) with the word *dis* (French for "say"): "Say, may I have this or that. . . ." In this context, *dis* was interpreted as an informal term of address among equals. Today it is currently used, e.g., in formulae of address in letters: *dis yangu . . . ,*

A vivid illustration of what that means in terms of Jamaa values and ideas is provided by a letter from Tempels to a local group (cited in Chapter 1). In the following passages from the Swahili text, one concept will remain untranslated: *ubaba/umama*, lit., the essence of being father/mother.

When a father who has only one child sees that his child starts to walk—is he not going to rejoice? And when the child then starts to talk?

You, father, you do not know how to read. Then you see how your child who goes to school learns to read, much better than you. Will you be jealous? No, you will be glad.

When a father sees his child growing up nicely, is he going to prevent him from growing up? No, he will rejoice, even if his child surpasses him in height and importance. When your only child gets married, are you, his father, going to tell him: "My child, you, too, shall have only one child. Do not try to surpass me by having two or three children." No, you hope that your child is going to have five or ten children.

This is true *ubaba*. A father, a real father, a real mother, rejoices when their child surpasses them. And this is the true *ubaba* we try to find in the Jamaa.

When we have a spiritual child [i.e., a candidate for initiation], he should know the Lord Jesus and the Virgin Mary as much as we know them; we hope and desire that our child will receive true *ubaba* or *umama* and in turn have spiritual children of his own. If we are unwilling for our child to have more spiritual children than we, then we do not have the spirit of *ubaba* and *umama*. To be unwilling for our child to have his children is jealousy, is sorcery [*uloji*], because it means to take away life/force [*uzima*] from our child, from our fellow Jamaa members. To be jealous of our children because of their fecundity [*uzazi*] is satanic.

In our Jamaa we do not want just one *baba* or one *mama* to do the initiation, nor any *baba* or *mama* to be the leader [*mukubwa*]. Our leader [*baba wetu mukubwa*] is Lord Jesus, our leader is the Virgin Mary. If our children want us to be their leaders, let us resist with all our force. We do not want to be "president" or "chief." Among us there should not be rulers and subjects.

My *dis.* . . . With the conception of the *dis* relationship, we are touching upon the highly interesting phenomenon of the development of "friendship ideologies" in urban Africa. A recent study deals with such an ideology among members of a government service (Jacobson 1968).

I myself have refused "presidency" or "chieftainship" in the Jamaa. Always I have referred you to your own priests; you should talk to them. Someone who rejects his own priest rejects the Lord Jesus. . . .

Someone who has children of his own, who locks his children up in his own enclosure [*lupango*], who keeps his children in his own separate group, is *baba* in neither the Jamaa nor the church. He does not aspire to the idea of *ubaba;* he is after power [*bumfumu*].

Our fecundity [*uzazi*] is a very holy matter; it unites us with the *ubaba* of God the Father himself.

A true *baba* cannot be after a position of power for himself; he cannot humiliate others [letter to the group in the C.E.C. at Kolwezi; undated; received in July, 1966].

Obviously, Tempels is dealing with those factions and tensions which characterize the group at Musonoi. Anyone who is somewhat familiar with the problems which the first propagators of Christianity had to face will be amazed by the similarities, not only of the conflicts but of the proposed solutions (cf., e.g., I Cor. 3:3 ff.). We may now refine and reformulate our definition of conflict in a Jamaa group.

A Jamaa, such as the group at Musonoi, is an association of followers of a prophetic message. For any given individual member this implies acceptance of a system of ideas and beliefs, both as orientation of, and norm for, action. The fact that this system is shared by a multitude of individuals and depends for its maintenance on frequent interaction results in the formation of a group. Any group based on voluntary association is likely to stress its outer limits as well as certain patterns of internal differentiation (leadership). These are commonplaces of small-group sociology. But leadership roles are defined in different ways according to the *content* of the shared system of beliefs and values, and this is where the Jamaa reveals some highly interesting features.

Relationships within the group are defined as relationships of *kizazi*, of (spiritual) generation/filiation. Such a genealogical model implies that every participant in the system has his position ascribed. On the other hand, *kizazi* in the Jamaa is not a network of actual biological generation. It is built around the central value of *uzazi*, fecundity, realized through spiritual *ubaba* and *umama*, i.e., transmission of doctrine through initiation. As defined in Jamaa teaching, *uzazi* is a "transcendental" value, an idea that must be "realized" but cannot be "possessed." On the other hand, fecundity, especially when linked with the notion of prestige and authority,[29] can easily be interpreted as a quality which can be maximized. The more "children" a Jamaa member "generates," the more he realizes and "has" *uzazi*. Thus, the kinship model of social relationships and the dominant value of spiritual *uzazi* can act as intrinsically opposed principles of action. This is very likely to generate conflict in any Jamaa group. The fate of a group, and of the charismatic movement as a whole, will depend on which of the possible solutions of this dilemma is adopted by a majority of the members. However, the development at Musonoi shows that the Jamaa has an astonishing ability to survive conflict and schism: *kizazi* seems to control *uzazi*.

POWER VS. MESSAGE

Finally, I should like to point to another inherent source of conflict in the Jamaa, less obvious than those we have dealt with but hardly less important. My informant, I. Kapongo, once quoted Tempels when we talked about the problems of leadership: *umfumu inaua mafundisho*—power, leadership, kills the doctrine. He insisted on this formula, even though I suggested that *umfumu* is more likely to kill *mapendo,* love, than doctrine. He had indeed touched upon a very profound connection: power and meaning are, if not mutually exclusive, two different domains of human activity. Especially in a prophetic-charismatic situation, their different exigencies may lead to conflict and tension. Jamaa doctrine, as far as it represents Tempels' message, is concerned with meaning, with providing the people who live in the industrial centers of Katanga with a way of seeing and understanding the world. Its ability to attract and convince people must in some way be due to the fact that it defines and solves their real problems. Hence it will continue to attract followers as long as it manages to provide a valuable solution of those problems. This implies, above all, an ability to change and to adapt to changes in the sociocultural environment. But this vital function will be seriously endangered as soon as *mafundisho* becomes a means of maximization of *umfumu*. In the

29. In the traditional context, the authority of the chief (the *mulopwe* among the Luba) is commonly phrased in terms of fecundity and filiation; cf. Theuws 1962:141.

development of Jamaa doctrine at Kolwezi there is much to suggest that routinization of charisma in Weber's sense—its conversion into traditional or bureaucratic authority by the laws of rational (i.e., economic) behavior—is not the only alternative. A process of "sealing off" the charismatic message from changing reality, as it were, by using it as a means of access to power over a group of followers may be equally important.[30]

THE URBAN JAMAA IN KATANGA AND KINSHASA

In both my field work and this presentation, the Jamaa group at Musonoi served as a paradigmatic case. Methodologically this implies that the Musonoi group should be typical enough to allow a study of all the significant elements in the formulation and acceptance of Tempels' message. That this was indeed so had to be verified by comparison with other groups in Katanga. The results justified the choice of Musonoi. The data in this and in the following section were selected from field notes, documents, and recorded interviews, not to provide a group-by-group comparison of history, membership, and activities, but rather to illustrate, in a series of short essays, the degree of diversity in the movement.[31]

Dogmatism at C.E.C. Kolwezi

In the Kolwezi area the only Jamaa which does not operate in a camp is the group in the *centre extra-coutumier* (C.E.C.). In our brief survey of settlements in this urban complex we defined the C.E.C. as the "free" city. Historically, of course, the idea of freedom was not the motive for the creation of this settlement type. Rather,

30. This puts the phenomenon of charisma into the context of current discussions about the prostitution of "culture" (read: academe) in the service of political and economic power (cf. Marcuse 1965).

31. My contacts with urban groups in Katanga and Kinshasa were limited to frequent but usually short visits. I had to concentrate on information from leaders and prominent members of these groups. This may result in a certain bias in the following presentation. It is possible that the attitudes that struck me as characteristic are those of the leaders I interviewed and not of the majority of the members. Still, they represent tendencies and trends in the Jamaa, and this is what I try to demonstrate in this section.

it reflects the efforts of the colonial administration to control the influx of population into the large industrial centers.[32]

In external appearance the C.E.C. is different from the camp, and one is tempted to conclude that it represents a different world. But countless "bars" and small stores, individual planning and decoration of houses, free access at any time of the day or the night—all this cannot conceal the fact that the realities of the Kolwezi area are as effective in the C.E.C. as in the other settlements. The C.E.C., as well as the core city and the camps, owes its existence to the Union Minière, which in some way or other controls almost all economic activities. In 1966–67 even the public mail was transported by the company.

Joseph Tshibangu seems to have brought the Jamaa to the C.E.C. in Kolwezi. Later he was assisted by Sylvain Mutombo and Mathieu Binga, two members of the *baba saba*. In 1966–67 all of them had left, and the group was led by Monica Kabole and Fortunat Kitenge. *"Mama* Monica," as she is called, has emerged as one of the most respected and influential personalities in the movement. She is by far the best "speaker" I met. Her *mafundisho* are classic in their fidelity to Tempels' message, but at the same time they are a testimony to her own intelligence and profound mind. Fortunat Kitenge, owner of a small grocery store, is the "political" leader of the group, the ambitious and authoritarian counterpart to *mama* Monica's charismatic authority.

Preoccupation with "doctrine," in both its positive and negative aspects, was what struck me as the common element in my observations of this group. The weekly *mafundisho* took place in three adjoining private houses, separately for the candidates of the three degrees of initiation. When I tried to establish my first contact with the group (in August, 1966, after six months at Musonoi), I was invited to attend the instruction for the first-degree candidates in *mama* Monica's house. The *mafundisho* was given by another member in a manner very reminiscent of the schoolroom, with

32. Actually, in planning and conception, the C.E.C. was a close relative of the camp. In any case, its reputation for being under less control than the Union Minière settlements was very convenient for the company; the C.E.C. could serve as an outlet for the private initiative of some of its most valuable employees, who received permission to build their own houses outside the camp. This permission is explicit company policy; see *Union Minière du Haut Katanga 1906–1956*:246, and the case of Daniel Mwangayi, cited above.

frequent references to "chapters" treated in previous sessions, repetition of important formulae, and summaries. Then one of the points was taken up by *mama* Monica and proposed for discussion. She then answered questions from the audience of some thirty or forty people and concluded the meeting with an improvised prayer, in which she summarized the main points of the *mafundisho*.

Several months later, after I had attended two or three of these meetings, I asked Monica Kabole whether she would be willing to discuss with me some major topics of Jamaa doctrine (which I intended to record on tape). She was not very enthusiastic but told me to come back later in the afternoon. When I arrived, I found not only *mama* Monica and her husband but also Fortunat Kitenge and another prominent member of the group. Then followed a most astonishing reversal of roles. Fortunat, after a short prayer, started by stating flatly that any communication between us would be impossible unless we first came to *kupatana* (had an encounter). This was followed by an examination of my intentions, my views about the Jamaa, the objectives of my work, and so forth. Fortunat ended the meeting with a lengthy speech in which he determined the conditions for further communications. In his somewhat confused way he dwelt on two basic errors in my approach. First, Jamaa teaching cannot be written down and must not be recorded. Jamaa is not a matter of doctrine and books. It calls for a change in one's life and can only be "learned" by practicing the *mafundisho*. Second, I was wrong in going to Musonoi and other places to find out about the Jamaa before I turned to the group in the C.E.C., because this was where the Jamaa first arrived from Ruwe. From now on, all my observations and findings should be subject to their (his and *mama* Monica's) approval.

This was the beginning of a series of ten sessions of intensive indoctrination, which put rather a strain on my professional patience, since I could have recited most of the "chapters" myself. Particularly annoying were long consultations between Monica Kabole and Fortunat Kitenge in Tshiluba, their native language, before or during the *mafundisho*—something I encountered nowhere else. The few conversations with *mama* Monica alone, however, were highly rewarding and represent some of the best information I was able to get.

The attitude I called "dogmatism" may well reflect an increased need of self-assertion in a group which does not enjoy the relative security of the camp. More likely it has developed as a response to the attitude of the local pastor. His authoritarian rule and lack of comprehension of the prophetic-charismatic character of the movement must have contributed a great deal to the defensive and intransigent reactions I found in this group. A side effect of this may be increased unity within the group. As far as I could observe, the Jamaa in the C.E.C. at Kolwezi is one of the few that are unaffected by open dissent and schism.

Pluralism at Lubumbashi

Open and diverse—this is the impression one gets of the Jamaa of Lubumbashi. My contacts were limited to two parishes: one in the Commune Albert (one of the wards of the former C.E.C.), the other at the camp of the B.C.K., a workers' settlement of the railway company and in every respect a copy of the Union Minière camps. In both groups a very influential leader cooperates with the local pastor, who is an initiated member of the movement.

Father D., the Benedictine missionary in the Commune Albert, is perhaps the most influential Jamaa leader in the clergy since Tempels left the Congo. He and his *baba* through initiation, Marcel Ndala, have made Lubumbashi a center of the movement which is certain to surpass Kolwezi in numerical importance as well as in influence on groups in other areas. Both are concerned with keeping Jamaa doctrine alive and open for further development. He is probably the initiator of a theme and leitmotif in the *mafundisho* at Lubumbashi which I did not hear at Kolwezi: the idea that the essence of *umuntu* (being man) and *ukristiani* (being Christian) is *kutafuta,* search for the truth, for fulfillment. Contrary to the spirit of *kutafuta* is everything that smacks of routine, ritualism, and pharisaical pretentiousness.

"Drive," initiative, and search for new avenues for the Jamaa characterize Marcel Ndala.[33] He is a tall, imposing "Luba-Kasai," at once self-assured and a very polite listener. We met several times; our first and our last encounters were particularly interesting, and I shall describe both briefly, for the sake of some valuable ethno-

---

33. Marcel Ndala is the informant "M." in my "Dreams and Charisma"; cf. there a brief characterization and the text of an interview with him (Fabian 1966:546–51).

graphic background they add to our description of leadership, its tensions and trends, at Musonoi.

Our first meeting took place at the residence of the Jesuits, rue Wangermee, in the "white" city. M. Ndala arrived in his own Volkswagen. Noticing that my Swahili was still somewhat shaky, he insisted on conducting most of our conversation in French, which he spoke quite well. I began by asking him about his beginnings in the Kolwezi area, where he had been an employee of the Union Minière. As a machinery operator and mechanic, he had lived at several camps, where he first heard about the Jamaa "sometime between December, 1950, and the year 1953." Accounts from people at Kolwezi confirm his claim to have been one of the first, and certainly one of the most influential, propagators of the Jamaa outside the *baba saba* (the seven founders). From the Union Minière he transferred to a company charged with the electrification of the railroad in south Katanga. This entailed relatively brief stays in many places, and wherever he was stationed he founded a group of the Jamaa. Today his "children" live in almost all major towns of Katanga and Kasai, and there are some even in Kinshasa. Many stay in contact with him through mail and frequent visits. Taking care of his correspondence and talking to his visitors takes all of his free time.

We discussed developments in the Jamaa, above all the chances for the future. On the whole, M. Ndala was optimistic. The Jamaa would continue to spread, not only geographically and numerically but also in terms of new tasks and objectives. "We are like soldiers," he said; "soldiers work everywhere for the nation." The Jamaa should try to influence people who hold key positions in the society, not in order to gain a position of power but to propagate the idea. As an example he pointed to a high official in the Sûreté (Criminal Investigation Agency) who had become a member of the Jamaa. He also talked of himself. As *chef de section* in the city's department of public works he has many opportunities to put Jamaa principles into action. Proudly he pointed out that he had started among his workers a movement for *uhaki* (justice, integrity) at work and as a result had almost completely eliminated theft of tools and material. Various Catholic groups invite him to lecture on Jamaa ideas, and this gives him another opportunity to promote the movement. M. Ndala had thought about the further development of the movement. In order to make it more attractive to people of all social strata, he told me, it was necessary to concentrate on the essentials, to curb excessive meetings and ritualistic tendencies. He compared his ideas and policies with the "backward" attitudes of the leaders in the Kolwezi area. In his opinion, the Jamaa there was going to lose influence; people attached too much importance to questions of doctrine and dogma, to external forms and practices, and were therefore unable to win new members among the progressive younger generation and the "intellectuals."

I must confess that, having known Jamaa leaders at Kolwezi, I was deeply impressed by M. Ndala, one of Tempels' earliest followers, who had been initiated by Tempels himself and had remained a fervent believer in his message; at the same time, he represented the type who is professionally successful, modern, and farsighted in his policies—a rather rare combination among leading Jamaa members. No one, with the exception, perhaps, of T. Maweja, seemed to have more potential for the transformation of the Jamaa from an enthusiastic and largely otherworldly group to a factor in the development of the Congo.

My last meeting with M. Ndala took place in February, 1967, this time at his own house in the Congolese city. Before I entered, I noticed that his Volkswagen had not been used for some time; all four tires were deflated—which was symbolic of the mood in which I found *baba* Marcel. He was resting on his bed. He had been treated for an ulcer and had returned from the hospital only a few days earlier. This time our conversation was in Swahili; we were no longer strangers to each other. Again we talked about the movement, its significance for the present and the future. To my great surprise, he seemed completely changed—very depressed and pessimistic. The gist of his remarks was that most of the so-called Jamaa people do not understand that only one thing counts: to have Christ in the heart. The rest is accidental and not really important. But most look for some secret knowledge in the Jamaa. They are eager to climb the ladder of initiation. Once they have reached the third stage, they do not know where to go from there. Many lose interest; others try to go on, try to *kupita u-kristiani,* transcend, surpass Christianity. This is what the dissident group at Musonoi tries, and I should not be surprised to find the same here at Lubumbashi. Who can tell where the Jamaa will end?

The case of Marcel Ndala demonstrates the tensions and conflicts that "progressive" Jamaa leaders are going to face. His determination to go ahead, to keep the movement open and attractive for a rising elite, to develop the essential idea, and to de-emphasize ritual implies that he has left the firm ground of complete identification with present Jamaa ideology in its standardized and semi-institutionalized form. As we have seen, a "ritual"—initiation—creates through the network of spiritual kinship the organizational matrix for the Jamaa. To a great extent, it is his position in this network that gives a leader his authority. Men like M. Ndala who—at least in certain situations and during certain periods—transcend the system of *kizazi* and see its virtues and flaws are faced with problems very similar to those which trouble the leaders of new nations: the choice between the comfort to be found in cultural traditions and the uncomfortable demands of "modernity" and change. Unlike the vociferous leaders at Musonoi who compete *within* a system which they do not question or challenge, M. Ndala appears as a lonely man, capable, perhaps, of saving the Jamaa from becoming an esoteric sect, but always close to resignation and despair.

An important factor which favors "pluralism" at Lubumbashi is a marked diversity in the attitudes and policies of the clergy. In Kolwezi, all parishes with the exception of the one at Ruwe are administered by members of the same religious order, most of whom have been in the area for many years and have, at one time or another, worked with Tempels. This is not the case at Lubumbashi. There the missionaries belong to a number of different orders, and some are secular priests from a Belgian diocese. They vary in age and cultural background (Flemish, Walloon, Spanish). Some have accepted Tempels' ideas with great enthusiasm, but others remain distrustful; only one, Father D., has the authority to unite, at least to some degree, the various tendencies and groups. But the Jamaa of Lubumbashi has no forum, comparable to the *pulan* meeting at Kolwezi, that could serve for discussing controversial issues and relieving tension.

Strangers at Kinshasa

I had the opportunity to study the Jamaa in the capital of the Congo during two visits of three weeks each in January, 1966, and March, 1967.

The precipitation of events that led to Congolese independence started in Kinshasa. Ever since, the city has been the center of "politics," as people in Katanga, both white and black, point out with contempt. In Katanga, the exigencies of industrial operations called for a continuity of the patterns set under colonial rule. Copper production, as the most important source of income for the new nation—and the old trusts—had to go on, even though this meant a considerable delay of "independence" for the Congolese in Katanga.

The breakdown of continuity in the capital was felt rather sharply in the mission church. If we are to believe the reports of those who have witnessed developments since 1960, the end of colonial rule brought the mission to the edge of catastrophe. In this situation, in which Christianity was in danger of being discarded as the white man's religion, the emergence of a genuinely "African" movement, such as the Jamaa in Katanga and in the Kasai, was greeted with great enthusiasm. Two Congolese priests, Fathers F. Edzu and J. Mambu, visited Jamaa groups in Katanga. As a result, several Jamaa families were literally imported to Kinshasa in the hope that they would become the core of a similar Africanization of Christianity. This was in 1961. In 1966–67 the movement had spread to at least six parishes, but it was estimated that less than a hundred couples were regular members.

One of the imported Jamaa people, Louis Ramasani, emerged as the most influential leader. He had the official support of the Congolese archbishop and of the clergy, but it was my impression that the situation in Kinshasa had become rather confused. Other Jamaa members from Katanga and Kasai arrived later (most of them as government employees) and apparently started their own groups, with or without the support of the church; some of them undoubtedly represented a "heterodox" faction. On the whole, the clergy who had not witnessed the origin of the Jamaa as a charismatic movement thought of it as just another pious organization; some pastors who had no Jamaa in their parishes were openly glad to have nothing to do with this uncomfortably independent group. At the time of my last visit, three of the most active supporters of the Jamaa—the two Congolese priests mentioned above and Father F. de Waele, author of a compendium of Jamaa teaching at Kinshasa—had left the city. A further disintegration of the movement seemed imminent.

Louis Ramasani, born in the Albertville region, was a teacher at a public elementary school at Lubumbashi before he came to Kinshasa. He now teaches religion at a high school. In our conversations he impressed me as an intelligent and open-minded man. Like M. Ndala, he pleaded for "flexible" *mafundisho,* adapted to the intellectual and social standing of the candidates. He also advocated Jamaa influence in politics and administration. At the same time, he had kept intact the original Jamaa teachings. His pronouncements about the necessity of initiation and spiritual generation seemed strangely rigid and much closer to the attitudes of the leaders at Musonoi.

In Kinshasa the language used in the weekly *mafundisho* is Lingala, a principle adopted from the very beginning. But the ethnic composition of the groups is hardly different from those at Lubumbashi or Kolwezi; the members are chiefly from Katanga and Kasai. Most observers, and L. Ramasani himself, think that one reason for the stagnation of the movement in the capital is its image as a group of strangers and troublemakers. Certainly this is the most obvious way in which the problem presents itself. But in one conversation L. Ramasani showed awareness of an inherent difficulty in the propagation of Jamaa doctrine beyond a relatively homogeneous social and cultural environment. He told me of his efforts to learn not only the languages (Lingala and Kikongo) but also the proverbs and customs of the region, because Jamaa doctrine must be taught as a continuation of the old customs. When I objected that this might have the undesirable effect of reinforcing "tribalism," he disagreed:

You did not understand. This has nothing to do with tribalism. It is just an attempt to grasp their aspirations [*faida*]. Is this not the way *baba* Placide did it? In order to impregnate the heart of people with his teaching, he himself had first to learn about their customs; he had to learn the mentality and the conceptions of the black people. When he did this, he was not trying to promote tribalism. On the contrary, he wanted to give them something of value which would end their tribalism; and this is what we try to do when we learn about all those customs, groups, and tribes. We want to impregnate their hearts with love for God so that they will be able to end tribalism among each other. I believe, once they understand this, it will be the end of tribalism [T 39].

These are classic Jamaa formulae—a direct continuation of Tempels' efforts in *Bantu Philosophy*. Why is it that, in Kinshasa, they attract only few followers beyond the small circle of those who regard the Jamaa as something from "back home" in Katanga and the Kasai? L. Ramasani came up with still another reason: it is not the ideas that the people at Kinshasa reject; what they fear is the consequences. The Jamaa members in Katanga are hard-working people who live in the protected but dull environment of the camp. Here everyone is after *furaha,* the distractions of the big city. No one has time to think, or get worried, about the meaning of human existence and the Christian faith, and all are afraid of the moral obligations that a conversion to the Jamaa would impose on them.

This probably comes very close to a sufficient explanation. Tempels' message is not accepted in the capital because it is not experienced as a liberating solution to the problems of daily life. To express this in terms of Adolphe Lubala's axiom, quoted at the outset of this chapter: the Union Minière is like the Jamaa; Kinshasa is not.

THE RURAL JAMAA IN WEST
AND CENTRAL KATANGA

In addition to the groups in the urban-industrial centers that we have so far been discussing, I also came in contact with, or received substantial information about, the Jamaa in more than forty places in Katanga and south Kasai. These, for lack of a better label, I have lumped together as "rural Jamaa." Actually they comprise the whole range of settlement types between the typical small village in the bush and the administrative and commercial district town. But all have certain traits in common which distinguish them from the social and cultural environment of the industrial region in which the movement originated:

1. The population from which the rural Jamaa recruits its members is culturally homogeneous and lives within the country of origin.

2. Economic activities usually are limited to agriculture (largely on a subsistence level), the crafts, and small commerce. The typical white-collar employee is the schoolteacher and the *commis* (clerk).

3. The area in which the rural Jamaa spreads is marked by regionalism in terms of cultural and political orientation. In many cases, traditional chiefs have reoccupied the power vacuum created by the termination of Belgian colonial rule. Some of them organize their own system of taxation and take charge of public works and welfare (roads, schools, medical care).

To characterize the Jamaa in this rural environment, I chose two areas in west and central Katanga. But before discussing them, I should like to mention briefly a number of groups which do not fit into either category, urban or rural.

These Jamaa groups are located in small towns along the railway between Kolwezi and the Angolan border—towns such as Mutshatsha, Kasaji, and Dilolo. The latter two, especially, are interesting for a sort of dual Jamaa stemming from the fact that these towns consist of two separate and quite different settlements. On the railroad itself there are small camps for the workers of the railway company, along with a commercial and a residential section for the European personnel, in which, again, a number of Congolese are employed. A substantial number, if not the majority, of the workers at the railway posts are strangers to the region. At some distance from the railroad there is a second settlement, the core of which is the Catholic mission with its schools and perhaps a small hospital. The population attracted by the mission comes from the surrounding country; the settlement is essentially a large village arranged in the traditional pattern, although some employees of the mission may be housed "Union Minière style." The chapels at the railway posts are considered mere outposts of the main mission. The Jamaa, however, is organized into two groups, one at the mission and the other on the railroad, and there is surprisingly little contact between them. The most obvious explanation for this seems to be the cultural and social differences between the two settlements. In the mission groups at Kasaji and Dilolo the language of the *mafundisho* is Tshokwe; in the railway camps at Kasaji and Dilolo the intertribal composition of the groups makes it necessary to use Swahili. But there is another distinction which is probably more important. In terms of *kizazi,* spiritual kinship, the groups at the railway stations are oriented toward Kolwezi or even Lubumbashi (more than five hundred miles to the east). Workers of the railway company come predominantly from the Kasai; they are often transferred or make use of their traveling privileges, so that frequent contact with the urban-industrial centers is assured. The groups at the missions are linked to the Jamaa in the interior—in this case to the Sandoa region.

There are two other groups which cannot simply be classified as "rural." Both operate in workers' camps attached to the tin mine at Kisenge and the coal mine of Luena. Both are at a considerable distance from the copper belt in south Katanga. In their setup, however, they are miniature editions, so to speak, of the Kolwezi area. Luena, for instance, consists of a camp for the miners, a white residential section (housing thirteen families), a commercial section, the mission, a hospital, and a *cité,* the Congolese section. The industrial operations are relatively small, which permits recruitment of workers from the surrounding country. The population in these camps is therefore more homogeneous than the population in the Kolwezi area.

After this very brief survey of some atypical groups outside the Katanga copper belt, we may now consider the Jamaa in two regions in which the traditional ways of rural life still prevail.

The Jamaa in the Heart of the Lunda Empire

Sandoa gained importance under Belgian rule as a district town (*chef-lieu du territoire*). It also has been the home base for the commercial operations of the Tshombe family. It is a pleasant small town overlooking the papyrus marshes of the Lulua Valley, about ninety miles north of Dilolo and half as far east of the Angolan border. Communication with Sandoa by road has become rather difficult, but through a small airport the city is in fairly regular connection with Kolwezi and Lubumbashi. Both the Catholic and the Methodist missions (at Majinga, a few miles to the south) run school systems and social programs which contribute to the importance of Sandoa for this part of Katanga. Culturally and in terms of traditional politics the region belongs to the "Lunda-Tshokwe empire"—a rather vague concept, incapable of adequately covering the extremely complex mesh of semi-independent political entities. It is enough to emphasize that Jamaa members in this region are typically bilingual and are often so "bicultural" that a distinction of Lunda *vs.* Tshokwe (*vs.* Ndembo) groups in the movement is impossible and unnecessary.

I must admit that it was frustrating not to be able to do "classical" ethnography in this area; both Lunda and Tshokwe culture await thorough anthropological investigation. Yet my story did not begin with Mwant Yav, emperor of the Lunda, but with Pierre Mwamba, a truck driver in the mine of Musonoi, and his wife, Therese Kapanga, who figured earlier in this book as prominent members of the Jamaa in Kolwezi. Both are Tshokwe from a village near Sandoa. Soon after they were initiated, they began to propagate the movement in this region, probably on one of their visits to the "village back home," as the workers in the camps say. Their most influential "child" (who could be their father in terms of age) became Nicodeme Kapenda. He also claims to have had instruction from *baba* Placide on one of his visits to Pierre and Therese at Musonoi. We may assume, then, that the Jamaa in the Sandoa region goes back to 1960–61.

Nicodeme Kapenda,[34] his wife Bernadette, and an old widow, Marie Tshisweka, are the leaders of the group at the mission post in Sandoa. Nicodeme was born "in 1909." With his father, one of the early recruits of the Union Minière, he moved to Elisabethville; there he worked as a houseboy until 1924. After his return to Sandoa he attended the mission school and later became a teacher there. At that time (around 1935) classes were taught in the local language or in Swahili; Nicodeme does not speak French. His age, his education, and the fact that he has been a practicing Christian most of his life make him a typical representative of his group—*jamaa ya wazee,* the "old-folks Jamaa" of Sandoa, as they are called by others. In my conversations with him at Musonoi and during my visit to Sandoa, Nicodeme Kapenda showed a somewhat naïve eagerness to prove that his Jamaa was a "real" Jamaa like the famous groups founded by the *baba saba.* Initiation, *mafundisho,* and the external form of the meetings were more important to him than *kutafuta,* search, and *kupatana,* encounter, ideas which preoccupy the leaders of urban groups. Much more than they, he had remained in his thinking under the influence of a very vital traditional culture, despite the fact that he had been exposed to Christianity for many years and had internalized its doctrine

34. N. Kapenda is the informant "N." in the paper "Dreams and Charisma" (Fabian 1966:546, 551–54).

to such a degree that the Jamaa ritual had made it possible for him to combine elements of the new religion and the old world view.[35]

More profound in his grasp of Tempel's message was Cyprien Yava, a retired schoolteacher living in a village near Sandoa. He had been introduced by a member of the group at Kisenge; in 1962 he was initiated into the third degree by Tempels at Musonoi.

Both N. Kapenda and C. Yava owe their authority as Jamaa leaders to the fact that they became heads of spiritual lineages. Both have founded, or are preparing the foundation for, groups in the surrounding country. Interestingly enough, they solved the problem of competition by dividing the territory: Nicodeme teaches groups to the north and east, Cyprien and his "children" to the west and south.

In Cyprien Yava's territory I visited two Jamaa groups, which I chose for a brief presentation since they are probably more interesting than Nicodeme's pious, elderly people at Sandoa.

Muteba, a large and well-kept village some twenty-five miles northwest of Sandoa, is the residence of a Lunda chief. Before entering the village proper, one passes a group of twenty-five or thirty exceptionally well-built adobe houses. This is the Jamaa village. The idea of practicing and demonstrating unity through communal living is neither unique nor new; not far from Kolwezi a village consisting entirely of followers of the Bapostolo movement was built during the time of my field work. But to my knowledge the group at Muteba is the only Jamaa group in Katanga which has realized this ideal. Undoubtedly the project was facilitated by the fact that practically all members of the group are elementary schoolteachers at the village school. I had the opportunity to discuss this Jamaa colony at length with Chief Paul Muteba. His main interest, he pointed out to me, is the development of his territory. The Jamaa village is a model of progress for his other subjects; this is why he gives the movement his support. Occasionally, when C. Yava visits, he even attends the *mafundisho* meeting,

35. This does not mean that his Jamaa was any more "syncretist" than other groups. From all available evidence, Nicodeme adhered in his teachings to standardized doctrine. But, while his answers were the same as those of urban leaders, his problems were determined by a living traditional culture. This appeared in his attitudes toward dreaming (cf. Fabian 1966), sorcery, and authority.

though the ritual obligations of his office make it impossible for him to practice Christianity, which was his religion before he succeeded his father. Chief Muteba is not concerned with the particulars of Jamaa ideology. His atitude toward the movement is sympathetic because he can count on the loyalty and cooperation of the Jamaa people. They in turn are proud of his support and use the prestige it confers on them to propagate Jamaa ideas.

A few miles west of Sandoa lies the residence and village of Samutoma, who claims the proud but somewhat incongruous title "Emperor of the Tshokwe." Originally he came to this region from Angola as the leader of a band of refugees from Portuguese rule. He was accepted as chief by the local Tshokwe and in the thirties was confirmed as "emperor" by the colonial administration in a move to counterbalance the influence of the Lunda paramount chief. Emmanuel Sukari, again a schoolteacher, is leader of a small but active Jamaa group at Samutoma village. When I visited him, he proudly pointed out the influence of his group, which counted among its sympathizers one of the wives of Samutoma and her daughter. She attended the *mafundisho* meetings and was planning to get separated from her husband in order to become a full member of the movement. Actually this turned out to be quite dangerous for the group. Samutoma, who had learned of his wife's inclinations, began to obstruct Jamaa activities wherever he could. A few days before I left the Congo, I received reports indicating that he had succeeded. In May, 1967, he had summoned the diviners of his court and had ordered them to cast a spell on the Jamaa. Emmanuel Sukari and several of his followers immediately fled from the village. Whether they believed in the effectiveness of the magic or not, they certainly had reason to fear for their lives.

Some 150 miles north of Sandoa lies Kapanga, in its setup and function very similar to Sandoa and perhaps surpassing it in cultural and political prestige. At Musumba, the royal kraal outside the city, the Mwant Yav has his residence. The mission, one of the oldest in the diocese, had to be ceded to another order when the Belgian Franciscans could no longer supply it with personnel. As a result, and because of the distance and poor road conditions, communication with the urban-industrial centers to the southeast is reduced to a minimum. The main mission at Kapanga has been visited by N. Kapenda from Sandoa, but so far no Jamaa group has been formed. However, there are at least two or three groups in village outposts to the north. According to the information I was given by the missionary in charge of this region, the movement was introduced from the mission at Tubeya, an important rural center in southern Kasai. Apparently there are no links whatsoever between these groups and those of the Sandoa region to the south—a highly interesting division, which is all the more puzzling since it cuts through one and the same cultural, economic, and political interaction sphere.

Baluba Fishermen at Kikondja

Roughly 150 miles northeast of Kolwezi, between the Lualaba River and the railway connecting Lubumbashi and Kamina, lies Bukama, a small district town. North of Bukama the Lualaba runs through a wide depression filled with crocodile-infested marshes and a chain of lakes abounding in fish. The savanna on the right bank of the valley was chosen by the Belgians as a game reserve (Parc National de l'Upemba). The ecological conditions of this region resulted in a special adaptation and, as the ethnographers assure us, a subculture which distinguished the riverine Baluba from their tribesmen to the east.[36]

Kikondja on Lake Kisale is a village typical of the region. The abundance of fish supports a surprisingly large population of some 15,000, according to the estimates in 1966–67; it is one of the largest nonurban settlements in Katanga. Kikondja is the residence of the *mulopwe* Kikondja, one of the most important Luba chiefs in the empire of Kasongo Nyembo. A Protestant and a Catholic mission maintain schools and dispensaries, and the government has even placed a police detachment in the village. Kikondja is one of the few rural regions which, once they had recovered from the short but ravaging war between anti-Tshombe Balubakat and the mercenaries and gendarmes of the secessionist movement, saw a modest postindependence prosperity. Under the auspices of the chief, who organizes the local fishing industry and tries to maintain viable roads for transportation, the products of Kikondja (dried, smoked, and salted fish) are sold in the markets of Kolwezi, Jadotville, and Lubumbashi. The incoming money can be

---

36. Cf. Baumann and Westermann 1948:171. In the camps they are called *Baluba ya mayi,* water-Baluba.

spent at a number of general stores owned by Greek merchants. Manioc, the staple food, which does not grow on the poor soil of the littoral, is obtained from villages in the interior.

While their tribesmen fought Tshombe in the north, the large number of Baluba-Katanga in the urban centers of the south became a possible threat to the regime. Many of them "disappeared"; the majority were imprisoned, in incredible conditions, in a huge concentration camp near Lubumbashi, from which some escaped. Among those who managed to return to their native villages were Jamaa people from Bukama, Kikondja, and Malemba-Nkulu (a district town north of Kikondja). The missionaries had left Kikondja in September, 1960. When they returned, they found all the buildings untouched; the chief had placed them under his personal protection. They also found a full-grown Jamaa at both Kikondja and Kalombo, a similar village fifteen miles to the southeast on Lake Lunda. Two *wakubwa*, big men, were competing for leadership: Symphorien Banza, a teacher from Malemba-Nkulu, and a certain Jourdain, who had joined the movement in the Kolwezi area. Father Modest, a veteran who had started his missionary career in 1929 on Lake Moero, had enough authority to make Jourdain leave the region. Since then the group at Kikondja has been led by Barthelemy Ngoi, a fisherman, and three other prominent members, two teachers and a clerk.

I visited the Jamaa of Kikondja in November, 1966. Despite certain difficulties in communication (the leader, B. Ngoi, speaks neither French nor Swahili), the results, especially concerning links between Jamaa doctrine and traditional models, were highly interesting. From the description of the economic situation given above, one might conclude that the cultural and social environment at Kikondja had remained stable and well integrated, but the external image of well-being and prosperity is deceptive. The return of great numbers of people from the urban centers in the years after independence has been a constant threat to traditional homogeneity. Before 1960 only the Catholic and Protestant missions had followers at Kikondja. In 1966–67 more than ten different denominations, sects, and movements were represented, not counting revived traditional and semitraditional "secret societies." Apparently this has been fertile ground for the Jamaa. According to the missionary, Jamaa people of Kikondja had been "ordinary" Christians before their conversion to the movement. The events and

troubles of 1960–62, however, had interrupted their placid association with the white man's religion; for several years they were left
alone. This is probably where Jamaa ideology came in and made
it possible for them to accept and live values of their traditional
culture, which had gained new prestige, without giving up their
Christian identity.

In terms of spread and regional alliance, the Jamaa of Kikondja
resembles the groups in the Sandoa region. Close links are maintained with Malemba-Nkulu; Symphorien Banza still is considered head of the spiritual lineage to which the group traces its
origin. Actual contacts through visits, however, are not frequent.
Shortly before my stay, S. Banza had seen his "children" for the
first time in a year. Kikondja itself has become a center of the
movement, since B. Ngoi and other prominent members have
founded groups in the villages nearby. Connection with groups and
leaders at Lubumbashi and the other centers is slight, despite the
fact that the fish trade assures fairly regular communication with
those cities. During my visit I was able to observe and interview
a certain *baba* Denis, a fish trader from Lubumbashi on a business
trip to his native Kikondja. Since he talked Swahili better than
most of the others, he assumed the role of representing the group
for me. Apparently he had the reputation of being a rather important member of the movement. When I questioned him about
the Jamaa at Lubumbashi, he seemed to know surprisingly little
about groups and leaders. I strongly suspect him to be "Jamaa"
only in his native village.[37]

PATTERNS OF GROUP-TRANSCENDING INTEGRATION

Tempels constantly maintains that Jamaa, if not entirely a personal affair, is restricted to local groups, to an encounter between
the priest and his parishioners, as he puts it. In line with this conception, I therefore limited myself, in the early part of this study,
to a more or less thorough description of local groups. The question

---

37. This, by the way, seems to be for many "migrants" a favorite way of
gaining prestige (and material support!) from the local Jamaa and the mission.
In one extreme case, a worker from Musonoi who had observed the Jamaa
in the camp but had never been a member returned to the village and started
to give improvised *mafundisho*.

now arises: Is Tempels right when he thinks that Jamaa is essentially the unpredictable and uncontrollable coalescence of a message and the ideas and aspirations of searching people? Is he right in believing that the formation of a Jamaa group is always a unique event, independent of preceding conditions, irrelevant for further development?

It must be admitted that any charismatic movement is likely to meet his claims *by definition.* The fact that it is new, that it lacks overt and differentiated patterns of organization, that it is *wirtschaftsfremd* (according to Weber it is a characteristic attribute of true charisma not to be oriented toward rational-economic goals)—all this makes it extremely difficult to grasp the reality it nevertheless represents. Action that is not institutionalized in a sense does not exist for the social scientist. To the degree that movements are incipient institutions they have always been a *crux sociologorum,* especially for those who tend to underestimate the orientational aspect of action.

Integration and Spheres of Interaction

On the other hand, "lack of institutionalization" is meaningful as a concept only in a relative, approximate sense. To be perceived, a social object must have shape of some kind. The question is, then, whether and to what extent we can conceive of the Jamaa as an institutionalized, i.e., organized, entity. At the outset it must be emphasized that, despite some attempts in that direction, Jamaa doctrine does not foresee any explicit organizational structures, either on the level of the group or for the movement as a whole. In the Congo, which inherited from the former rulers their preoccupation with associations, committees, hierarchies, and titles and which is known, especially in the context of the Catholic mission, for a proliferation of "movements" and pious societies, this is a remarkable exception. Or so it seems, because, *contrary to the prophet's claims,* there are organizational links between the followers. Let us recapitulate the evidence:

1. Our analysis of the Jamaa at Musonoi has demonstrated beyond any doubt that the "prophetic event," the conversion to Jamaa ideas, results in the formation of a group of followers—a *group* of people who interact regularly according to group-specific norms, not just a category of people who share some diffuse social

attribute (such as being smokers, football fans, or even "Catholics"). A Jamaa group has observable outer limits (membership, activities) and internal structures marked by a differentiation of roles and statuses (leaders *vs.* followers, priest *vs.* lay leaders, etc.). Definition of these roles and statuses is derived from the crucial principle of Jamaa doctrine: *umuntu,* the essence of being man, is *uzazi,* fecundity. Consequently, human relationships are phrased in terms of achieving and transmitting fecundity, i.e., in terms of generation/filiation (*kizazi*).

2. Groups more or less identical in their setup and activities with the paradigmatic case at Musonoi operate within a large geographic area, in varying social and cultural environments. Historically, all these groups are linked together by a common source of ideology, the Jamaa doctrine developed by Tempels and his first group at Ruwe. Those links were established by a small number of propagators who spread the message. No case is known in which a group was formed in response to mere free diffusion of ideas, without the intervention of personal "carriers."

3. The main factors which favored transmission of the doctrine via personal carriers and formation of new groups are the three vast and largely overlapping interaction spheres created by the Catholic mission, the mining industry, and the traditional cultures. Patterns of spread in the Congo indicate that some combination of these three factors seems to have been a necessary condition for the formation of Jamaa groups. However, our brief survey of urban and rural groups in Katanga brought out the interesting fact that those three structural prerequisites apparently define the outer limits for the spread of Jamaa groups but seem largely irrelevant for the establishment of group-transcending links within the movement. To illustrate this, I shall enumerate a number of "transgressions"—cases of group-transcending integration which do not correspond to the structural boundaries of the three interaction spheres.

a) Contrary to the principles proclaimed by Tempels, Jamaa groups do not limit themselves to the parish as a unit of ecclesiastical organization. Members in the groups at Musonoi and Kamina,[38]

---

38. Kamina, about two hundred miles north of Kolwezi, is one of the most important urban centers in Katanga outside the Lubumbashi-Jadotville-Kolwezi copper belt. Culturally it is situated in the heart of the Baluba-Shamba region

for instance, are recruited from several parishes. On the other hand, two independent and largely unrelated groups coexist within one mission at both Kasaji and Dilolo. Cases of open schism are by no means exceptional.

Nor is orientation and interaction between groups confined to the larger ecclesiastical unit, the diocese. Groups at Kamina and near Kapanga, both belonging to the Kamina diocese, are linked with Lubumbashi and south Kasai, respectively. In this context one should also point to the fact that the formation of a Jamaa group—again contrary to Tempels' claims—does not depend on the local pastor's being a member of the movement. Spread of the movement, then, is not simply correlated with acceptance of Jamaa ideas by the clergy. Very vital groups, such as the one at Malemba-Nkulu, operate without assistance from the local pastor. Some groups were formed in the absence of missionaries (like the ones at Kikondja and Kabondo-Dianda); others show open opposition to the hierarchy (like the group at the C.E.C. in Kolwezi).

b) We have stated that the environment created by the social policies of the mining company was the original world for the Jamaa. But Jamaa groups were formed and flourish in urban sections not controlled by the Union Minière, as well as in rural areas down to the bush-village level. People who never lived in a camp became leaders in the movement; examples are N. Kapenda at Sandoa and B. Ngoi at Kikondja. One could object to this that the camp is but the most thoroughly organized form of the general colonial situation. This is probably true; but then we would have to explain why the movement does not expand beyond the zone of influence —or, rather, recruitment—of the large companies in Katanga.[39] On

---

(the residence of the "emperor" Kasongo Nyembo is a few miles outside the city). It owes its present importance to its position on a railway junction (connection to the Kasai and northeast Katanga) and to the former Belgian air base, which now serves as a garrison for the national army. It is also the seat of the Catholic bishop to whose diocese Kolwezi belongs. The Jamaa is represented in four parishes and contains groups with homogeneous membership (using Kiluba as the language of instruction) and others with intertribal composition (using Swahili).

39. In this context I should like to point to the fact that, in the immediate rural surroundings of Kolwezi, the Jamaa has had very little success. I was not able to conduct a thorough investigation of the matter. The suggestions made by knowledgeable informants were of several kinds. First, it was said that the villages near the mining centers had been "depopulated," in the sense that the young and able people (from whom the Jamaa usually recruits its

the other hand, groups in the interior are not necessarily allied with those in the nearest industrial center (Kamina is much closer to Kolwezi than to Lubumbashi). The strongest case for a correlation between the propagation of the Jamaa and the operations of a large company could be made for the "railway Jamaa," but the function of the railway as a means of communication is too obvious to make this correlation a significant one.

  c) Similarly, it would be difficult to prove that cultural affinity plays a decisive role in the constitution, spread, and group-transcending patterns of alliance of Jamaa groups. Again, it may well be that the distribution of cultural themes on which Tempels built his ideology defines the outer limits for the acceptance of his message. But in terms of group alliance within the movement, the cultural factor is not necessarily the basis of close links. As we have shown for the Lunda-Tshokwe territory, two clusters of groups, around Sandoa and north of Kapanga, have no connection with each other. On the other hand, groups in traditionally hostile regions of the Luba empire are linked together; examples are the Jamaa of Malemba-Nkulu and the one at Kabongo. Overcoming of *bukabila,* tribalism, after all, is one of the most explicit affirmations of Jamaa doctrine.

  d) A spatial factor, finally, cannot be excluded, but it is certainly not decisive. Clusters of Jamaa groups like those around Sandoa and Kikondja owe their existence to physical proximity. A village-based Jamaa leader who decides to found a new group in the nearby country is limited by the amount of time he can be absent from his job and by the conditions of communication with his prospective "children." N. Kapenda, for instance, has a hard time keeping contact with his foundation at Kafakumba, some one hundred miles east of Sandoa. But his own group was founded by people from Musonoi, more than three times farther away.

  In summary, patterns of interaction within the three systems— the Catholic mission, the large companies, and the cultural units

---

members) had left to seek employment in the mining industry. Others pointed out that depopulation had resulted in a "demoralization" and frequent relapse into paganism—again not a favorable climate for the Jamaa. (It is true that, for example, the Catholic mission at Kanzenze near Kolwezi had lost its congregation almost completely.) Some informants thought that the rural people considered the Jamaa as something "foreign," a concern of the inhabitants of the camp, most of whom were strangers in the area.

—do, in varying degree and combination, structure the spread of the Jamaa. But none of them sufficiently accounts for group-transcending integration within the movement. In other words, the Jamaa is neither a pious Catholic society nor a voluntary association typical among industrial workers nor a cultural movement of "Bantu philosophers."

Spiritual Kinship and the Idea of Unity

What is the organizational basis which links Jamaa groups together? In Chapter 1, I mentioned Tempels' continuing influence through the directions and advice he gives to important leaders of the movement. The effectiveness of this leadership from a distance should not be underestimated. But as far as ordinary, everyday decisions are concerned, the leader in Belgium is far away. Tempels' continuing influence is not a sufficient explanation for the integration of the movement. Actually, the answer is quite close at hand: the structural frame on which Jamaa groups are formed and by which they are linked together to form a movement is, above all, the network of *kizazi*—spiritual generation/filiation. Earlier in this section I pointed out that not a single Jamaa group was formed as a mere response to the diffusion of ideas. Neither, I might add, is the preaching of a peripatetic prophet considered sufficient to constitute a Jamaa. Always it requires that an initiated member "give birth" to a group of "children" in a long period of instruction in the doctrine (normally one year for the first degree). Once it has been established, a paternal/filial relationship is to last forever. Links to a *baba* and a *mama* are not severed when their "children" move to another place and join the local group. Most of the communication between groups (through visits, mail, and messages) follows these lines of *kizazi*.

Kizazi links groups, or members of groups, but it also implies a certain degree of segmentation in the movement. However, this tendency is counterbalanced by another, equally important principle of Jamaa doctrine: *umoja,* unity. The concept is used widely; in concrete terms, it applies most often to unity among groups and unity of the doctrine. As we have seen in the description of the Jamaa at Musonoi, unity is enacted and demonstrated in the regular *mafundisho* meeting in which the local leaders play an important role as "speakers." "Speaker" is an adequate translation of the term "prophet," and it is in this sense that I call the authority of Jamaa leaders "prophetic." It remains true that prestige and position of leaders derive from their "fecundity" in the network of *kizazi,* but it is spiritual generation that counts—transmission not of biological life but of spiritual life through instruction in the doctrine. It is to be expected that local leaders, as "speakers" of the doctrine and concerned with its integrity, will develop interests in the movement which transcend their own *kizazi* or their own local group (often the two are identical).

These somewhat deductive considerations are strongly supported by facts. Whenever Jamaa leaders go beyond the limits of their local groups and relate to other leaders and groups, the issue will be *umoja,* unity of the doctrine and unity within the movement. Prominent Jamaa leaders travel frequently and visit other groups, very often with the explicit goal of preserving and restoring unity and to assure that the "right" doctrine is being taught. In making these expeditions, the leaders are clearly trying to enlarge their spheres of influence; they collect followers rather than "children," and this is the point where an organizational principle quite different from *kizazi* may eventually unite the movement, or clusters of groups within the movement. The data do not suggest that such a shift is imminent. In 1966–67 there were signs of a separation of alliance systems around leaders in the Kolwezi area and those at Lubumbashi, but these had not reached the level of overt organizational divisions. Another indicator for the direction of the development are supraregional meetings. Like the weekly *mafundisho,* the Easter rally, and similar meetings, these are demonstrations of unity—in this case, group-transcending unity. But my information shows a marked decline in the importance, and an increased localization, of these meetings. At this moment it is impossible to predict whether segmentary *kizazi* or holistic *umoja* will become the most influential principle in the development of the movement.

PART II

The Doctrine

3 ❧ THE SYSTEM OF
JAMAA DOCTRINE

CLARIFICATION OF CONCEPTS

Two reasons made me choose a theory of charisma as the conceptual framework for the description and analysis of the Jamaa. First, such a theory can be viewed as a nontrivial and practical approach to sociocultural change.[1] Second, if it is understood in terms of Max Weber's intentions, a theory of charisma directs research toward concern with the intellectual basis and direction of social process. It deals with the dynamics of ideas in situations in which strictly behavior-centered approaches (no matter whether they are of the structuralist or quantitative variety) are bound to fail simply because their categories and operations depend on the availability of data indicating regular, established patterns of action.

So far I have tried to describe the "conversion" that changed the missionary Placide Tempels into *baba* Placide, founder of the Jamaa. I have discussed the sociocultural background for this event, patterns of intragroup organization and intergroup alliance, and leadership and trends in the development of the movement in Katanga. In order to locate exactly the juncture between this and what is now to follow in Part II, I shall have to recapitulate briefly the main elements in the theory that serves as its conceptual frame:

1. Charisma becomes socially visible as *a type of authority,* in Weber's terms, or as a mode of integration of a group consisting of a leader (or leaders) and followers.

2. Negatively, the relationships obtaining between a charis-

---

1. "Nontrivial" because it is devised to cope with specific and often dramatic forms of departure from everyday action. "Practical" because these phenomena are, much more than other phenomena of change ("urbanization," "modernization," etc.), likely to be manageable in size and temporal extension. Cf. Fabian 1965:15 f.; 1969a:160 f.

matic leader and his followers are characterized by the fact that they differ from those in established, "everyday" forms of authority. Legitimation of charisma is not based primarily on traditional office, rational competence, economic power, and so forth. Positively, these relationships are based on the acceptance of *new orientations* and, in the case of prophetic-charismatic movements, usually on new definitions of the issues *felt to be of vital importance* for a given group of people in a given situation.

3. Because it is enactment of new orientations, charismatic behavior constitutes, in terms of a general theory of action, a privileged approach to the "causes" of *cultural change*.

4. To be useful as an analytical tool, the theory of charisma must be applied to *limited* phenomena: a given leader, his direct followers, and, above all, their orientations, which must have attained a stage of *objectivation* that makes them *accessible for analysis.*

In an immediate and fairly obvious sense, "limitedness" is required by the economy of anthropological research techniques; "degree of objectivation" refers to the quality of "data"—in this case, to the degree to which Jamaa ideas are, or can be, verbalized by informants and recorded by the investigator. Both criteria are of a strictly methodological nature. But there is more involved than methodology. Limitedness and objectivation may be viewed in an epistemological perspective, in which case they translate as boundedness and communication. Very briefly, the argument runs as follows.

The presentation of our findings is divided into Part I, which deals primarily with the Jamaa as a historical and social phenomenon ("The Founder," "The Movement"), and Part II, which describes it as an ideology ("The Doctrine"). This division into parts springs from the necessity to narrate in a temporal sequence what in reality cannot be separated. I do not think that this division could be upgraded to an "analytical" separation of the social and the ideological ("cultural") aspects. Such a distinction is possible and valid only if one could start out with a strictly scientific and analytical theory of movements and rely on the availability of "data" to be tested or subsumed under such a theory. It is a central argument of this study that movement phenomena are not "available" in the sense that the data of empirical science are "available."

To perceive them at all, one must enter the total context to which they belong. This context cannot be construed; it must be identified (or "discovered"), and in this task one must cope with two major problems: (*a*) the problem of the boundaries that define a total context and (*b*) the problem of the medium that makes it possible to enter such a context.

In our attempt to demonstrate the boundaries of the phenomenon Jamaa in terms of historical events and observable patterns of action, we were constantly forced to refer to tenets of Jamaa doctrine as the only means of understanding the events and structures we isolated. We had to insert Swahili terms such as *kizazi, uzazi,* and *umoja* and interrupt our presentation with reflections on semantics. All this pointed to the second of the two epistemological criteria: language. The total context which makes up the Jamaa movement is "given," to both the participant and the observer, through language as the one medium which represents *and* constitutes such a context.[2] This turn to language as both the medium and the goal of knowledge provides the epistemological foundations for a study of social phenomena which is not and, as we have pointed out repeatedly, cannot be based on an "objective" (i.e., detached from the subjects involved) availability of data. In this sense I wholeheartedly subscribe to Dell Hymes's proposition that "ethnographic objectivity is intersubjective objectivity" (1964:14).[3]

The "turn to language" is one of the most conspicuous trends in current anthropology. Since, in our analysis of Jamaa doctrine, we are going to employ analytical procedures which have grown out of this trend, it will be useful to clarify our own position. First, I should reiterate what I consider to be the crucial point. Turning to language as a key to understanding social phenomena is for me

2. Language has a crucial function in terms of the means and ends of fairly orthodox ethnography. It is, of course, not the only medium of communication and, therefore, not the only medium of access to a context of communication.

3. The approach I am outlining here is in many respects quite similar to the program which Dell Hymes formulated for an ethnography of communication (1964), even though I think that he did not confront the problem of intersubjectivity in its most radical manifestation (i.e., intersubjectivity between investigator and investigated). In any case, I feel that my work is closer to his concerns than to those of "formal semantic analysis," as might be suspected from my use of componential analysis (cf. Hammel 1965).

the result of epistemological considerations, not just a matter of methodological expedience.[4] This distinction implies that analysis of a body of language material in terms of formal-structural methods of some kind is for me not the end of understanding. To me, the claim of recent "cognitive anthropology" that a culture (or a segment of culture) is adequately described when one is able to formalize the taxonomic or paradigmatic principles of its organization is unfounded (cf. Tyler 1969:3, 5). Above all, I cannot accept what seems to be the underlying philosophy of language in these approaches. This is expressed in the following definition of the concerns of "cognitive anthropology": "Nearly all of this work has been concerned with how other peoples 'name' the 'things' in their environment and how these names are organized into larger groupings" (*ibid.*, 6). Emphasis on denotation and classification presupposes the availability of already constituted "data" ("material phenomena"; cf. *ibid.*, 3). Such an approach is, in my view, unable to deal with elements of an ideology in which the function of language is, above all, articulation and communication. To give an example, the doctrinal concept of *umuntu* (being man) can in no conceivable way be treated as an arbitrary label for a discrete element of experience; nor can its taxonomic relationship to other terms, such as *upeke* (solitude, loneliness), *uzima* (life/force), render its meaning if it is described solely in terms of logical relations of opposition, inclusion, hierarchy, and so forth. What *umuntu* means cannot simply be read from a taxonomy or paradigm of Jamaa terms but must be *interpreted* by a genetic-historical method which re-enacts its formation in the minds of the prophet and his followers.[5]

For me, successful application of an analytical method like componential analysis is not equal to understanding a culture from the "inside." On the contrary, it is just one of the procedures that helps one to work one's way from the outside to the inside of a be-

---

4. The latter is expressed in Burling's paper, "Linguistics and Ethnographic Description" (1969).

5. Elsewhere I have insisted on taking account of the classificatory and the articulatory functions of language in reference to the role of names in kinship terminologies, even though the contrast I proposed may be misleading in its formulation (i.e., a contrast between "naming" and "classifying"; cf. Fabian 1965b:712). The same paper contains further considerations regarding the uses of componential analysis which, I felt, were not necessary to repeat in this context (*ibid.*, 701–3).

lief system embodied in language. And even this it does only up to
a certain point. It allows us to classify terms and concepts of Jamaa
teaching by starting with morphological and grammatical features
(of Katanga Swahili) and lexical features (of Jamaa Swahili).
Thus, it works from the general context of an African language to
the specific semantic domain of a doctrinal language. One of the
immediate results of componential analysis is that it demonstrates
that terms which Jamaa language shares with Katanga Swahili in
general, or with the doctrinal language of the mission church, are
organized in a specific and distinctive way. This gives us a clue to
the fact that their meaning may be different from the meaning
the same terms have in the two other domains. But to know that
their meaning is different is far from saying exactly *what* they
mean. Their actual content can be determined only when the
formal classificatory principles of Jamaa doctrine (its "components") are reconcretized and related to the creative process of
ideology formation. In other words, componential analysis will be
employed as a *method* which helps to formalize and structure a
belief system. I never regard it as a "theory," [6] either in my own
head (because I believe that understanding poses epistemological
and hermeneutic, not merely logical, problems), or in the head of
the "natives" (who, I assume, think, articulate, and produce, and
not merely "classify," ideas).

These considerations explain why, apart from passing references, I shall make no further effort to relate the following analysis
to the work that goes under the name of "ethnoscience," "cognitive
anthropology," or "formal semantic analysis." My methodological
debts to these approaches are evident; my theoretical affinities to
them are minimal.

Finally, the division of this study into its two parts may create
the impression that we are progressing from an "etic" to an "emic"
description. Indeed, in terms of K. L. Pike's criteria for that distinc-

6. Reduction of the concept of "theory" to the sum total of rules organizing
a culture is implicit in Tyler's considerations. Total confusion of three concepts usually separated by theorists of science, together with a behaviorist
view, is evident in the following statement: "Consequently, this *description*
[of the rules of a culture] itself constitutes the "*theory*" for that culture, for
it represents the conceptual *model* of organization used by its members. Such
a theory is validated by our ability to predict how these people would expect us to behave if we were members of their culture" (Tyler 1969:5; my
italics).

tion, it would be hard to avoid this conclusion. From a general description of the Jamaa as a "movement," we proceed now to an analysis of its *specific* message; we try to *discover* rather than create the *system* of the doctrine; we aim at showing the *integration* of concepts in a *total* system (cf. Pike 1966:153 f.). All these are typical of an emic approach, and there is no need to dwell on our sympathies for its professed aims. But I am reluctant to adopt the etic-emic distinction as a rationale for dividing this study into its two parts. As I pointed out before, the turn from "sociological" to "linguistic" analysis was taken as a result of epistemological considerations. And it is an epistemological foundation which seems to be lacking in Pike's distinction. Let me explain this with reference to one of his main criteria. An etic investigator takes an external view of a system, whereas emic analysis sees it from the inside (Pike 1966:153; cf. also Tyler 1969:11). As far as I can see, this distinction simply restates the one between the two major variants of a scientistic approach in the social sciences. Etic research works in analogy to "empirical" science (theory construction–data collection–verification), while emic approaches have an affinity to logicomathematical science.[7] Both proceed on the uncritical assumption of a subject-object, theory-data dichotomy; neither is able to show why and how it is possible to enter an alien belief system and understand it from the inside because neither of them contains a theory of intersubjectivity and communication. This brings us back to the assertion we made earlier, that componential analysis (undoubtedly an emic procedure) offers a method, not the theoretical foundation, for a language-centered approach.

SELECTION AND EVALUATION
OF THE MAIN DOCUMENT

To become a fully initiated member of the Jamaa normally takes at least three years of *kufwata mafundisho*, instruction in the doctrine. Assuming that participation in the public meetings and private instruction requires about four hours per week (a minimal estimate) and granting that half of this time is spent on

---

7. Cf. Tyler's statement: "For the cognitive anthropologist cultural anthropology is a formal science" (1969:14).

repetition and discussion, the actual presentation of Jamaa doctrine would take about three hundred hours of *mafundisho*. All the recordings made in the field, including the interviews, add up to some twenty hours. The mere processing of one minute of recorded text (by transcription and translation—the time spent on learning the language, preparing and carrying out recording sessions, preparing the processed material for analysis by filing and indexing, etc. is not counted here) requires up to one hour of work. In other words, though a full course of *mafundisho* takes about 300 hours, it required 1,200 hours to process the recorded texts, which represent about 20 hours of Jamaa teaching, or roughly 7 per cent of the material which would be presented to a Jamaa member in a full three-year course. Does this apparent discrepancy between efforts and results mean that, for a single researcher with the time usually spent on field work, it is impossible to collect enough data to represent the system of Jamaa doctrine as a totality, not just in some of its aspects? The answer, as might be expected, is no.

The dilemma can be solved by distinguishing two kinds of totality:

1. Totality of the intentional scope. Jamaa doctrine is, as an orientational system, a means of perceiving and structuring reality. Reality as the "stuff" for Jamaa doctrine is potentially coextensive with the total "world" of the members of the movement, something which, for all practical purposes of research, is unlimited. Furthermore, to understand the actual scope of Jamaa doctrine would require knowledge of those orientational systems and their "stuff" which went into the making of the Jamaa. This includes, among many other things, elements of certain traditional cultures and of Catholic theology. This sort of knowledge, even if it can be acquired only approximately, is a necessary prerequisite for a historical and ideological critique of Jamaa teaching. In such a critique a doctrine is judged *qua* pronouncement about, or representation of, reality. But this is not our concern at the moment.

2. Totality of systematic integration; the totality of structural patterns or "rules" to which any given statement in Jamaa language can be reduced (and by means of which it can be generated). The data available to us are more than sufficient to isolate the structural framework, or the grammar, of the doctrine. And this is what we try to do now.

Applying these considerations to the material listed in Appendix III, I decided that the most economical solution would be to focus on the only written document, the *kitabu* (book) of Musonoi. Additional information, of course, will be drawn from recordings and field notes.

According to my information, the *kitabu* was completed in 1961. It is said to be the result of discussion among members of all Jamaa groups in the Kolwezi area. The discussions took place in regular meetings (every second Sunday) at Musonoi. According to their function, these meetings were called *pulan,* from the French *plan* (outline). As was described in the first part, the meetings continue to be held and are still called *pulan.*

It is possible that initially the authors of the document had more ambitious aims. Perhaps they planned to work out a catechism of the entire teaching. The part that eventually was completed contains only the outline of topics to be treated in the *mafundisho* leading to the first degree of initiation. It may be that the *kitabu* remained fragmentary simply because the authors did not have enough energy or interest to continue. A certain clumsiness of expression, inconsistency of organization, and other shortcomings suggest that the project did surpass the capacities of semiliterate people, even though most of them show astonishing rhetorical talents in the oral *mafundisho.* But another explanation is possible if we take a clue from a remark at the end of Tempels' manuscript on "How Religious Instruction Originates and Grows." Although much more sophisticated and elaborate, this document covers the same topics and arranges them in the same way as our *kitabu.* There the founder says:

> Only when they are ready to experience love, love for the fellow man in all its aspects and in every sphere, when anger, hatred, envy, and discord are banned from their hearts . . . only then can one go on with the *initiation* about [*sic!*] the living-together of, or the encounter between, Christ and Mary. But this then becomes personal instruction [*inlichting*] about the encounter between a certain human being and her god . . . a sacred event, *about which one must keep respectful silence, about which one cannot talk publicly, and about which one cannot write* [*loc. cit.,* 46; my italics].

If our assumption is valid that this manuscript and the *kitabu* are identical in scope, we may infer that the latter covers everything that is regarded as "public" in Jamaa doctrine. (The attribute "public" will be clarified in a later discussion of "secret knowledge" in the Jamaa.) This interpretation is corroborated by surveys of the topics in fifty recorded and about seventy unrecorded *mafundisho*.

The *kitabu* is written in Swahili by people who probably never had any formal training in this language. Some words and constructions are incomprehensible; orthography and punctuation are not consistent. Yet, on the whole, the text is clear and readable. Compared to other efforts in Katanga Swahili, the *kitabu* is impressive for its literary qualities. If more of the letters written by Tempels in Swahili were available, it might be possible to demonstrate his influence on the style of the *kitabu*. In any case, one must assume that most of the standard expressions and formulae go back to the founder.

I should add that all chapters of this outline of Jamaa doctrine are formulated as *spoken mafundisho*. The typical terms of address, *bababa na bamama,* are used constantly.

The scope as well as the particular flavor of the *kitabu* is best represented by the following list of the chapter titles. In presenting this, I shall suggest the original in the use of capital letters, underlining, etc. Some of the concepts remain untranslated.

MAFUNDISHO ABOUT THE CATHOLIC JAMAA — PART ONE.
Explanation of this *mafundisho* of mutual understanding among the *wa baba* and *wa mama* of the Jamaa.
MAFUNDISHO ABOUT THE CATHOLIC JAMAA—PART TWO.
MAFUNDISHO ABOUT THE CATHOLIC JAMAA — PART THREE.

SECOND PART OF THE JAMAA

MAFUNDISHO IN PART FOUR (4) — THE JAMAA AMONG THE APOSTLES!

MAFUNDISHO IN THE FIRST PART OF UMUNTU [being man]. WHAT IS MAN?
MAFUNDISHO IN THE SECOND PART *OF UMTU*.
ABOUT THE THOUGHTS OF UMTU:

MAFUNDISHO IN THE *THIRD PART* OF THE THOUGHT OF UZAZI [fecundity] WHICH GOD GAVE TO MAN. THERE ARE TWO

KINDS OF UZAZI: UZAZI OF THE BODY AND UZAZI *OF THE SPIRIT*.

MAFUNDISHO IN THE PART ABOUT MAPENDO [love].
THE MAPENDO GOD GAVE: *TO MAN*. THERE ARE TWO KINDS OF MAPENDO: MAPENDO OF THE BODY AND MAPENDO OF THE SPIRIT.

MAFUNDISHO IN THE PART ABOUT THE UBABA [being father] OF GOD.
MAFUNDISHO IN THE SECOND PART ABOUT THE UBABA OF GOD. *THE THOUGHT OF UBABA/*.

MAFUNDISHO IN THE PART ABOUT THE UMWANA [being child] OF G O D. THOUGHT OF THE UMWANA OF GOD AS IT WAS IN THE THOUGHTS (OF OLD).————

MAFUNDISHO IN THE THIRD PART ABOUT HIS UBWANA [being husband]: GOD. THOUGHT OF THE UBWANA OF: GOD. AS IT WAS FROM THE BEGINNING.

MAFUNDISHO IN THE PART ABOUT THE SIGN OF THE *CROSS*.
MAFUNDISHO IN THE PART ABOUT THE SIGN OF THE CROSS.

MAFUNDISHO IN THE PART ABOUT THE THOUGHTS OF THE VIRGIN MARY: FIRST BEFORE ALL CREATURES.

MAFUNDISHO IN THE FIRST PART ABOUT THE BEGINNING: *CREATE THE ANGELS*.
MAFUNDISHO IN THE FIRST PART ABOUT THE THOUGHTS OF CREATING THE ANGELS.
MAFUNDISHO IN THE FIRST PART ABOUT *CREATING THE ANGELS*. [Two subtitles: Second part about the angels. FOURTH PART ABOUT THE ANGELS]
FIFTH PART OF THE MAFUNDISHO ABOUT THE ANGELS.

MAFUNDISHO IN THE FIRST PART *ABOUT ADAM AND EVE*.
MAFUNDISHO IN THE PART *ABOUT ADAM AND EVE*:
MAFUNDISHO IN THE FOURTH PART: *ABOUT ADAM AND EVE*.
MAFUNDISHO IN THE FIFTH PART: *ABOUT ADAM AND EVE IN NR. 5*.

MAFUNDISHO IN THE SIXTH PART ABOUT *ADAM AND EVE.*
MAFUNDISHO (OF THE JAMAA) IN THE SIXTH PART:
ABOUT ADAM AND EVE HOW GOD DESCENDED ON EARTH FOR THE FOURTH TIME TO EXPEL THEM BECAUSE OF THEIR SIN. MAFUNDISHO IN THE SIXTH PART ABOUT ADAM AND EVE. HOW GOD DESCENDED ON EARTH FOR THE FOURTH TIME *TO EXPEL THEM FOR THEIR SIN.* . . .
MAFUNDISHO IN THE SEVENTH PART ABOUT ADAM AND EVE. HOW GOD THOUGHT OF THE REDEEMER. . . .

MAFUNDISHO IN THE PART ABOUT THE UZAZI OF ADAM AND EVE.

MAFUNDISHO IN THE FIRST PART: ABOUT NOAH.
MAFUNDISHO IN THE SECOND PART: *OF THE MAFUNDI-SHO ABOUT NOAH./*
MAFUNDISHO IN THE SECOND PART ABOUT: Noah.
MAFUNDISHO NR. 4 ABOUT NOAH.

MAFUNDISHO IN THE FIRST PART / ABOUT ABRAHAM.
MAFUNDISHO IN THE SECOND PART. MAFUNDISHO ABOUT *ABRAHAM.*

MAFUNDISHO IN THE *FIRST PART: ABOUT MOSES.*
Nr. 2 MAFUNDISHO OF THE SECOND PART ABOUT MOSES.

Mafundisho in the first part about the birth of the *Virgin Mary.*
MAFUNDISHO ABOUT THE BIRTH OF THE VIRGIN. MARY.

MAFUNDISHO ABOUT THE UBIKIRA [being virgin] OF MAMA MARIA.
MAFUNDISHO IN THE THIRD PART OF THE MAFUNDISHO ABOUT THE VIRGIN MARY.
MAFUNDISHO IN THE FOURTH PART OF THE MAFUNDI-SHO ABOUT THE VIRGIN MARY. WHEN SHE *GOT MARRIED TO JOSEPH.*

MAFUNDISHO IN THE FIRST PART ABOUT: THE ANGEL GABRIEL AND THE MESSAGE FROM GOD.

MAFUNDISHO IN THE FIRST PART. ABOUT THE WABABA AND THE WAMAMA WHO INITIATE CHILDREN INTO THE FIRST WAY OF THOUGHTS.

DEFINING THE DOMAIN: JAMAA LANGUAGE

Strictly speaking, Jamaa teaching is not *a language;* it is expressed *in a language.* Utilization of linguistic concepts and techniques, therefore, cannot be but analogous and derived in the analysis of a body of doctrine.

Jamaa doctrine is formulated in Swahili; [8] the vocabulary and

---

8. The problem of Swahili as a vehicular language in south Katanga is too complex to be treated in this context. Here I wish to note only some observations directly relevant for our purposes. While in the northeastern part of the present Congo Swahili has been used for a long time by an Islamic, arabized population (the "Wangwana"), it is a recent import to Katanga, and it would seem to owe its present importance there to the fact that it was favored and promoted by the mission and the big companies. Its "vehicular" function and character are therefore much more marked and have resulted in considerable changes of the original substrate. In comparison to forms of East Coast Swahili, these changes brought about what is commonly referred to as a "simplification" of noun classes and especially of the use of concordial prefixes. Other changes affected the phonology (influence of phonological patterns from autochthonous languages). Not surprising in a vehicular language is the ease with which vocabulary from other languages is borrowed (from the languages of the region, and from French, English, and Portuguese). Another characteristic of Katanga Swahili is the development of not only regional but "social" dialects. Popular classification distinguishes four kinds:

1) *Kiswahili bora* (*bore*), "fine" Swahili: used in translations of the Bible and liturgical texts, to some extent also in radio broadcasts and newspapers; this kind is relatively close to East Coast Swahili.

2) *Kiswahili ya bantu:* the Swahili spoken by the people (i.e., the Congolese); the Katanga Swahili in the sense described above.

3) *Kiswahili ya wazungu,* or simply *kizungu:* the work and kitchen language used by the whites. Very influential in the development of this reduced form has been a guide by Verbeken (1965), often reprinted, and adopted as official "textbook" by the Union Minière.

4) *Kiswahili ya monpère,* Kiswahili of the missionaries: the variety used by missionaries, usually based on a study of grammar and vocabulary of classical Swahili and often influenced by prior knowledge of an autochthonous language in much the same way as the *kiswahili ya bantu.*

I should like to add—although I can go only on my own superficial observations—that in category 2 I found considerable differences between the talk of men (who are exposed to *kizungu* at work), of women (who are closest to the native languages), and of children (who show the influence of primary education in French).

Concerning the regional differences, I observed a stronger influence of both "fine" Swahili and French at Lubumbashi than at Kolwezi. The place of Jamaa language in this classification would be somewhere between categories 2 and 4, i.e., it is basically a language of the camp, influenced in its standardized formulae by the *kiswahili ya baba Placide,* the missionary language spoken by Tempels and his successors in the clergy.

I do not know of any comprehensive study of the Katanga variety of

grammar it uses are part of this linguistic system. We must assume that the rules of Swahili govern any statement in Jamaa doctrine. But it can be demonstrated that, on a higher level of abstraction and within a certain domain, elements of Swahili are integrated into a system whose mode of integration is not that of the Swahili language. We shall be able to isolate structures (or "rules") which include the rules of Swahili but which represent relationships between words and between statements that cannot simply be derived from linguistic analysis of Jamaa documents. This *intentional system* of Jamaa doctrine (as I shall call it in order to avoid misunderstandings which may arise from terms like "ideology") and the *linguistic system* of Swahili, however, cannot be separated neatly as belonging to different levels of abstraction. Both are, if we may use another linguistic concept, *code* for the Jamaa message. In attempts at explanation they must be treated as interrelated variables. The possibilities of making a statement expressing Jamaa ideas are defined by the rules of Swahili; on the other hand, certain morphological and lexical idiosyncrasies of Jamaa language can be understood only in terms of the "underlying" doctrine.

If we succeed in applying these considerations to our data, we will have reached the core of the problem this study is concerned with: the impact of ideas on social action—"ideas" being understood as autonomous systems of symbols governed by rules which cannot be derived from the needs of the social system in which they operate. Jamaa doctrine, even though it was "abstracted" from the world in which Tempels and his followers lived, will then appear as an independent source of orientation and change via orientation.

To make available a minimum of material for analysis, I have compiled, mainly from the *kitabu,* a list of words which can be considered basic vocabulary for the Jamaa language. In selecting these terms I have admittedly followed my "intuition" in the sense that assumptions about frequency of use and relative weight of these terms derive from my knowledge of the recorded material and my experience in the field. Obviously one could think of a more rigid method of establishing such a list (based on statistical oper-

---

Swahili. E. Polomé has published a number of papers which constitute steps toward this task (1963, 1968, MSS). An interesting comparison with the language situation in the Zambian copper belt could be based on Epstein (1959).

ations on frequency, context, correlation, etc.), but this is beyond the scope of a preliminary investigation. Nor did I try to compile the following list according to the standards of lexicography, for the simple reason that it should represent the "crude" material and be as little formalized as possible. The lexical items, or clusters of such items, are arranged alphabetically, the way they appear on file cards. Names, nouns, and verbs are listed indiscriminately, preference being given to the form most often used in the *kitabu* and other documents. Translation and comment try to take account of two things: contrast to "everyday" Swahili use, and context within Jamaa doctrine.

Basic Vocabulary of the Jamaa Language

1. *Adam na Eva,* Adam and Eve. God created *Adam* by putting his "three big thoughts" (cf. *mawazo tatu*) into the body of red clay (*udongo mwekunda*) (cf. *mwili/roho*). When Adam had finished "naming" the other creatures, he began to feel lonely (cf. *upeke*); he thought of a companion (cf. *mawazo, muntu mawazo*). God gave him *Eve.* They lived in perfect union until Eve was seduced by *Lucifer* (cf. *Lucifer, shetani*). Both had to leave the paradise. From then on they had to work (cf. *kazi*) and suffer under the yoke of the body. *Eve* became *Adam*'s slave (cf. *mutumwa*), but because he had pity on her (cf. *huruma*), God decided to have mercy on mankind (cf. *Bwana Yezu Kristo*).

2. *ku-agana* (v.), to make an agreement, a pact.

3. *amri* (n.), order, rule. *Amri ya Mungu,* God's commandments. In the *kitabu* the expression used most frequently is *amri yetu ni . . . ,* "our rule is . . . ," followed by an axiom summarizing the preceding instructions.

4. *baba* (n.), father; *mama* (n.), mother; *mutoto, mwana* (n.), child. Apart from signifying the biological relationships (and their "classificatory" extensions in kinship language), *baba* and *mama* are commonly used in Katanga as respectful terms of address for adult married people. In Jamaa language they are obligatory between husband and wife, expressing the relationship of "mutual generation" (cf. *ubaba, umama, umwana, ku-zala*). The same relationship is reflected in *mutoto,* child through initiation (cf. *ku-ingia, ku-endelea*). A priest will be called *baba* if he is somehow connected with the Jamaa. Other contexts: *bababa na bamama,*

standard address in the *mafundisho* meeting; *baba mukubwa,* leader (cf. *ukubwa*); *baba/mama ya Jamaa,* member of the Jamaa; *Mungu baba,* God Father (cf. *Mungu*); *mama wetu,* our mother, standard reference to the Virgin Mary (cf. *Bikira Maria*).

5. *Bikira Maria,* Virgin Mary. The first human being conceived by God as his *jamaa* (cf. *muntu mawazo, jamaa*), born from human parents and named *Myriam* (cf. *Myriam*). After several years of service in the Temple (cf. *ubikira*), she was married to Joseph (cf. *Joseph*), received God (cf. *ku-pokea*), and gave birth to the redeemer *Bwana Yezu Kristo* (cf. *Bwana Yezu Kristo*).

6. *bwana* (n.), lord husband; *bibi* (n.), wife. In Jamaa language never used as terms of address (cf. *baba, mama*); most often used in reference to marriage as realization of the "three big names" (cf. *ndoa, nyumba, majina tatu*). The Virgin Mary is *bibi* in relation to God (cf. *ubwana*).

7. *Bwana Yezu Kristo,* Lord Jesus Christ. Son of God (cf. *Mungu, mwana*), born as the redeemer (*mukombozi*) of the Virgin Mary (cf. *Bikira Maria*), realized with her the perfect Jamaa on earth (cf. *jamaa*). An exact evaluation of the role of *Bwana Yezu Kristo* is extremely difficult and must await further investigation. Even though he is talked about, referred to, and quoted in much the same way as in the Catholic teaching, his role in creation and salvation seems to have been taken over by the Virgin Mary.

8. *ku-chunga* (v.), to tend, take care of, be faithful to. Describes (often in the associative form *ku-chungana,* take care of each other) the attitude expected from a Jamaa member to (*a*) a spouse, (*b*) the group (cf. *umoja*), (*c*) the doctrine.

9. *dunia* (n.), world, earth. Used (*a*) as correlate and contrast to heaven (either with a cosmological or a moral connotation; cf. *mbingu, mwili*); (*b*) as "scenery" for the spread of the movement, *mu dunia muzima,* all over the world.

10. *eklezia* (n.), most often *eklezia katolika,* the Roman Catholic church; often identified with the Jamaa (cf. *jamaa*).

11. *ku-elezea* (v.), to make clear, explain. Related to teaching (cf. *ku-fundisha*), but with stronger emphasis on actual information *vs.* recitation of standardized doctrines.

12. *ku-endelea* (v.), to progress; *ku-endelesha,* to make someone progress. Technical terms for the process of initiation into the movement (cf. *ku-ingia, njia*). The noun *maendeleo* is not restricted to the technical meaning.

13. *ku-fanana* (v.), to be like, resemble. The basic connection between God and man. The noun *mufano* is frequently used in instructions, mostly with the meaning of "example" (for illustration or imitation).

14. *ku-fundisha* (v.), to teach (cf. analysis of the concept in Appendix III, *"Mafundisho"*).

15. *furaha* (n.), joy; *ku-furahisha* (v.), to make someone feel joy. In a restricted doctrinal sense used to signify (*a*) the purpose of creation, e.g., *wamalaika wanafurahisha Mungu,* the angels cause joy to God; (*b*) the purpose of the husband-wife relationship. The noun may have a negative connotation, "the joy of this world."

16. *ku-fwata* (v.), to follow. Employed in a technical sense: *kufwata mafundisho,* to be a candidate for initiation (cf. *ku-fundisha*).

17. *Gabriel.* One of the three prominent angels, God's messenger to the Virgin Mary (cf. *Lucifer, Mikael*).

18. *ku-geuka* (v.), to change; *kugeusha* (v.), to cause to change. In Jamaa usage: to convert to the movement by changing one's way of life.

19. *ku-hurumia* (v.), to have mercy, compassion; *huruma* (n.), mercy. This concept is best conceived of as a correlate to *furaha* (cf. *ku-furaha*) in the sense that it designates (*a*) God's mercy with the creation and (*b*) Adam's—the husband's—mercy with his wife.

20. *Ibrahimu,* Abraham. Together with Noah and Moses, one of the three models for the Jamaa before the advent of Mary and Christ (cf. *Noah, Moses*); pictured as the obedient servant of God, who was able to "change" because he left his tribe (cf. *ku-tumikia, kazi, ku-geuka, ukabila*).

21. *ku-ingia* (v.), to enter; *ku-ingiza* (v.), to cause to enter, to introduce. Very closely related to *ku-endelea* (cf. *ku-endelea*) as a technical term for initiation, perhaps somewhat narrower (referring to actual reception into one of the degrees of initiation). The term is also used for "the spread of the Jamaa": *kuingiza Jamaa kwa wantu wengine,* to propagate the Jamaa among other people.

22. *jamaa* (n.), family. In the *kitabu* the term is introduced with two basic meanings: (*a*) the unity and community of all Christians (cf. *umoja, eklezia*) and (*b*) the Jamaa as a group and movement (cf. *nkundi*). In the system of Jamaa doctrine, Jamaa refers to the models for, and the realizations of, two kinds of unity: unity within the group, and unity of husband and wife. Source and model for

both is God, who wanted to share his richness with a companion (cf. *Bikira Maria*), with a group in heaven (cf. *malaika*), and with people on earth. Adam, God's *jamaa* on earth, resembles his creator (cf. *ku-fanana*); he, too, thinks of a companion to be his *jamaa*. He and Eve then realize the unity of husband and wife, *jamaa*. This line of Jamaa thinking is resumed in the teaching about the Holy Family at Nazareth (cf. *Joseph*), the union between God and the Virgin (cf. *bwana/bibi*), and Christ and Mary as the models for marriage on earth (cf. *ndoa*). A second line runs from the *jamaa* of the angels as a model in heaven for the visible Jamaa on earth through various historical prototypes (Noah, Abraham, Moses-Israel, the Apostles), down to the first group at Ruwe (cf. *nkundi*).

23. *Joseph* (*Jozefu, Yusufu*). Husband of the Virgin Mary (cf. *Bikira Maria*); their union was based on *mapatano*, encounter (cf. *ku-pata*).

24. *ku-jua* (v.), to know, to master. Often used to separate Jamaa people from others as *mwenye kujua*, those who know, i.e., are initiated. *Kujuana* (v.), to know each other, is one of the tasks of the Jamaa (cf. *kazi, ku-pata*).

25. *ku-katala* (v.), to refuse, to reject. In Jamaa language, the epitome of evil intentions and evil action, since it is diametrically opposed to unity and mutual agreement (cf. *umoja, masikilizano*); often synonymous with *ku-kata* (v.), to cut, separate, start a schism.

26. *kazi* (n.), work, duty; *ku-tumik(i)a* (v.), to work (for). The term will be explained in a separate study. Here I should like to comment on some expressions typical of Jamaa language: *kutumikia mawazo*, to realize an idea (cf. *mawazo*); *kutumikia Mungu*, to work for God; also, to "realize" God, live the thoughts of God (cf. *mawazo tatu*); *kazi ya kugeuka*, the process of initiation.

27. *ku-kosa* (v.) and *kosa* (n.) have two connotations: (*a*) lack, and (*b*) sin, do wrong. Connotation (*b*) is predominant in the terminology of the mission church in both the moral and ritual sense (i.e., *kosa* as "matter" for confession; another term for *kosa* is *zambi*, which is the name of God in some autochthonous languages, e.g., Tshokwe). In Jamaa language, as always, the ritual connotation is incorporated, but emphasis is put on aspect (*a*): *kosa* is lack of fulfillment, e.g., *Adam alikosa mwenzake*, Adam was without a companion and was therefore a *muntu kipande*, an

incomplete human being. When Adam and Eve did wrong, their sin (*kosa*) is described as *walikatala kuletana* (*mwili*), they refused to give each other (their bodies) (cf. *ku-katala*). *Lack* of unity, rather than *violation* of some rule, has been the source of evil ever since (cf. *ukabila*). Similarly, *Lucifer*'s sin was *ku-katala* or *kusimamia,* standing up against God. It resulted in a schism among the angels, prototype of all separation among men in general and within the Jamaa in particular (cf. *Lucifer, malaika, nkundi, ukabila, ukubwa*).

28. *ku-kumbuka* (v.), to recall something, think about something; *ku-kumbusha* (v.), to make someone think. The emphasis is on concentration and "meditation"; thus, *ku-kumbushana,* to make each other think, is often used to describe the function of the *mafundisho* meeting. In the expression *Mungu ametukumbushana mawazo yake,* God made us think his thoughts, this meditative, i.e., communicative, function is very clear. Occasionally the term is used in the sense of "being concerned about," but most often it is closely linked to the doctrine of *mawazo* (cf. *mawazo*).

29. *Lucifer*. Most powerful and most gifted of the angels. He refused to carry out God's order: to serve men on earth (cf. *malaika, kazi, ku-katala*). He brought separation into the group of angels (cf. *nkundi*) because he sought power (cf. *ukubwa*). God punished him, not by taking away any of his gifts and power, but by condemning him to solitude (cf. *upeke*). *Lucifer* persuaded Eve to "enjoy her body alone" (*kucheza naye peke yake*) and was chased, together with her and Adam, from the paradise. It is interesting that in the *kitabu* neither the snake symbol nor the concept of Satan (cf. *shetani*) plays a role in the account of the original sin. Lucifer is called *mulozi,* sorcerer, the power-hungry human destroyer of unity par excellence.

30. *majina tatu* (n.) *ya Mungu,* the three names of God. An important doctrinal concept, parallel to that of the "three thoughts (cf. *mawazo tatu*). The difference seems to be that *majina tatu* refers to more concrete manifestations of divinity and is also used in ritual invocations (cf. *msalaba*). The *kitabu* has two versions of the *majina tatu:* (*a*) *baba, mwana, roho mutakatifu,* Father, Son, and Holy Ghost; (*b*) *baba, mwana, bwana,* father, child, husband.

31. *malaika* (n.), angel(s). The *kitabu* speculates very little about the nature of angels. They are created as *roho tupu,* pure spirit, or *mawazo pasipo mwili,* thought without body. More im-

portant is their purpose and function: the angels were created as God's Jamaa in heaven to serve God's Jamaa on earth (cf. *jamaa, kazi*). When *Lucifer* refuses to serve (cf. *Lucifer, ku-katala*), the angels split up into two groups (cf. *nkundi*). Those led by *Mikael* become guardian angels; the others are condemned to solitude (cf. *upeke*). In the doctrinal system, the angels serve as a model for the Jamaa on earth in the two aspects distinguished above (cf. *jamaa*): (*a*) like the good angels, a husband and member of the Jamaa "guards" his wife, the movement "guards" the other people outside; (*b*) the Jamaa, the movement, was "united" from people of many tribes (the angels also were originally "nine" groups with different languages); the Jamaa experiences discord from within because some members seek power (the angels were split up by Lucifer) (cf. *ukubwa*).

32. *mapendo* (n.), love; *ku-penda(na)*, (v.), to love (each other). One of the "three thoughts" (cf. *mawazo tatu*). In the instructions, two kinds of love are distinguished: corporal *vs.* spiritual (cf. *mwili/roho*).

33. *masaidiano* (n.), mutual help; *ku-saidia(na)* (v.), to help (each other). Another of the "three thoughts" (cf. *mawazo tatu*).

34. *masikilizano* (n.), mutual understanding; *ku-sikilizana* (v.), to understand each other. The meaning is both "to comprehend each other" and "to have an agreement." Another of the "three thoughts" (cf. *mawazo tatu*).

35. *mawazo* (n.) (the singular form *wazo* is seldom used), thought(s); *ku-waza* (v.), to think. The most important and most typical concept of Jamaa doctrine, an adequate analysis of which will require a separate study. Here I should like to quote a summarizing definition which I attempted elsewhere:

Mawazo . . . is best characterized by its function as a "common denominator" between various elements of *Jamaa* theology and anthropology. God is "creator" but, in relation to man, much more "thinker." Before man was created as Adam and Eve, he was already present in God's *mawazo*. This preexisting *muntu mawazo* is invariably described as someone who is neither male nor female, neither young nor old, neither white nor black. Being *mawazo*, he is in perfect communication with God. Therefore, *muntu mawazo* and God make the primordial *Jamaa*. Then God created man as *mwili na mawazo* (body and *mawazo*) because he wanted someone on earth with whom he could be *Jamaa*. He also wanted that perfect union between God and man to be dependent on perfect union between man and man, above all, between husband and wife. There are endless *mafundisho* on the modalities and intricacies of this union, which alone can give what man desires: *uzima uzazi na mapendo,* "life/force, fertility, and love." In this, *mawazo* is the principle of unity, whereas *mwili* causes diversity. For husband and wife to become *kintu kimoja,* "one thing," it is not sufficient to unite their bodies; they must penetrate each other in their *mawazo.* It is because of the body that mankind is split up by *bukabila,* "tribalism." Because they are united in their *mawazo,* people of different tribes are together in one *Jamaa.* Even the different stages of initiation are often called *wazo* since they are steps to the perfect union. Sometimes speakers end their *mafundisho* with the standard formula: "These are some *mawazo* I had"—even if their instruction was nothing but a recitation of standardized doctrine. Finally, dreams are called *mawazo* because they make it possible for man to communicate with God and other men beyond the limits set by his body [Fabian 1966:558 f.].

For further contextual references cf. *mawazo tatu, mwili/roho, kukumbuka, ku-pata, muntu mawazo.*

36. *mawazo (makubwa) tatu* (n.), the three (big) thoughts. In the *kitabu, mawazo tatu* (cf. *majina tatu*) serves as a key formula for: (*a*) the essence of the doctrine—Jamaa doctrine is a *mawazo* doctrine; (*b*) the essence of human being and human aspirations (cf. *umuntu*): life/force (cf. *uzima*), fecundity (cf. *uzazi*), and love/unity (cf. *mapendo*); (*c*) the realizations of these aspirations through mutual understanding (cf. *masikilizano*), mutual help (cf. *masaidiano*), and love (cf. *mapendo*); (*d*) the essence or nature of God and of what God has given to man (cf. *Mungu, muntu mawazo, Adam na Eva*); (*e*) the presence of God in man and in the Jamaa.

37. *mbingu* (n.), heaven. Occasionally the term refers to the origin and goal of human existence; the *kitabu* speaks of *yetu inchi ya mbingu,* our country in heaven. In the doctrinal system, however, the term is most frequently just the correlate to *dunia,* earth (cf. *dunia*), marking a distinction between two realms without implying a contrast between natural and supernatural; most often it refers to the relationship between model and realization rather than that between source and recipient.

38. *Mikael(i),* Michael. The third of the prominent angels (cf.

Lucifer, Gabriel), opponent of Lucifer as the obedient servant of God.

39. *mitume* (n.), Apostles (always in the plural form). One of the historical prototypes of the movement (cf. *jamaa*). Model for conversion to, and spread of, the Jamaa (cf. *ku-geuka, ku-ingia, ku-tuma*). The Apostles are exemplary "followers"; in the chapter which deals with them, this seems to be the most important aspect (cf. *ku-fwata*). They are treated as a group; not one of them is named; no connection with *eklezia* is explicitly mentioned.

40. *Moses (Musa)*. One of the historical prototypes of the Jamaa (cf. *Ibrahimu, Noah*). Moses is pictured as the liberator of *Israel*, also a model for the Jamaa, the implications being: (*a*) Jamaa/Israel is the "chosen people," united by God (cf. *nkundi, ukabila*); (*b*) Jamaa/Moses is the liberator of God's people, i.e., of other Christians and of pagans (cf. *kazi, nduku*).

41. *msalaba* (n.), cross. In the *kitabu* this is introduced in the chapter about *ishara ya msalaba,* sign of the cross, which is the ritual reminder for Jamaa people to live the "three names" of God (cf. *majina tatu*).

42. *Mungu,* God. As a name, it signifies the divine being who is the origin of everything. In a way that is not quite clear, the term comprises, in an attributive function, the persons of the Trinity, each of whom is the embodiment of one of the big thoughts (cf. *majina tatu, mawazo tatu*). Very frequently used are expressions like *Jamaa ya Mungu,* the Jamaa of God, *mafundisho ya Mungu,* God's *mafundisho. Mungu* is the husband of the Virgin Mary (cf. *Bikira Maria, bwana/bibi*); he talks to *Noah, Ibrahimu, Moses,* and *Joseph;* he is the one who watches over the Jamaa on earth. In short, the use of the terms seems to be the same as in Christian theology (except, of course, the husband/wife connotation). More thorough analysis of a great number of documents, however, might reveal a somewhat different structural position of the concept in the system of Jamaa doctrine. My hunch is that the absolutely transcendent character of *Mungu* (stressed in the Judeo-Christian-Islamic tradition) is much less emphasized. Jamaa people do not speculate about *Mungu* unless this is directly relevant to man (cf. *umuntu*). As *mbingu,* heaven, has no "supernatural" connotation (cf. *mbingu*), so *Mungu* is part of the same universe to which man belongs. He is never pictured as a perfect, self-sufficient being; he

created the world and man because he felt lonely (cf. *upeke*). During recordings and conversations I made a very interesting observation: Often informants would say *muntu* (man) instead of *Mungu,* without being bothered by the error. The phonetic affinity of the two terms does not sufficiently explain this. However, considering the fact that both God and man will occur most often in the same context, i.e., whenever the "three thoughts" are talked about (cf. *mawazo tatu*), the "error" can be ascribed to an equal value of the two concepts in the system.

43. *muntu mawazo* (n.), "thought-man." An extremely difficult concept, about which the doctrinal statements seem to contradict one another: (*a*) *muntu mawazo* is the being conceived by God before creation of the world and of Adam and Eve. God gave this *muntu* all his *mawazo,* i.e., his own nature (cf. *mawazo tatu*), and both were in perfect union; (*b*) often *muntu mawazo* is pictured as the perfect or "common" human being, unaffected by any of the distinctions that separate men on earth—he was neither male nor female, neither tall nor short, neither young nor old, etc.; (*c*) the *kitabu,* however, reveals the identity of *muntu-mawazo* with *Bikira Maria* (the Virgin Mary), the companion-wife of God, *mbele ya vyumbe yote,* before all creatures, his *wake moja,* his only one.

44. *mutumwa* (n.), slave; *utumwa* (n.), slavery. Frequently used to describe the human condition before the advent of the Jamaa or before conversion to the Jamaa. Except in the Jamaa, the wife is her husband's slave because Eve was condemned to be *mutumwa wa huyu bwana,* slave of this husband. Israel lived in slavery, and so do the Christians and pagans who have not joined the movement (cf. *nduku*).

45. *mwanzo* (n.), beginning, origin. At least three connotations must be distinguished: (*a*) beginning in historical time, e.g., *mwanzo ya Jamaa ku Ruwe,* beginning of the Jamaa at Ruwe; (*b*) the primordial time of origins, most often referred to by the expression *tangu zamani,* in times of old—the time in which God created; (*c*) origin in the sense of principle, source, ontological ground—at one point the *kitabu* calls the "three thoughts" *mwanzo yetu,* which can mean anything between "our origin" and "our nature, essence."

46. *mwili* (n.), body; *roho* (n.), spirit, soul. Except in the expression *roho mutakatifu,* Holy Spirit (cf. *roho mutakatifu*), the two terms are always used as correlates: (*a*) *mwili/roho* signifies

the constitution of man: body and soul. But in Jamaa language this formula of the official catechism of the mission is rarely used. Most often it is said that man is *mwili na mawazo,* body and thought (cf. *mawazo, nyama*). (*b*) *mwili/roho* is used consistently in speculations about the "three thoughts" (cf. *uzima, uzazi, mapendo*). In this case the two concepts are thought of as the two principles, sources of good (*mawazo, roho*) and evil (*mwili*) in a metaphysical sense (the morally good or evil always is traced to man's intentions, not to his nature; cf. *ku-katala, ku-kosa*). Each of the chapters about the three thoughts is divided into two sections: corporal and spiritual. The body is the principle of separation and division among men, from the separation of the sexes to the separation among cultures and societies (cf. *ukabila*). The spirit is the principle of unity (cf. *umoja*).

47. *Myriam,* Mary. The esoteric name for the Virgin Mary (cf. *Bikira Maria*), not employed in the teaching of the mission. The name is mentioned in the *kitabu* together with a translation *mambo ya kushangaa,* something astonishing, but without any further comment. *Myriam* is an important element in Tempels' doctrine of encounter (representing the "feminine pole" in spiritual encounter), with which we are not concerned in this context.

48. *ndoa* (n.), marriage. *Ndoa* is the realization of Jamaa (cf. *jamaa*) below the level of the group (cf. *nkundi*). Membership in the movement is restricted to *wantu wa ndoa,* married people, to whom all instructions are addressed (the exception being religious people who are not allowed to marry). On the whole, the conception of *ndoa* is ontological rather than legal (it makes man "complete"; cf. *ku-kosa*). In speaking of the legal and ritual aspects, the French word is often used: *kufanya mariage,* to get married in the church (which, by the way, is a requirement for admission to the Jamaa).

49. *nduku* (n.), brother, relative. Widely employed in Katanga Swahili to describe anything between actual sibling relationship and tribal or cultural affiliation. In the *kitabu* the term is used in this general sense, most often in formulae like *wanduku wetu wakristiani,* our Christian brethren. In terms of complementary distribution, it separates outgroup from ingroup relationships. Jamaa people do not call one another *nduku* but *baba/mama* or even *wazazi,* parents (cf. *baba/mama*).

50. *njia* (n.), way, road. A very typical Jamaa expression, with three major connotations: (*a*) in a general sense it means "a way

out" of the problems of human existence, a solution, a guide; (*b*) in a more strict sense it has about the same meaning as *kazi,* work, order (cf. *kazi*), i.e., the Jamaa "way" of doing things, of solving problems; (*c*) as a technical term it refers to initiation into the movement (cf. *ku-endelea, ku-ingia, ku-zala*), e.g., *njia ya kwanza,* first way, first degree of initiation.

51. *nkambo* (n.), grandparent, ancestor. When asked what had attracted them in Tempels' teaching, many informants would point out that he explained things in the *namna ya bankambo,* in the way of the ancestors. In the *kitabu* the term is used in this original sense (e.g., for the addressee of pagan offerings) and in order to express the relationship between the present Jamaa and its models and prototypes, e.g., *nkambo yetu Ibrahimu,* our ancestor Abraham (cf. *jamaa, Ibrahimu, Noah, Moses*).

52. *nkundi* (n.), group. The concept is treated most extensively in the chapter about the angels (cf. *malaika*). In contrast to *kabila,* tribe (cf. *ukabila*), it has mostly a positive connotation, e.g., in *nkundi yetu ya Jamaa,* our Jamaa (group, or movement). The difference seems to be that *kabila* is always based on some "natural" and necessary common attribute (such as race, language, social status), whereas *nkundi* refers to the voluntary congregation of the "followers."

53. *Noah* (or *Noe*). One of the prototypes of the Jamaa, but attention centers not so much on his person as on the ark, which becomes a symbol for the Jamaa.

54. *nyama* (n.), animal. Of some importance in Jamaa reasoning in the context of the doctrine about the "three thoughts." To seek nothing but corporal fecundity, however legitimately and honorably, would be to live like an animal (cf. *uzazi, mwili/roho*). *Nyama* expresses not so much the corporal component of human nature but the nonilluminated, nonconverted human being.

55. *nyumba* (n.), house, household. Occurs often in doctrinal language. Whereas *dunia* (cf. *dunia*) is the space in which the Jamaa spreads as a movement, *nyumba* is the place in which the marital Jamaa is realized (cf. *jamaa, ndoa, bwana/bibi, baba/ mama*).

56. *pagano* (n.), pagan; *kristo, kristiani* (n.), Christian. In the *kitabu* the two terms usually occur together in contrast to ingroup references. Thus, for both, the same formula may be used: *wanduku wetu wakristiani,* our brethren the (other) Christians, and *wanduku*

wetu wapagano, our brethren the pagans. Both are included in efforts to propagate the Jamaa (cf. *nduku*). In other contexts, however, the two terms may be used in opposition. In these cases, reference will most often be to *kipagano,* pagan things (rituals, beliefs), rather than to *wapagano* (persons who are not baptized).

57. *ku-pata* (v.), to receive, obtain; *ku-patana* (v.), to receive each other. The associative form *ku-patana* is the translation of Tempels' "encounter"; *ku-pata* is frequently employed to designate the communication and realization of Jamaa ideas, e.g., *ku-pata mawazo,* to dream, *ku-pata umoja,* to reach unity (cf. *mawazo, ku-pokea*).

58. *ku-pokea* (v.), to receive. Very closely related to *ku-pata* (cf. *ku-pata*), but with a stronger emphasis on actual "taking in." In the ritual context one employs the expression *kupokea komunyo,* to receive communion. The term clearly has a sexual connotation. In the chapter about the conception of the redeemer the Virgin Mary prepares herself *sawa bibi anataka kupokea bwana,* the way a wife gets ready to receive her husband; the same connotation may be found in the formula *komunyo wa ndoa,* "communion" of marriage (i.e., marriage as a ritual of mutual receiving). Finally, the term also expresses acceptance of Jamaa teaching: *tukipokee mafundisho,* let us receive the *mafundisho*.

59. *ku-potea* (v.), to lose, to get lost. This is what the Jamaa is all about: *tutafuteni kintu kikubwa kinatupotea,* let us search for the great thing we lost (as a rare exception an idiomatic expression of classical Swahili is used: *kinatupotea,* the literal translation of which would be "the great thing that lost us"). The "great thing" is the essence of being man, symbolized in the "three thoughts" (cf. *ku-tafuta, umuntu, mawazo tatu*).

60. *rafiki* (n.), friend. Signifies the free attachment to a person as opposed to links of kinship and culture or society (cf. *nduku, ukabila*). The term is not important in the *kitabu,* but some of the recorded *mafundisho* about marriage stress the idea that husband and wife should first be united by *urafiki,* friendship. This serves to underline the personal character of the union in contrast to traditional arrangements between extended families.

61. *rangi* (n.), color, color of the skin. In the *kitabu* God is said to have formed Adam's body out of red clay (*udongo mwekunda*); Adam was neither *mweusi,* black, nor *mweupe,* white (*muzungu,* "white man," has a pejorative connotation). In many

mafundisho this color triad is employed to mark the major racial divisions among men (cf. *ukabila*). The interesting point is that all informants insisted on a triad rather than a black-white opposition, even though most of them were not sure whom they meant by "red people." All this indicates that an outright racial function has not yet superseded the symbolic function of the traditional color triad.[9]

62. *Roho Mutakatifu,* Holy Spirit. Unlike his role in many other movements with a Christian background, the third person of the Trinity does not play a prominent part in Jamaa teaching. *Roho Mutakatifu* is identified with the third "big thought," *mapendo,* love; he is mentioned in the Annunciation scene; as far as I can see, documents show no evidence of Spirit-possession.

63. *saserdos, mupadri* (n.), priest. In the *kitabu* the term occurs in only two contexts, with a somewhat negative connotation in both: (*a*) Before Christians discovered unity in the Jamaa, the priests used to think of themselves as the *wakubwa wa eklezia,* the rulers of the church; they alone had the right to teach, and people accepted this (cf. *ukubwa*). (*b*) When the Virgin Mary served her years in the Temple (cf. *ubikira*), the priests accused her (*wakaanza kumshtaki*) of trying to surpass them in piety and devotion. Obviously, this reflects the difficulties and tensions in the relationship between the movement and the church hierarchy. Other documents point out the positive role of the priest in Jamaa teaching and ritual (cf. our analysis of the internal constitution of a Jamaa group).

64. *shetani* (n.), Satan. The opponent of God (cf. *Mungu*) and lord of evil. Jamaa members must avoid *mambo ya shetani,* the things of Satan. At one point the *kitabu* depicts Christ (cf. *Bwana Yezu Kristo*) and *shetani* as leaders of two hostile tribes (cf. *ukabila*). *Shetani* is said to be the name that Lucifer was given when he refused to serve God (cf. *Lucifer*), but patterns of complementary distribution of the two names suggest two personages rather than one.

65. *ku-shituka* (v.), to be startled. Used consistently to describe reaction to the experience of the divine. Eve, Moses, and the Virgin Mary *akashituka,* were startled, when God appeared and talked to

9. For the traditional foundation of this tripartite division see V. Turner's "Color Classification in Ndembu Ritual" (1966).

them. The same term is typically employed (*a*) by informants who speak of their first reaction to Tempels' message and (*b*) as a standard formula concluding the account of a dream (*minashituka*, I wake up).

66. *ku-shuka* (v.), to come down, descend. Used with two major connotations: (*a*) It describes descent from heaven; God *akashuka*, descended, on earth several times when he created Adam and Eve and when he punished them. He also "descended" on the house of Joseph and Mary to become their child. As in *ku-pokea*, to receive (cf. *ku-pokea*), there is a sexual connotation (the Oxford *Standard Swahili Dictionary* cautions against employing the causative form *ku-shusha* and derivatives, "as they are words used for an orgasm in coition"). The term may also refer to the origin of man: *tulishuka hapa dunia*, we descended on earth. (*b*) Derived from (*a*) is the reflexive and causative form *kujishusha*, to lower oneself, to be humble. Jamaa people should be *mwenye kujishusha*, humble, and they should imitate God, who lowered himself to become the child of human parents (cf. *umwana*). Related expressions often used in Jamaa teaching are: *ku-tupa* (v.), to throw away, to abandon; *ku-acha* (v.), to leave, to abandon (i.e., all the prerogatives of one's social status, as a condition for entering the Jamaa); *ku-jitolea* (v.), to sacrifice oneself.

67. *ku-sumbulia*, *ku-zungumuza* (v.), to converse, to discuss. Both words are frequently used in everyday language. In the Jamaa they have a somewhat restricted and technical sense: *kusumbulia mafundisho*, to talk about the *mafundisho*, is listed as one of the two basic duties of husband and wife in the Jamaa (the other is praying together). The importance of this "discussion" is expressed in the title of the chapter in which God "descends" on the Virgin Mary (*cf. ku-shuka*): *masungumuzo ya Mungu na Bikira Maria*, conversation between God and the Virgin Mary. Similarly, *kusumbulia/kuzungumuza* is used with reference to the establishment of human contacts leading to "encounter" (cf. *ku-patana*). Except for the actual sexual component (cf., above, "discussion" between husband and wife as enactment of the Jamaa), the terms are rather vague. One is tempted to translate them with the fashionable "to have a dialogue," since both expressions are loaded with ideological significance and are practically void of specific content.

68. *ku-tafuta* (v.), to search for. Describes the efforts of Jamaa people (*a*) in the sense of "looking for a solution" and "trying to

understand" (often in the reflexive form *kujitafuta,* to search for oneself, to try to understand oneself—a condition for conversion) and (*b*) in the sense of "to strive for": *kutafuta kuwa umoja,* to strive for unity.

69. *ku-tuma* (v.), to send. Refers to the "mission" of the Jamaa: *Mungu alitutuma,* God sent us (cf. *kazi*).

70. *ubaba* (n.), being father. One of the "three names" (cf. *majina tatu*) associated with the ideas of fecundity and mercy (cf. *uzazi, huruma*).

71. *ubikira* (n.), virginity. In the *kitabu,* virginity is treated only in connection with the service of the Virgin Mary at the Temple (cf. *Bikira Maria*). Interestingly enough, it is translated as *umaSoeur,* from the French *ma Sœur,* the term of address for a nun. In other words, *ubikira* refers to a state of unmarried life and dedication to religion but is not concerned with virginity "before, during, and after giving birth," as in the Catholic dogma.

72. *ubwana* (n.), being husband. Another of the "three names" of God (cf. *majina tatu*). Like the other two basic human relationships (cf. *ubaba, umwana*), this one is pre-existent in God and then enacted as a model for the Jamaa in God's relationship with the Virgin Mary (cf. *Bikira Maria, bwana/bibi*).

73. *ukabila* (n.), "tribalism." The term is listed in its abstract form (prefix -u) because it is most often used in contrast to another central idea, *umoja,* unity (cf. *umoja*). The Oxford *Standard Swahili Dictionary* translates *kabila* as "tribe, clan—a smaller division than *taifa* and larger than *ufungu, jamaa.*" In Jamaa language the term is one of the most important concepts of the doctrinal system. Its connotations, however, vary a great deal; sometimes they seem to be diametrically opposed: (*a*) *kabila* may signify "tribe" or "traditional." To abandon the customs of *kabila yetu,* our tribe, is one of the conditions for conversion (cf. *ku-shuka, ku-acha*). This was exemplified by Noah and Abraham, who left their *kabila* to carry out God's orders (cf. *Noah, Ibrahimu*). (*b*) *kabila* sometimes is used in a positive sense: *kabila yetu Jamaa,* the Jamaa, our tribe, as opposed to *kabila ya pagano,* the pagans. (*c*) Negatively, *kabila* can refer to every conceivable distinction or difference that separates people, including *kabila ya ubibi na ubwana,* the roles of husband and wife, or *kabila ya umwanaume na umwanamuke,* the separation of mankind into two sexes. In this latter sense, however, the connotation can be positive.

As the *kitabu* points out, God created man and woman different so that they could realize *ubwana/ubibi,* being husband/wife, one of God's "three names" (cf. *majina tatu, ubwana*). (*d*) The meaning of *ukabila* is always negative when it refers to separation and discord as the sources of evil, the condition of humanity which the Jamaa tries to overcome (cf. *umoja*).

74. *ukubwa* (n.), being big, having a position of authority and power. If *ukabila* is a violation of the principle of *umoja* (cf. *ukabila*), *ukubwa* is contrary to the principle—and to the actual links—of spiritual generation/filiation (cf. *uzazi, umwana, ku-shuka*). Whenever a Jamaa member seeks *ukubwa,* this is a sign of the presence of Lucifer, who became the example of everything that is disruptive (cf. *Lucifer, malaika, nkundi*). Occasionally, *ukubwa* may be applied to "power" and "the powerful of this world" in general. God chose to be born in the humble family of Mary and Joseph, against all expectations of the *wakubwa,* the powerful in Israel. The implication is that the Jamaa people, too, were blessed with a message and a way to heaven (cf. *ku-fundisha, njia*), even though most of them are humble people. This is also aimed against the representatives of the hierarchy (cf. *saserdos*). Yet at one point the *kitabu* promises that those who accept the thoughts of the Jamaa like *mutoto kidogo,* a small child, will be the *wakubwa wa mbinguni,* the powerful in heaven. This is the only hint at a reversal of conditions in the other world, otherwise a prominent theme in the teaching of prophetic-charismatic movements.

75. *ku-umba* (v.), to create. God created the angels, the earth, Adam and Eve, but not his Jamaa: *Mungu alianza Jamaa yake katika mawazo,* God "began" his Jamaa in thoughts (cf. *mawazo*).

76. *umoja* (n.), unity. The final goal of all the separate activities of the Jamaa, as well as of the separate aspects of the universe, is union and unity (cf. *masikilizano, ukabila*): *njia yetu ni kujitolea kwa umoja,* our way is to sacrifice ourselves for unity (cf. *njia*). Often used are expressions like *tukuwe kintu kimoja,* let us be (become) one thing, *tukuwe muntu moja mu Jamaa ya Mungu,* let us be one man in God's Jamaa. Absolute equality based on mutual understanding and love should be attained at every level: between husband and wife (cf. *mutumwa*), in a Jamaa group (cf. *nkundi, ukubwa*), and between the Jamaa and all other people (cf. *nduku*). Because *umoja* expresses the two aspects of unity and

equality, it is in contrast to *ukabila,* separation (cf. *ukabila*), and to *ukubwa,* domination (cf. *ukubwa*).

77. *umuntu* (n.), being man. The doctrine of *umuntu* is central in Jamaa teaching. Whereas the chapter about *jamaa* focuses on what one could call the dynamic aspects of the relationships between God and man, man and fellow man, husband and wife, etc., *umuntu* stands for the essence and nature of man. Since man was conceived by God after his likeness (cf. *ku-fanana*) and since God communicated everything he had to man (cf. *muntu mawazo*), the doctrine of God and the doctrine of man are practically identical (cf. *Mungu*).

78. *umwana* (n.), being child. One of the "three names" of God (cf. *majina tatu*), the relationship which God established as a model for humanity when he descended to be born (cf. *ku-shuka*).

79. *ku-unga* (v.), to unite; *ku-ungana* (v.), to unite each other. Widely used because closely related to the central idea of unity (cf. *umoja*). The meaning can vary between "bring/get together" and "identify oneself with": Michael accuses Lucifer before God: *anakatala kuungana na mawazo yako,* he refuses to accept your thought. The term may also have a sexual connotation.

80. *upeke* (n.), being alone, solitude. Basically, the meaning of the term is negative; it is contrary to Jamaa values of unity and community. Its function in the doctrinal system, however, is somewhat ambivalent: (*a*) If it were not for *upeke,* God would not have thought of a Jamaa (cf. *jamaa, mawazo*), Adam would not have thought of a companion (cf. *Adam na Eva*), and people would not be motivated to join the Jamaa in their quest for human fulfillment. (*b*) On the other hand, *upeke* is the worst thing that can happen to anyone. When God punishes Lucifer, he allows him to keep his *ukubwa,* power, but he condemns him to solitude and isolation, which equal death. Another meaning of *upeke* is "egotism" (this is what made Eve commit the original sin; cf. *Adam na Eva, ku-kosa*).

81. *uzazi* (n.), being parent, fecundity. One of the "three thoughts" (cf. *mawazo tatu*). In the doctrinal system two kinds of *uzazi* are distinguished: spiritual and corporal (cf. *mwili/roho, nyama*). The concept is most closely linked to initiation, organization, and spread of the movement (cf. *ku-zala;* see also our remarks about *uzazi* in Part I).

82. *uzima* (n.), life/force. The third of the "three thoughts,"

also distinguished as spiritual *vs.* corporal (cf. *mawazo tatu, mwili/roho*).

83. *ku-yala* (v.), to become full of; *ku-yalana* (v.), to become full of each other, penetrate each other. The *kitabu* uses this term to describe the complete union between God and the Jamaa and between husband and wife.

84. *ku-zala* (v.), to give birth, to engender. Refers in a technical sense to initiation. The passive form *ku-zaliwa* is related to the idea of *ku-shuka* (cf. *ku-shuka*) and the thought of *umwana* (cf. *umwana*). Because husband and wife realize in their union the "three thoughts" of the Jamaa, the *kitabu* can say *Bwana azaliwe kwa Bibi; na Bibi azaliwe kwa Baba,* the husband shall be born of his wife; the wife shall be born of her husband. Consequently they call each other "father" and "mother" (cf. *bwana/bibi, baba/mama*).

STRUCTURING THE DOMAIN: ELEMENTS OF A "GRAMMAR" OF JAMAA LANGUAGE

We are now confronted with a list of words. These words were chosen regardless of their morphological appearance and grammatical function. They were selected only for their (estimated) frequency and weight in the *kitabu* and were then listed alphabetically for convenient reference.

Like the analyst of a set of kinship terms (or of other systems of "primitive classification"), we shall first try to rearrange the arbitrary sequence of terms in such a way that relationships between the concepts can be reduced to a minimum number of categories. The second step will be to determine the relationships between those categories and reformulate them as the basic rules of structural integration for the entire domain. The resulting paradigm may then be called the "system" of Jamaa doctrine.

Once more it should be made clear that the projected mental operations on Jamaa language are *logical,* not *epistemological.* In other words, the "structures" and "rules" of structural integration we hope to find will be regarded as valid to the extent that they conform to the logical requirements set by the analysis and not because they represent "true" statements about reality which conform to real or assumed universal structures of the human mind.

Epistemological problems which might concern the anthropologist (i.e., those which are linked in some way or other to the problem of cultural factors in cognition) cannot be treated within one given system of doctrine. They belong to the critique of ideology, based on synchronic and diachronic comparison of doctrinal systems.

Furthermore, it should be kept in mind that the following classification, even though it starts out with linguistic units, is not one of elements of the code (words), but of elements of the message (ideas). However, we have said before that the relationships between code and message, in the sense these terms are used here, are not random. We assume that these relationships are manifold and intricate, and we shall try to make them explicit to the extent that this is possible; but they are not, as such, the object of our investigation.

Clues from Morphology and Grammatical Function

In analyzing a list of kinship terms, the first step is usually to lump words with a similar external appearance together into categories. We shall start with this procedure, except that we shall take as "external appearance" not so much the form of the words but rather their grammatical function in the linguistic system to which they belong (unlike kinship terms, doctrinal terms will not belong to just one grammatical category). With few exceptions, the words on our list are either nouns or verbs. (See Figures 2 and 3.) Several subdistinctions in the category of nouns are easily recognizable: one between proper names and "the rest," and, within "the rest," between those which have very obvious common morphological features (u-, ma- prefix) and the others. For reasons which will be clear later, the proper names are now listed in a "historical" sequence. No translation is given, but each word carries its number in the vocabulary for easier reference.

We can now rewrite the paradigm in a more formalized way:

N = nouns, subdivided into
    N_1 = proper names
    N_2 = others, distinguished as
        N_{21} = nouns of the u-class
        N_{22} = nouns of the ma-class
        N_{23} = "the rest"
V = verbs

PROPER NAMES	OTHERS	
Mungu (42)	amri (3)	majina (30)
muntu mawazo (43)	baba/mama (4)	mapendo (32)
Bikira Maria (5)	bwana/bibi (6)	masikilizano (34)
malaika (31)	dunia (9)	masaidiano (33)
Lucifer (29)	furaha (15)	mawazo (35, 36)
shetani (64)	huruma (19)	
Mikael (38)	kazi (26)	
Adam/Eve (1)	kosa (27)	
Noah (53)	mbingu (37)	
Ibrahimu (20)	msalaba (41)	ubaba (70)
Moses (40)	mutumwa (44)	ubikira (71)
Gabriel (17)	mwanzo (45)	ubwana (72)
Roho M. (62)	mwili/roho (46)	ukabila (73)
Myriam (47)	ndoa (48)	ukubwa (74)
Joseph (23)	nduku (49)	umoja (76)
B.Y.K. (7)	njia (50)	umuntu (77)
mitume (39)	nkambo (51)	umwana (78)
eklezia (10)	nkundi (52)	upeke (80)
jamaa (22)	nyama (54)	uzazi (81)
pagano/kristo (56)	nyumba (55)	uzima (82)
saserdos (63)	rafiki (60)	
	rangi (61)	

FIG. 2.—Nouns

Schematically, this can be presented as in Figure 4.

1. The division between N_1, proper names, and N_2, "other" nouns, needs no comment, except for the fact that we chose to include in N_1 some terms referring to personages, groups, and functions even though the terms are not proper names in the strict sense, e.g., *muntu mawazo* (43), pre-existent man; *malaika* (31), angels; *pagano/kristo* (56), pagan/Christian; *jamaa* (22), name of the movement; and *saserdos* (63), priest. The function of N_1 concepts in the doctrinal system is not quite so easy to determine. Even though they are proper names grammatically, they do not simply refer to individual actors. Adam and Eve, Lucifer, Moses, and even the Virgin Mary are treated as symbols, prototypes, or models for the Jamaa. We may, therefore, tentatively describe the underlying idea (or "function") of category N_1 as *symbolization*.

2. Equally obvious are the morphological contrasts within the

ku-agana (2)	ku-kumbuka (28)	ku-umba (75)
ku-chunga (8)	kumbusha	ku-unga (79)
chungana	kumbushana	ungana
ku-eleza (11)	ku-penda (32)	unganisha
elezea	pendana	ku-yala (83)
ku-endelea (12)	ku-pata (57)	yalana
endelesha	patana	ku-zala (84)
ku-fanana (13)	ku-pokea (58)	zaliwa
ku-fundisha (14)	ku-potea (59)	
ku-fwata (16)	ku-saidia (33)	
ku-geuka (18)	saidiana	
geusha	ku-shituka (65)	
ku-hurumia (19)	ku-shuka (66)	
ku-ingia (21)	shusha	
ingiza	ku-sikilizana (34)	
ku-jua (24)	ku-sumbulia (67)	
juana	ku-tafuta (68)	
ku-katala (25)	ku-tolea (66)	
ku-kosa (27)	ku-tuma (69)	
	tumika (26)	
	tumikia	

Fig. 3.—Verbs

N			V
N₁	N₂		

N₁	N₂₁	N₂₂	N₂₃

Fig. 4.—Grammatical/Morphological Classification of Jamaa
Concepts

N_2 category of nouns. Nouns with *u-* or *ma-*class prefixes are easy to distinguish from the rest.

N_{21} terms, nouns of the *u-* class, are usually thought to express "abstraction." [10] But if we look at the concepts on our list, it would be more appropriate to call the underlying concept *projection,* i.e., projection of basic human values and modes of existence to a transcendental level. If Jamaa doctrine speaks of *uzima* (82),

10. To be more precise, of the two *u-* classes in classical Swahili, we are talking only of the one corresponding to the *bu-* class in other Bantu languages

life/force, or *ubaba* (70), being father, it does not aim at "abstract" ideas of life and fatherhood but at the transcendental sources of life and fatherhood. Those "sources" are the *mawazo* (35, 36), thoughts which God has not only "revealed" but "given" to man (cf. the expression *ku-leta mawazo,* to give *mawazo,* and *ku-pata mawazo,* to receive *mawazo*). N_{22} terms, nouns of the *ma-* class, are linked partly to N_{21}, in that *majina tatu* (30), "three names," and *mawazo tatu* (36), "three thoughts," are generic names for *u*-class concepts (the "three names" are *ubaba, umwana, ubwana*), and partly to category V, verbs, since they are derived from verb stems, e.g., *ma-sikilizano* (34), *ku-sikilizana.*

N_{23} is a morphologically heterogeneous category. It contains nouns which in Katanga Swahili belong to almost all classes (some of them could take prefixes of several classes, e.g., *u-rafiki,* friendship, *ba-rafiki,* friends). Semantically, however, the range of N_{23} concepts is more limited than morphological heterogeneity might suggest. Most of them refer to social attributes, functions, groups, norms (e.g., *rangi* [61], color, race; *baba* [4], father; *nkundi* [52], group; and *kosa* [27], sin). It is interesting to see which terms are left over if "social" is taken to be the dominant connotation in this category: *dunia* (9)/*mbingu* (37), earth/ heaven; *mwili/roho* (46), body/spirit; *mwanzo* (45), origin; and *njia* (50), way. All these terms express cosmological notions and are best conceived of as conceptual links between categories N_{21} and N_{23}; they set the scene, as it were, for the relationships between transcendental "thoughts" and their realizations in the movement.

3. Category V, the verbs, is semantically a medley of activities, states, and moods. But the words were listed in such a way that a striking common morphological characteristic becomes visible. In the *kitabu* as well as in other documents one observes a tendency to use most of the listed words not in their simple but in a derivative form. Let us have a look at the derivations most frequently employed.[11] These are:

(in Katanga Swahili *u*- and *bu*- are, in fact, used rather indiscriminately). Ashton describes the underlying idea of the class as follows: "Words which admit of no singular or plural concept, such is abstract nouns denoting qualities or states. These often have a common root with nouns of the M-, WA-, and MA- Classes, or with adjectives or with verbs" (1961:104).

11. We are following the classification of derivative forms by Ashton (cf. the table in Ashton 1961:214).

a) Causative: *ku-kumbuka* (28), to think; *ku-kumbusha,* to cause to think.

b) Associative/reciprocal: *ku-kumbusha; ku-kumbushana,* to make each other think.

c) "Prepositional," perhaps better called "incorporative" (reflecting direction toward an object): *kutumika,* to work; *ku-tumikia (Mungu),* to work for (God).

d) Passive: only one such form occurs on our list: *ku-zala,* to give birth, *ku-zaliwa,* to be born.

Again, the underlying common idea seems obvious to me: These verbs do not presuppose merely a subject/actor and an object; the particular derivative forms in which they are used usually imply the presence of other participants who share, receive, or give whatever the verb signifies. This function, which I would call *association,* links the verbs to most of the nouns of category N_{23}, i.e., to those which refer to "social" entities.

Structural Foci of Jamaa Doctrine

Taking our clues from a classification of doctrinal concepts according to morphological and grammatical criteria, we have vaguely determined three major "underlying ideas": (*a*) projection, (*b*) symbolization, and (*c*) association. These terms, outside their proper context, might suggest that we are interested in analyzing the mental operations implicit in the formulation of Jamaa doctrine. This, however, is not our aim. Confronted with a body of doctrine, we are trying to understand how this domain is structured and how those structural components that might become visible in the process of formal analysis are interrelated.

A first step toward this goal is to see whether those three rather abstract "underlying ideas" might not have a more concrete function as structural foci in the system of Jamaa doctrine. I propose the following considerations:

1. The concepts that express "projection" are in fact the ensemble of the transcendental sources of action. Similar to Plato's "ideas," they are universal but not really "abstract," in the sense of abstract principles or rules. The best word to cover the functions of "projective" concepts I can think of is *ontology:* the sum of doctrinal

statements about the origin, essence, and meaning of being (human being, as far as the Jamaa is concerned).

2. Most of the concepts to which we have ascribed the function of "symbolization" are proper names. Jamaa doctrine, however, is not interested in the persons to which the names refer *qua* individuals; they are seen as actors in paradigmatic situations. Accounts of such paradigmatic actions are most commonly called myths; the sum of such accounts may be called *mythology*.

3. Finally, in a number of nouns and some morphological particularities of verbs we have observed a "social" or "associative" function. This was taken to express the fact that enactment of Jamaa ideas is essentially incorporative; it always involves more than just one actor. A term to express this social aspect is near at hand: *movement*. Jamaa doctrine is not formulated (contrary to what the prophet tells us) as a vague universal philosophy but as a program for social action.

A simple procedure of classification has given us valuable clues to "underlying ideas," or structural components, of Jamaa doctrine. Yet our commentary on the resulting paradigm has shown that the divisions which marked contrast and opposition and which separated the three categories were not really exact and definite. For instance, we have said that words of the *ma-* class, category N_{22}, "lean" to both category N_{21}, nouns of the *u-* class, and category V, verbs. In order to reduce this ambiguity, the paradigm can be refined by taking the three basic functions distinguished above—projection, symbolization, and association—as the dimensions of a "property space" of Jamaa doctrine. If we rewrite projection, symbolization, and association as P, S, and A, and arrange them in a three-by-three table, as in Figure 5, we should be able to distinguish six

	P	S	A
P	P	SP	AP
S	SP	S	AS
A	AP	AS	A

FIG. 5.—The Property Space of Jamaa Doctrine

classes of Jamaa concepts, three of them "pure," three "mixed." (Since the sequence of combination has no distinctive function— PS = SP—we can eliminate three of the nine possible combinations.)

As we shall see, a rearrangement of our Jamaa vocabulary following the new distinctions will in fact lead to a more thorough and more interesting organization of the domain. Of course, such attempts should be made with some caution. We now have to rely exclusively on lexical information; opposition and contrast of connotation cannot be determined so easily and exactly as in the case of morphological or grammatical features. Terms with multiple meanings will have to be listed in more than one category. A few concepts that would demand more comment and explanation than the present context allows will be omitted (such as *shetani,* Satan; *nyama,* animal). In any case, "classes" should be taken as structural foci, not as rigid categories. Here, then, is the rearranged vocabulary:

	PROJECTIVE	PROJECTIVE-ASSOCIATIVE	SYMBOLIC PROJECTIVE-
	umuntu (77)	(*mapendo*) (32)	*Mungu* (42)
	umoja (76)	*masaidiano* (33)	*Bikira Maria* (5)
	ukabila (73)	*masikilizano* (34)	*muntu mawazo* (43)
	ukubwa (74)	(*mawazo*) (35)	*ku-umba* (75)
	upeke (80)	*furaha* (15)	*ku-shituka* (65)
	ubaba (70)	*huruma* (19)	
	umwana (78)	*ku-fanana* (13)	
	ubwana (72)	*ku-shuka* (66)	
	uzazi (81)	*ku-potea* (59)	
	uzima (82)		
	(*mapendo*) (32)		
	majina (30)		
	(*mawazo*) (35, 36)		

SYMBOLIC

malaika (31)
Lucifer (29)
Mikael (38)
Adam/Eve (1)
Noah (53)
Ibrahimu (20)
Moses (40)

SYMBOLIC-ASSOCIATIVE

eklezia (10)
jamaa (22)
pagano/kristo (56)
saserdos (63)
msalaba (41)
ku-endelea (12)
ku-fundisha (14)

Gabriel (17)
Myriam (47)
Joseph (23)
B.Y.K. (7)
mitume (39)

ku-ingia (21)
ku-pata (57)
ku-zala (84)
(ku-fwata) (16)
(ku-geuka) (18)
(ku-jua) (24)
(ku-kumbuka) (28)
(ku-pokea) (58)
(ku-tafuta) (68)
(ku-sumbulia) (67)
(njia) (50)

ASSOCIATIVE

ku-chunga (8)
ku-eleza (11)
ku-katala (25)
ku-kosa (27)
ku-penda (32)
ku-saidia (33)
ku-sikilizana (34)
ku-tolea (66)
ku-tumika (26)
ku-unga (79)
ku-yala (83)
(ku-fwata) (16)
(ku-geuka) (18)
(ku-jua) (24)
(ku-kumbuka) (28)
(ku-pokea) (58)

amri (3)
(baba/mama) (40)
bwana/bibi (6)
kazi (26)
kosa (27)
mutumwa (44)
ndoa (48)
nduku (49)
nkambo (51)
nkundi (52)
nyumba (55)
rafiki (60)
rangi (61)

In commenting on these new "classes" of Jamaa concepts, generated by a simple logical device, we shall now try to conceptualize and identify the concrete functions of P, S, and A and their variants.

Category P, "pure projective" concepts, is exclusively made up of words of the *u*- and *ma*- classes. The *ma*-class terms *majina*, names, and *mawazo*, thoughts, serve, as we have said before, as generic names for *u*-class concepts. We also included *mapendo*, love, which invariably is listed as one of the "three thoughts," together with *uzazi* and *uzima*.

Those words of the *ma*- class which, despite their morphological affinity to P concepts, refer to action as well as to "principles" (*masaidiano,* mutual help, *masikilizano,* mutual understanding, *mapendo,* love) can now be assigned to category PA, projective-associative concepts. Also included in this category are a number of terms previously identified as "associative": concepts like *huruma,* mercy, *furaha,* joy, *ku-fanana,* to be similar, have a transformational function in the system of Jamaa doctrine. For instance, the "three thoughts" are the essence and nature of God *and* man, because man was conceived to *kufanana Mungu,* was conceived after God's likeness. Angels and mankind are united in the same goal of existence: *kufurahisha Mungu,* to cause joy to God. God is moved to have mercy on mankind (*huruma*) because Adam has mercy on Eve. A transformational concept par excellence is, of course, *mawazo,* thoughts, which was defined as "a common denominator" between various elements of Jamaa doctrine (cf. *mawazo* in the vocabulary; also *ku-shuka, ku-potea*).

What are the common characteristics of PA concepts? They are both action- and principle-centered. I prefer to call it principle- rather than norm-centered because the "projective" concepts of the *u-* class are not concrete norms for action. PA verbs and nouns, therefore, do not express any specific actions or attitudes. Nowhere is the concrete content of *furaha,* joy, or *masikilizano,* mutual understanding, described. A *mafundisho* on *mapendo,* love, can go on endlessly praising this great virtue without defining what it really means. This "joy of emptiness" and the constant preoccupation with "union" (with one's fellow man, with God, with the universe) express in my eyes a strong *mystical* component of Jamaa doctrine.

But mystical union, not mediated by rites, norms, or practical goals and therefore ineffable and void of concrete content, is, if we may put it this way, a short cut between the levels we have called "ontology" and "movement." The main road to fulfillment leads through the country of "symbols."

Again, our new combination of logical possibilities will enable us to make more refined distinctions. First of all, we decided to separate, as category PS, projective-symbolic, those names and concepts which are linked with the P level because they express something that existed before the creation of this world: *Mungu,* God, *Bikira Maria,* the Virgin Mary, *muntu mawazo,* pre-existent "thought-man," and the verb *ku-umba,* to create, always reserved to *Mungu.* As we can see, category PS includes the "high god" and those "supernatural beings" who, for some historians of religion, represented a premythical stratum of primitive religion, a state of pure belief before it was covered with exuberant mythology and demonology. Fortunately, we do not have to speculate on historical strata. For us, category PS is not a stratum, a deposit of ideas and symbols, but a structural focus of Jamaa doctrine. It allows us to separate from other concepts with symbolic function those which link the level of transcendental ideas (P) with the level of paradigmatic realizations (S)—"ontology" with "mythology."

It is not easy to find a fitting label for category PS. "Theology" would seem the most obvious term if it were not for the fact that this level also includes, in the doctrine about *muntu mawazo,* "thought-man," the "anthropology" of the Jamaa. I propose to leave the category unnamed (and to use circumlocutions when necessary) in recognition of its unique character.

Category S, symbolic concepts, is now restricted to those personages or groups of personages who are the actors in the exemplary situations of Jamaa mythology: Lucifer and Michael in the fight of the angels; Adam and Eve in the story of creation, sin, punishment, and promise of salvation; Noah, Ibrahimu, and Moses as models for the movement; Gabriel, Myriam, Joseph, the Lord Jesus Christ, and the Apostles in the story of salvation, i.e., in the instauration of God's Jamaa on earth.

A very useful subdistinction which our new paradigm allows us to make is the one between categories A and SA. The "mixed" category SA, symbolic-associative, contains terms that previously were listed with S concepts, even though they are not proper names in the strict sense. They can now be grouped with the A concepts that were said to express "technical" aspects of the enactment of Jamaa doctrine. In other words, category SA contains terms with a *ritual* connotation: they refer to the congregation of followers (*jamaa*) and to the standardized ways and means of obtaining membership in the movement and the "goods" promised in Tempels' message (i.e., all the technical terms connected with instruction and initiation). Also included is *msalaba,* or *ishara ya msalaba,* sign of the cross, treated in the *kitabu* as a ritual presentation of the "three names" of God.

It is rather difficult to draw a line between the "mixed" SA class and "pure" A concepts. Since the Jamaa is a prophetic-charismatic movement, all terms referring to the social-action aspect ("associative," as we have called it) are likely to have "symbolic" (and ritual) connotations. Let us take as an example the term *ku-kumbushana,* to make each other think. It may signify the *effects* of instruction in the doctrine ("make each other think") but it could also mean the *ritual evocation* of the doctrine (through "common meditation"). Similarly, *ku-geuka,* to change, can have a ritual significance if it is taken to refer to tangible prerequisites for initiation (e.g., to get married in the church, to do away with ancestor worship and magic). Therefore, terms which cannot decisively be attributed to either category A or SA were listed in both.

Category A, associative, includes concepts which signify personnel, organization, activities, moral code, and expected attitudes of the movement.

We are now left with a group of terms which do not fit into any one of the six permutations of P, S, and A:

dunia (9)
mwanzo (45)
mbingu (37)
(*njia*) (50)
mwili/roho (46)

(*Njia,* the way, was also included in category SA, since it can mean the ritual of initiation.) These "cosmological" terms, as we have called them before, heaven/earth, body/soul, beginning/fulfillment, seem to link all three levels: *mwanzo* is God's time before creation of the world; *mbingu* and *dunia* are the world in which angels and men dwell; *mwili/roho* is man's constitution which links him with God and the angels; *njia* adds a directional, dynamic dimension to the constitutive elements of Jamaa cosmology. I still think that we should conceive of these terms as the "scenery" or the "stage" for the entire doctrine.

SUMMARY: STRUCTURAL COMPONENTS OF JAMAA DOCTRINE AS UNITS FOR COMPARISON— PRELIMINARY OBSERVATIONS

Through several steps of formalization and reconcretization of classes of Jamaa doctrinal concepts we have been able to isolate a number of structural components of the doctrine. Our method employed logical devices of opposition, contrast, distribution, and combination. In an attempt to conceptualize the relationships *between* the resulting classes of concepts (i.e., their "functions" within the system) we formulated the following seven structural foci:

a) Category P, projective: an *"ontology,"* the sum of statements about the ultimate principles and sources of being;

b) Category PA, projective-associative: a number of concepts implying a direct, *mystical* realization of the ultimate principles;

c) Category PS, projective-symbolic: a *"theology,"* the doctrine of God, the Virgin Mary, and pre-existing "thought-man";

d) Category S, symbolic: the list of *mythical* actors and situations as prototypes and models for the Jamaa;

e) Category SA, symbolic-associative: those concepts concerned with the standardized enactment of the mythical models: *ritual;*

f) Category A, associative: terms that signify the internalization/ institutionalization of Jamaa doctrine in the Jamaa *movement;*

g) A group of terms embracing all levels, tentatively referred to as *"cosmology."*

Apart from providing the analyst with the intellectual pleasure of being able to reduce a complicated domain to a few components, what is the use of such formalization? The answer to this question is largely beyond the scope of this study, in which we have sought to limit ourselves to investigations permitting us to present and understand Jamaa doctrine as a system. However, as a conclusion to this chapter, I should like to suggest at least some ways in which analysis could continue.

First, the "use" of formal analysis of symbol systems, such as we have attempted, is to prepare ethnographic data for comparison. Naturally the fact that we came up with a "holy seven" number of levels is of no theoretical importance. Those seven categories could again be combined to form a seven-by-seven property table—and so forth. The decision to stop and accept a certain number of categories as analytical tools is a practical one.

The seven foci distinguished above allow us to compare Jamaa teaching with other doctrinal systems (*a*) in terms of their scope and (*b*) in terms of particular issues and their integration into the system. I shall very briefly touch on some of the promising issues for later comparative study.

As to the scope of the doctrine, it will have become clear that the Jamaa in fact aims at a total definition of reality and a total orientation for its followers. Our conclusions in the first part of this study are now confirmed: it is impossible to conceive of the movement as a pious association within the mission church. Such an association would be characterized by some limited goals and activities (charities, veneration of the Sacred Heart, etc.). But *kuwa Jamaa,* to become Jamaa, means, as the *kitabu* and many other documents state, to find *umuntu,* what it means to be man. With its emphasis on *umuntu,* Jamaa doctrine is in fact more inclusive (albeit much less articulate) than Christian teaching which centers on revelation and the history of salvation! (I am talking, of course, of the sort of teaching a Congolese candidate for Christianity would be confronted with.) Nothing indicates that Jamaa doctrine shares with Christian doctrine the concern for limits between the natural and the supernatural, the divine and the human, religion and morals, philosophy and theology, faith and reason.

The fact that the Jamaa could stay "within" the mission church (at least for all practical matters) can now be better understood, too. A glance at the structural foci we distinguished shows that Jamaa doctrine and church teaching (or rather, the languages of Jamaa doctrine and of church teaching) overlap most in the S category, on the level of myth and symbols. We should add that this is also the case with a large number of SA, or "ritual," concepts not listed in our vocabulary, i.e., those that refer to the ritual of the church and are accepted as a whole, even though they are not very prominent in the *mafundisho* (e.g., communion, confession, prayer). Because levels S and SA have, in Jamaa doctrine, a structural position which differs considerably from the one they occupy in Catholic teaching, the "orthodox" association of the movement with the church could go on indefinitely (in the same way as, in our society, "practicing" members of a church are listed as faithful believers even if they accept but a small portion of the dogma).

Our structural frame for comparison enables us to see another reason that makes an open clash between Jamaa and church unlikely. It will be remembered that most terms referring to the doctrine and to instruction in the doctrine were listed in category SA, the level of "ritual." Jamaa teaching is standardized access to the "promised goods," a verbal ritual, not discursive argument. The missionary zeal of Jamaa people is motivated by the basic value of fecundity (*uzazi*) and not so much by the urge to convince candidates of some truth.

Eventually our distinction of structural foci will allow us to evaluate the relative importance of Tempels' contribution and of the modifications through his followers. A straight line leads from category P, Jamaa "ontology," to the prophet's speculations in *Bantu Philosophy*, whereas he would probably deny authorship of the very peculiar "theology" expressed in category PS.

"Encounter," one of the most important and most contradictory of Tempels' ideas, can now be seen in a different light: *ku-patana*, to have an encounter, was listed among the *ritual* terms of Jamaa doctrine. Thus, the entirely "personal" in what we have called the prophetic event is "socialized" through ritualization. Now we can also appreciate the double meaning of a statement like "the Jamaa cannot be founded; it must arise from the encounter between the priest and his parishioners." It appears to insist on an entirely informal, personal and casual relationship, whereas in reality (at least for most Jamaa members), it requires the priest to undergo formal initiation.

Equally significant could be the results of our formal analysis of Jamaa doctrine for a typology of movements. The structural components we distinguished could serve as the dimensions of a classification. In this context I should like to comment briefly on the most interesting among recent attempts, Kopytoff's paper on "Classifications of Religious Movements: Analytical and Synthetic" (1964). I fully share his skepticism regarding the possibilities of an over-all classification of movements. I also think that he gives an excellent statement of the problem when he writes: "The question has never been whether we should or should not classify, but rather what we should classify and how" (*ibid.,* 87). But it seems to me that only an idea- (or ideology-) centered study could combine a formal analytic approach with an emphasis on the specific content and historical uniqueness of movements; or, to put it in terms of Kopytoff's discussion, only an idea-centered approach could be synthetic without being "platonic" (*ibid.,* 82). Since it is our basic assumption that such an approach implies some theory of charisma, it will be understandable that we disagree with Kopytoff on an important point. We hold that "prophetism" is by definition more important than "nativism" as a "diagnostic trait" (cf. *ibid.,* 81) and that there must be an "emphasis on dramatic features" (*ibid.*, 87), because this is a logical implication of a theory of charisma which deals with the extraordinary in contrast to the established.[12]

Finally, an observation on a seemingly insignificant point in Kopytoff's paper causes me to touch on a question that I have so far carefully avoided. Kopytoff, if we go by the title of his paper, is concerned with the classification of "religious" movements—an attribute presupposing a classification which we are asked to accept as evident and nonproblematic. In our study the term "religion" is hardly ever used, in any case not as an analytical concept. This expresses my conviction that a "theoretical" definition of religion, i.e., a definition that would allow the formulation of hypotheses for research similar to those which can be derived from the concept of charisma, is currently not available. Horton's (1960) and Spiro's (1966) attempts to revive Tylor's "belief in Spiritual Beings" are, in my opinion, really aimed at reducing religious action to some sort of social "interaction" which in turn is a prerequisite for their more or less functional (need-satisfaction) view of religion. Goody (1961) sets out with a critique of Durkheim's "inclusive" definition and ends up with a reduction of religion to a subcategory of ritual. Geertz proposes to see religion as a cultural system—an interesting view, but it only pushes the problem further back, because Geertz does not give us a satisfactory definition of *what* should be treated as a cultural system, other than symbols of boundary experience (1966). On the whole, anthropologists still seem to accept a definition based on unexamined or little-examined categories derived from our own culture.

In a sense, and for the time being, we accept this situation as a fact and may call the Jamaa a "religious" movement because it operates in the context of what is commonly called religion. However, our own analysis of the Jamaa, with its emphasis on the "boundaries" of both the action and the symbol systems involved, would set much more rigorous standards for comparative statements than those that are often applied. Methodologically it would be a questionable procedure to compare the doctrine of a movement with something as vague as the "theology of the mission church" or with "traditional religion." In this study we have limited ourselves

---

12. For my own previous discussion of typologies and an approach centered on diagnostic features see Fabian (1963, 1965a).

to drawing comparisons and showing connections only on specific points. In a sense we accept Durkheim's postulate of a "church" as an essential element in a definition of religion: comparison between different religious systems must take account of the "social referents." In our specific context—the rise of movements in a (post) colonial situation—the claim of the mission church to represent a unified system of belief and action is often too easily accepted. The only differences recognized are usually those between denominations, but, to my knowledge, there is no study available which shows the marked differences in orientation and teaching between different mission orders, missionaries with different cultural background and education, home church *vs.* mission church, etc. Perhaps the most serious gap, however, is that we know almost nothing about the faith of orthodox mission Christians, and I strongly suspect that improved information on that point would make many statements about the "deviance" of "sects" and "separatist movements" look rather simplistic. (For a broader treatment of these problems see Fabian, in press).

All this, of course, applies to the study of religion in general, and especially religions in our own society, whose claims to unity and uniformity we are prone to accept. In this sense the study of the Jamaa and similar movements may open for anthropology a back door to the cathedrals of Christian theology.

4 ❀ LEARNING, TRANS-MITTING, AND SHARING THE DOCTRINE

The purpose of our formal analysis of Jamaa doctrine has been to demonstrate that it constitutes a system of beliefs, values, symbols, and norms which has its own mode of integration. Such a system does not, however, float somewhere in the thin air above the world of social action. In our description and analysis of the founder and the movement we have repeatedly pointed out that Jamaa doctrine is eminently practical in that it directly defines and influences patterns of behavior and organization. In this final chapter we shall again be concerned with the "links" between orientation and action and will assemble some of the data on problems of the institutionalization and internalization of Jamaa doctrine. Our discussion will be restricted to problems and topics connected with our previous presentation. Neither our theoretical aims nor the nature of our data permit a treatment of questions of internalization in terms of a theory of personality and culture. Investigation into the psychological processes of accepting and "learning" a prophetic message, technical (i.e., psychoanalytical) interpretation of dreams, and attempts to understand the personality structure—and specific changes in the personality structure—of leader and followers are outside the scope of this study.

INITIATION: BEING BORN INTO THE MOVEMENT

A Wall of Silence

The presentation of Jamaa teaching in the *kitabu* concludes with this rule:

This is the essence of our way [*njia*], the Jamaa. It will make us strong so that we can progress; do not give it away to anyone who is not a member of our Jamaa.

Quite a surprising conclusion, we might think, since in so many chapters of the *kitabu* it is said that "the way" (*njia*) should be known to the entire world. Everyone, Christian or pagan, is considered a candidate for the Jamaa and should be made to progress on this way (*ku-endelesha*). Enthusiastic consciousness of "the way," of a message and its universal relevance, pervades Jamaa teaching at all levels. Nothing is more abhorrent than to pursue this way alone (*upeke*) or "in a corner" (*mpembeni*). Isolation is the mark of Satan. Yet, here stands the warning, "Do not give it away," which seems to erect a solid dam against the flood of enthusiasm.

Not always is the wall of secrecy that surrounds the Jamaa so visible and obvious as in this warning. In my field work I ran against it many times, often realizing it only much later. Tempels, the founder, would speak at length about the "natural" secrecy and discretion that should surround personal "encounter," the prophetic event. If asked about specific points of the doctrine, he would refer me to the Jamaa people in the Congo. In the field, when I had learned the language of the movement and could discuss the doctrine with my informants, many of them, sometimes in the middle of our conversation, would ask who my *baba* and my *mama* were. The relationship established whenever two human beings discuss questions that matter to them was not deemed sufficient as a common ground for our conversation. They wanted to know my place in a genealogy, and, when they discovered that I had no such place, they either retreated or tried to "give birth" to me. Once at a *pulan* meeting the Jamaa people surrounded me with stubborn silence until they realized that I was not quite aware of what was going on (it was during the first months of my field work); they then proceeded without taking any further notice of me. On another occasion I was discussing Jamaa problems with Father B. and Monsignor Malunga at Musonoi. Both were frank and cooperative, but suddenly they excused themselves and left me because they had to attend a Jamaa ceremony to which I could not be invited. In all these situations the "wall" which separated me from the

Jamaa people stood for the fact that I had not gone through *formal initiation.*

At several points in this study we have touched on the problem of initiation and have discussed some of the relevant observations. Let me briefly recapitulate these:

1. First of all, there was the founder's insistence on "encounter" as a basic experience. Encounter is the "liminal" experience in the process of "becoming one," the aim of Jamaa teaching.

2. Other evidence came from patterns of group organization and alliance. We found that relationships between members of the group were conceived of as spiritual generation/filiation. To introduce a new member is to become his "parent." Membership can be obtained in no other way.

3. We have briefly mentioned some of the rules and practices of instruction or *mafundisho* (e.g., presentation of "candidates" at the *pulan* meeting, private sessions in which only two couples participate, etc.).

4. Finally, we found a body of linguistic evidence, a terminology expressing the "technicalities" of entering the Jamaa; cf., in our vocabulary, *ku-endelea* (12), *ku-ingia* (21), *njia* (50), *mawazo* (35, 36).

These seemingly disconnected aspects of Jamaa initiation must be understood in terms of the *ritual* of *ku-ingisha*, introduction to the movement.

The "Three Ways": The Ritual

Asked about their position in the movement, Jamaa members will claim to be in one of the "three ways," e.g., *niko mu njia ya mpili,* I belong to the second way. But there will be no external signs of hierarchical differentiation and order, no badges, no (visible) privileges. All that this "second (or first, or third) way" means is that the candidate and his wife have chosen their spiritual parents. They have been following instructions in the doctrine for a certain time (one or two years for each degree). They have shown to their "parents" and to the group sufficient evidence of "conversion" (legal, or legalized, marriage, renouncement of paganism, and active participation in the life of the group). And they have gone through the ritual of *ku-ingisha*. This ritual is "performed" by a priest (i.e., an active member of the hierarchy of the mission church). That a priest has to do this is explained partly by the nature of the rites (cf. below), partly by the fact that, in the early times of the Jamaa, the act of receiving members into the movement was reserved to the founder. For priests who become members of the movement, Tempels has formulated specific instructions as to when and how to conduct the rite of *ku-ingisha*. My own information comes from one of the leading priests in the movement and consists of a summary of the rite written in Swahili. Since I was asked to treat this as a confidential matter, I shall have to restrict myself to some essential points.

In its external form the rite is basically the same for all three degrees. The officiating priest proceeds as follows: (*a*) He starts with an *examination* of the candidates, the purpose of which is not so much to see whether they have memorized the *mafundisho* but to produce evidence of their "conversion" (cf. *ku-geuka* [18]). (*b*) Then follows an *instruction* about the meaning and the importance of the step the candidates are going to take. An essential part of this section is a kind of "revelation": the candidates are taught the meaning of an esoteric prayer they had learned before. (*c*) Instruction is followed by a *prophecy*, in which the initiates are told what to expect in their new state. (*d*) Then the priest gives some *directions* regarding the initiatory experience (cf. below) which is expected to confirm the ritual during the following night. (*e*) The ritual concludes with prayers and blessings, recited by the priest alone or by both priest and initiates.

Under this common form each degree of the ritual actualizes one of the "three big thoughts" (cf. *mawazo tatu* [36]). This explains why the usual term for degree, *njia*, can be replaced by *wazo*. The sequence runs as follows:

1. *Njia ya kwanza*, the first way: The candidates receive the thought of *uzima* (82), life/force, by "uniting" themselves with *Bwana Yezu Kristo* (7) and *Bikira Maria* (5), respectively. They are told to prepare for this union through prayer and meditation and to keep the secret of their new state. The *proof* of their admission to the first degree will be their initiatory experience, union with *Bwana Yezu Kristo* and *Bikira Maria* in a *dream*. Information on how this union is thought to take place can be found in our comments on such concepts as *ku-shuka, ku-pata,* and *ku-pokea*.

2. *Njia ya mpili*, the second way: The candidates receive the

thought of *umoja/mapendo* (76, 32), to be actualized in a total union between husband and wife, now taking the roles of *Bwana Yezu Kristo* and *Bikira Maria.* Again, there are admonitions to pray and to meditate about this "thought." The initiatory experience of this stage is not mentioned in my document, but it is obvious that the logic of the rite calls for ritual intercourse between husband and wife, a *komunyo ya ndoa,* communion of the marriage, which elevates their everyday marriage to the level of *jamaa* (22).

3. *Njia ya tatu,* the third way: The candidates receive the thought of *uzazi* (81). Husband and wife, now in the roles of Mary and Joseph, are to give birth to Jesus Christ, represented by the priest. This is the point where the ritualized "encounter" between priest and candidates is supposed to happen: the "exchange" of their deepest feelings and wishes, of the story of their lives, and their conversion. The idea is that in this "confession" the priest humiliates himself before his parishioners to become their child. He re-enacts God's descent on the Holy Family (cf. the implications of *ku-shuka.*). Having given birth to the priest, the initiates have now acquired *uzazi,* parenthood, which gives them the right to introduce other candidates to the movement.

Ideas and Symbols

The ideas behind these three stages of initiation are easily identified. In the "first way" the candidates are expected to acquire a lively and life-giving (*uzima*) consciousness of their vocation. In the "second way" they are to realize complete union, i.e., complete *jamaa,* between husband and wife. The "third way," encounter between the couple and the priest, gives them complete union with, and full integration into, the group. In each of the three stages we find the use of familiar symbols: a ritual examination, a dream, ritual intercourse, and ritual confession (with strong overtones of a descent-ascension, death-rebirth symbolism). All these are known as universals in the ethnography of initiatory rites. But the fact that "universal" symbols are employed makes it difficult to identify their specific function in Jamaa initiation.

Jamaa initiation does not mark transition between stages in the life cycle. All candidates are adults and are married; presumably they "have settled down" psychologically and socially *before* they are admitted to the first degree. Yet the symbolic content of the three degrees of initiation is pictured as a progression from birth to marital union to parenthood. In many instructions the "thoughts" that mark the various degrees are presented as developmental stages. G. Kasongo developed this idea in the following way:

When a child is born, it is like clay. His body is like clay; but inside he is not clay, he is man. When such a child grows up, what will be the first thing he thinks of? Love. Whom does he love first? His father and mother. You see how his *bumuntu* [being man] develops? Why does the child love his father and mother? Because he knows that it is from them that he got his life [*buzima*]. . . . You see, the first thing we desire is *buzima*. But after that, after he has grown up, he will think of love. He will say to himself: I want to love, and I shall look for a wife. And when he has found a wife? He will think of parenthood: Now I want to have children. . . . Now all three thoughts have entered him. When he thought of children, what was his idea? *Uzazi* [parenthood, fecundity]. And when he thought of a wife? Which of God's thoughts did he think then? *Mapendo* [love]. And when he thought of his father and mother? He thought of *uzima* [life/force] [T 14; abridged translation].

The distinction between the function of ideas and symbols as *models of* and as *models for* action could help to clarify the situation (though we must not lose sight of the fact that these functions are not mutually exclusive). "Normally," initiation rites appear to *reflect* (symbolize) stages of transition in the life cycle. Jamaa initiation gives the impression of working the other way around; it *induces* states of transition. And the fact that it does have this effect must probably be explained in terms of the content of the central idea of *umuntu* (being man). If this assumption is correct, it could reduce the ambiguity that still surrounds Tempels' concept of "encounter." This prophetic event, as we have called it, is usually described as a sudden, unpredictable, and uncontrollable experience or "discovery" of unity with a fellow human being. But in Jamaa initiation "encounter" is ritualized; the ineffable is put into words; the nonextended and the sudden is extended into three stages marking a progress that takes many years; the entirely personal is socialized. Out of the prophetic *event* developed a *technique* by means of which people are induced to identify themselves with the prophet's message. It is easy to see that more thorough investigation into the working of Jamaa initiation could further support one of the basic assumptions of this study: that charisma is an important force for sociocultural change because it "mobilizes" ideas; it makes possible their acceptance and their implementation.

I should like to add a remark on the rule of "secrecy" mentioned earlier. By now it will have become clear that Jamaa initiation is not just introduction to a body of secret lore (characteristic of associations with specific goals, such as many of the traditional "secret societies"). "Secrecy" in the Jamaa is a symbolic device which dramatizes identification with the group and, above all, the value put on the *personal* character of conversion. Functionally it is not very effective, since it is a "rule" without sanctions and since there is *de facto* no body of secret knowledge different from the doctrine taught in the *mafundisho* meetings to candidates of all degrees. Even the actual rite of initiation, which is never performed in public (i.e., in the presence of the entire group), is covered by personal discretion, not formal secrecy.

This is perhaps the best moment to point to a highly interesting line of inquiry. Further insight into the symbolism and the function of Jamaa initiation may be gained if one looks for the (historical) sources from which Tempels derived, or simply assembled, his ideas and symbols. I must emphasize that such a vast problem as the influence of Luba culture on Jamaa doctrine lies beyond the limits set for this study, but I should like to present at least one illustration directly relevant to the questions we are discussing.

There are many reasons for believing that Tempels "invented" ideas and symbols of Jamaa initiation with a concrete model in his mind: the *buyanga*, a society of hunters among the Baluba Katanga. Many informants confirmed that this *buyanga* was one of the founder's favorite *mifano*, examples, in propagating his message. From the description that Tempels' confrere Theuws gives, I should like to mention these major points:

1. Despite the fact that the *buyanga* is an association of hunters, its organizational basis is not really that of a professional guild. The major link between the members is not so much some specialized knowledge or lore but a participation in the force of *buyanga* (symbolized by spirits and by magical implements). This reminds one very much of the role of *bumuntu*, the central "force" in the Jamaa. In one of Theuws's formulations the parallelism appears very clearly:

A *diyanga* [member of the *buyanga*] occupies in the village about the same position as the notable. The members do not live together and are dispersed over distant villages, but they form a closed group through the magic force in which they alone participate, in which they alone are solidary. They alone were "born" as children of the same force, born to the same life [1962:192].

2. Another trait common to the *buyanga* and the Jamaa is a certain elite consciousness. Even though Tempels and his followers usually deny any desire to surpass their fellow Christians, it is obvious that the same (culturally defined) logic operates on the Jamaa and on the *buyanga:* differentiation implies rank. Tempels himself has made profound remarks about this principle of Luba ontology (cf. 1959:41–43).

3. No one can become a *diyanga* by just taking possession of the symbolic representations of *buyanga;* rather, he must be initiated by a member of the society (Theuws 1962:188). The same idea occurs in the Jamaa: no one can be Jamaa by just learning the doctrine ("taking possession of the symbolic representations of *bumuntu*"); rather, he must be introduced by a member.

4. In the *buyanga,* as in the Jamaa, initiation creates a parent-child relationship between initiating and initiated: "During initiation the older member is 'father' and the candidate 'child' or 'son.' The older member 'gives birth' to him in the *buyanga*" (*ibid.,* 189).

5. Most remarkable is another similarity between the *buyanga* and the Jamaa: initiation includes the wives of both the older member and the candidate; membership in the *buyanga* is in couples (*ibid.,* 189). It will be remembered that the Jamaa member addresses his wife as *mama,* mother, not as *bibi,* wife (cf. *baba/mama* [4] and *bwana/bibi* [6]). After the initiation the wife (i.e., the first wife in a polygamous marriage) of a *diyanga* is called *inamakola, ina* meaning "mother" (cf. van Avermaet and Mbuya 1954: 194; Theuws 1962:191).

6. Initiation into the *buyanga* is completed by presentation of the candidate to the village chief in a way which reminds one very much of the role of the priest in Jamaa initiation (Theuws 1962: 190 ff.).

7. Two of the most typical social rules of the Jamaa have close parallels in the *buyanga:* traveling members of both will be housed by a fellow member, not a relative (*ibid.,* 191), and the success

of a *diyanga* as a hunter depends on his wife's cooperation—while he prepares for the hunt and during the time he is out in the bush she must observe certain taboos (e.g., confinement to her hut) and is supposed to accompany her husband in her "thoughts" (*ibid.,* 191, and private communication). The latter point, especially, is a very prominent topic in Jamaa instruction. The document quoted above includes the following "rule," given to the candidates at the end of the "second way": "You, *baba,* when you go to your work, on the road: guard your *mama* in your thoughts [cf. *ku-chunga* (8)], talk to her, be close to her in your thoughts. And you, *mama,* do the same" (T 14).

Ritual and Conflict

The ritual of initiation into the Jamaa provides "channels" through which the system of Jamaa doctrine becomes internalized and institutionalized. However, it would be wrong to think of this channeling function as a completely "routinized" and automatic process. In many instances and situations the very ritual that is supposed to bring about integration into the group and complete unity becomes a source of conflict or dramatizes already existing conflict.

There is, first, the fact that initiation into the Jamaa is dependent on a complete consensus among several individuals: husband and wife, candidates and initiating couple, candidates and initiating priest.

It was interesting to note the reactions if one confronted Jamaa people with the following simple problem: What if the husband decides to join the Jamaa, but his wife is not interested in the movement? Usually the first reaction was impressive testimony to the power of those ultimate definitions of reality we have called "Jamaa ontology": some informants would not even understand the question. The idea of an individual seeking only for himself the goods promised by the Jamaa seemed inconceivable to them. "Ontologically" man does not exist as an independent individual. Someone who is not a child, a parent, or a spouse is considered a *muntu mufu,* dead man. As a second reaction, the informants would admit that there are indeed many practical difficulties to face. All of them were eager to stress one point: Jamaa members must be free in their choice. Unlike the husband in traditional society, the husband here is not allowed to use physical force; the wife should not try the subtle means of "passive" resistance. Magic, one of the most commonly employed methods of resolving marital conflict, is, of course, excluded altogether.

It is very impressive to see how many couples have reached a lasting harmony *in* the Jamaa and, undoubtedly, *through* the Jamaa. Yet the data suggest that Jamaa doctrine and initiation bring about "unity" not by eliminating conflict but rather by "dramatizing" tensions and by elevating them to a symbolic level on which they can be "solved" through constant confrontation with the ideas and norms of the doctrine. (We shall have more to say about this in the following section.)

Another possible source of conflict is the parent-child relationship between the initiating and the initiated. The choice of one's "parents" in the Jamaa is free. But the idea of *kizazi*, spiritual kinship, implies that, once the choice has been made, the relationship becomes a "necessary" one, much like the relationships of biological generation. One may leave and abandon one's parents, but this does not change the *fact* of generation/filiation. Many tensions and quarrels in a Jamaa group arise when members refuse to acknowledge the "necessary" character of spiritual kinship and change their alliance. The ritual of initiation may then act as a control mechanism. The governing idea is the progressive "birth" of the candidates; changing one's parents in the process of "being born" is never considered just a technicality; it is a serious offense, since it interferes with the growth of *uzazi*, fecundity.

In a similar way, the requirements of initiation may cause or aggravate conflict between a Jamaa group and the local pastor. As we have said, the presence of a priest, at least in the third stage, is a necessary element of Jamaa initiation. However, the great majority of Jamaa groups have not been able fully to incorporate a priest through initiation. The problem that this situation poses is handled in various ways. Sometimes only the leader and one or two others are fully initiated while the other members are kept waiting, so to speak, until the priest will agree to become a member. Other leaders are known to have sent their candidates to the few Jamaa priests for initiation (e.g., to Musonoi and Lubumbashi). As late as 1966 entire groups of candidates made the 1,000-mile trip by train from the Kasai to Kolwezi to be initiated by Father B. These expeditions, of course, do not increase understanding between a local missionary and his parishioners, especially if the former does not understand that people are compelled to such "unloyal" behavior by the rules of initiation—the very ritual that should unite a local pastor with his Jamaa group.

Conflict may come from the fact that performance of the ritual of initiation and the change of attitudes it is supposed to symbolize are two different things, each following its own rules. There are no reasons to doubt that Tempels saw initiation as a *means* of "teaching" and "learning" the message. On the other hand, it is rather difficult for the average Jamaa member not to take initiation as an *end*. Hence the difficulty many leaders have in keeping their candidates from trying to "go on" after the third stage is reached. M. Ndala at Lubumbashi complained to me about this tendency of *kupita ukristiani,* (of trying) to surpass Christianity. For him it had become a threat to the survival of the Jamaa. He and several other leaders, therefore, began to play down the importance of the ritual and to stress conversion and practice.

MAFUNDISHO: TEACHING THE MESSAGE

Ambivalent Attitudes toward "Teaching"

In the preceding section we introduced the topic of initiation by pointing out an apparent contradiction between the claim for universal relevance and the rules of secrecy. A similar situation presents itself when we look at the data regarding *mafundisho,* instruction in the doctrine. It will be remembered that the founder expressed an aversion for "manuals" and formal indoctrination. Jamaa, he maintained, cannot be taught; it must spontaneously "arise" from the prophetic event of personal "encounter." Yet he propagated his ideas as a peripatetic teacher in the camps near Kolwezi, and he is remembered as *mwenye kufundisha,* someone who knew how to teach. He coined Jamaa doctrinal formulae and put them into a system, *swahili ya père Placide,* "the Swahili [i.e., the language] of père Placide," as one informant referred to it. He initiated, or at least sponsored, codification of his message in the *kitabu* of Musonoi. From his exile in Belgium he continues to supervise the teaching of the doctrine (by pronouncing on disputes, sending outlines, etc.).

Like the founder, Jamaa people often show an ambivalent attitude toward "teaching." There can be no doubt that *mafundisho* constitute an important part of the activities of a group. On the other hand, one often hears leaders complain about the burden of *mafundisho* and about little-enlightened followers who think that the Jamaa consists of nothing but "instruction." One can think of two major reasons for this ambiguity:

1. By definition, a charismatic message is likely to have a spontaneous impact. Enthusiastic "testimony" and "conversion" rather than planned teaching and learning are the expected responses to the new system of orientations. Many Jamaa leaders are aware of an inherent contradiction, or tension, between the surprising, overwhelming effect of Tempels' message at the beginning of the movement and the present elaborate system of initiation and *mafundisho* taking several years to complete.

2. Clues from linguistic data show that, despite the importance of concepts related to *kufundisha,* to teach, Jamaa terminology excludes technical terms of everyday Swahili such as *masomo,* school, education, and *mwalimu,* teacher. This is explained by the specific situation in which the movement operates. Critics of the mission in the Congo often point out that the church has become *une église de gosses,* a children's church. In the Congo (and many former colonies), preoccupation with schools and children created an image of the mission as some sort of educational institution. Baptism and participation in the ritual life were regarded as necessary concomitants (or evils) of the way into the white man's world. In a sense, the Jamaa movement can be understood as a reaction against a religious situation dominated by the concern for teaching and education. This recurred very often as a theme in conversations with Jamaa people. Many informants told me that only conversion to the Jamaa had made them realize that Christianity was a religion for adults.

Despite this ambiguous attitude toward the concept of "teaching," Jamaa people spend a considerable amount of their time in teaching or being taught. In the public *mafundisho* meeting and in private instructions the system of Jamaa doctrine is consciously transmitted, following a certain order (of "chapters") and rules of progressive initiation. In the process of being transmitted, it is often manipulated, changed, or used for the realization of specific goals.

Teaching and Authority

Jamaa doctrine and organization do not as such provide avenues for the formation of a class of teaching specialists. Still, every group has one or several prominent members whom we have called "speakers," since their prominence is based on their role in the *mafundisho* meeting; they alone will usually recite the instruction in the doctrine. Now we are in a better position to understand this informal class of specialists. In terms of the basic conceptions of the Jamaa, transmission of doctrine is *transmission of life*. Someone who, because of his rhetoric and because of the impact of his personality, is able to attract a large number of candidates will be recognized as a leader. But it is important to see that his authority is interpreted as the authority of a father of many children. Such authority is not contestable. Laurent Mujanshi at Musonoi, for instance, probably was surpassed by many members of the group in intelligence, rhetorical style, and pleasant personality. But he maintained his position as a prominent teacher and almost monopolized the *mafundisho* meeting because he had "given birth" to more candidates than anyone else. Obviously, in his case (and in many others), teaching had become an expressive rather than an instrumental activity. When Anaclet Tshikala began to compete with Laurent Mujanshi (cf. Chapter 2) for leadership in the group, he had, consciously or unconsciously, to accept the terms or "weapons" in which the latter expressed his position. Tshikala's contributions to the *mafundisho* meetings became attempts to "outteach" Mujanshi about the same topic and in the same style.

On the whole, Jamaa leaders are surprisingly conscious of the temptation to manipulate the charismatic message as a means of increasing their authority. Earlier we have quoted Tempels' rule: *ukubwa inaua mafundisho,* power kills the *mafundisho.* Marcel Ndala of Lubumbashi repeatedly told me that the leaders of the Kolwezi area used their "teaching" to enlarge their influence and power among other groups in the movement. This also was his reason for not accepting the *kitabu* as an authoritative document on Jamaa doctrine. He himself differentiated between *mafundisho* and education and maintained that "teaching," the way most groups were practicing it, was the most serious obstacle for the Jamaa in attracting followers among *les intellectuels.*

Teaching and Context

The strong tendency to use "teaching" as a means of *expressing* one's position in the group rather than *transmitting* orientations corroborates our findings in the formal analysis of Jamaa doctrinal language. Terms connected with "teaching" and "instruction" for the most part had to be included in the category of symbolic-associative, i.e., ritual, concepts. We shall now examine some observations which give further support to this view.

Late in April, 1967, I attended a *pulan* meeting at Musonoi. It turned out to be a particularly stormy session. The issue under discussion was an invitation from a Congolese priest to ten couples from each Jamaa group of the area to participate in a *carrefour,* a sort of workshop, about the Jamaa. The majority seemed to be in favor of accepting the invitation, particularly since the priest was the child of Jamaa parents. However, Anaclet Tshikala and Paul Ngama took it as an occasion to propagate their own favorite idea: "Before we go to anyone and explain to him what the Jamaa is, we should first *be* Jamaa—revive our forgotten ideals and practice what we are preaching. Above all, we should not pretend to act unanimously when in reality we are divided by factions." All this sounded very general and vague but in fact was aimed at the members of the group at Luilu, who had gotten into violent conflict with their local pastor. Another speaker immediately attacked Anaclet Tshikala on his weakest point—his struggle with Laurent Mujanshi for leadership of the group at Musonoi. For the first time in more than a year of observation, I saw a meeting of the Jamaa threaten to get out of hand. Discussion degenerated into wild shouting and gesticulating until, all of a sudden, a *baba,* not a very prominent one, started to give a *mafundisho*. Very calmly he recited doctrinal formulae which had no connection with the preceding discussion. He talked about God, the angels, and the Virgin Mary and concluded, after fifteen minutes of meandering through many chapters of Jamaa teaching, with a rather obscure practical application. I was stunned by the effect of the "instruction." The audience listened attentively, not giving the slightest sign of impatience (which might have happened under other circumstances). After the *mafundisho* had ended, calm and equilibrium seemed to have been restored. Several other matters were discussed quietly before the meeting was terminated.

It seems obvious that an explanation for the success of this *mafundisho* must be sought in the ritual-symbolic function of teaching. The actualization of Jamaa doctrine through recitation had forced the participants to calm down because it transferred interaction from an instrumental to a symbolic level. Conflict was not negated (cf. our remarks on "dramatized conflict" in the ritual of initiation earlier in this chapter), but its terms were redefined in Jamaa language, and this redefinition included a solution.

Further light on this is shed by an experience I had in November, 1966, when a *mama* of the Jamaa at Musonoi asked me to lend her some money; her family had gotten into a difficult situation (probably through debt). I gave her half the amount she asked for, since that was all I had with me. Two days later I was approached by her husband, who asked for "the rest." Usually calm and dignified, he was now very nervous and even gave the impression of having strengthened his spirits with a few drinks. His embarrassment and shame at being obliged to ask a young white man were almost physically noticeable. Suddenly, as soon as we had finished the financial transaction, he began to recite a *mafundisho* about *ubaba,* fatherhood, and *masaidiano,* mutual help, vaguely related to the situation in which we found ourselves but largely consisting of a juxtaposition of quite disparate doctrinal formulae. At the end of it he had completely regained his composure. Here, again, it seems to me that the *mafundisho* served to project a situation which implied shame and humiliation to a symbolic level on which the relationship between us was redefined in "metaphysical" terms of love, parental care, and mutual help, unaffected by the inequalities of everyday life.[1]

The ritual-symbolic function of Jamaa teaching explains some typical reactions of Jamaa informants. Only on very rare occasions was I able to speak to one informant alone (the exception being some very prominent leaders and close friends). Monica Kabole (cf. above, pp. 94 f.) would refuse to talk about the Jamaa (at least most of the time) unless Fortunat Kitenge or another member of

---

1. Evidence from similar situations excludes an alternative explanation: that the person was trying to "pay" me with information in exchange for the money he had borrowed.

the group was present. In some similar situations informants pointed out that other members would become "jealous" if they talked alone. Once, at Sandoa, a *mama* suddenly stopped in the middle of a *mafundisho* and gave an explanation which probably came closer to the truth. She told me it was not right to teach *upeke,* alone, in isolation. "Teaching" is a communal rite, never just transmission of information.

Routine and Method

At this point we can make an important distinction. If we accept most of Max Weber's premises for a theory of charisma, we might be tempted to conclude that ritualization equals "routinization" (and that the presence of nonspontaneous, ritualized behavior is a sign of the waning of charisma). From our study of the Jamaa we can adduce two reasons against such a view. First, I think, the formal analysis of the doctrine and our brief presentation of the ritual of initiation have demonstrated conclusively that "mythological" and "ritual" conceptions were an integral part of Tempels' charismatic message from the very beginning. The development up to the time of field work does not indicate that the orientational content of this message has become less important than its ritualized forms. Second, in a certain sense "ritual" and "routine" can be understood as counteracting forces. Besides the laws of rational (i.e., "economic") behavior, the *factor of time* plays an important role in the processes of routinization of charisma: lasting relationships between the charismatic leader and his followers eventually must submit to the demands of everyday life (Weber 1964:182). As our account of the ritual function of teaching in the preceding section has shown, the effect of ritual symbolic behavior can be the *conquest of time* (i.e., of the time and its laws in which everyday life is situated). Through the recitation of Jamaa doctrine the "everyday" struggle for power between Anaclet Tshikala and his opponents was transformed into a "universal," timeless situation of discord for which the Jamaa provides universal solutions. Clearly, in this instance, the verbal ritual of *mafundisho* served to counteract, if not neutralize, tendencies to routinize the Jamaa as a means of obtaining influence and personal power.

Jamaa people themselves are conscious of "routine" in the teaching of the doctrine, both in a negative and a positive sense. Ignace

Kapongo once remarked to me that, after ten years of weekly *mafundisho,* the instructions became *sawa wimbo ku misa,* like the hymns during mass—everybody joins in the familiar words and melodies without thinking about the sense. Outsiders, especially among the clergy, are very much aware of the "routinization" of Jamaa teaching and make it one of their favorite objections against the movement. Jamaa people sometimes defend themselves by maintaining that the regular and public *mafundisho* meetings are not really held to instruct (*kufundisha*) but to counsel (*ku-shauria*), and to some of the high-school students at Kolwezi the Jamaa appeared as a *société conseillère,* especially in matters of marriage (cf. Appendix II). There are reasons to believe that the shift from *mafundisho* to *mashaurio* is not a late development. In stressing the function of "counsel" (especially in matters of marriage, which are so important in the Jamaa), Tempels may consciously have incorporated an element of Luba culture.[2]

"Routine" in a positive sense—facility in speaking, for example, and a command of proverbs and imagery—is much appreciated in traditional culture as well as in the Jamaa. In giving a *mafundisho* the speaker is free to insert *mifano,* short illustrations of a point taken mostly from everyday situations, or *arisi,* full-length stories "invented" after traditional patterns of fables and narratives (cf. Appendixes VII and VIII). Some informants showed a certain pride in their authorship, or even "ownership" of their *mafundisho* and *arisi.* After listening to the recording of a *mafundisho* he had just spoken on tape, M. Binga once jokingly accused me: *unaiba mafundisho yangu,* you steal my *mafundisho.*

The use of proverbs (which is extremely important in traditional rhetoric) is almost completely excluded in the urban centers, where the language of the *mafundisho* is Swahili. According to my observations, the adoption of Swahili as a lingua franca in Katanga has not led to the integration of such elements of Swahili literature and oral tradition as proverbs. Only occasionally have I heard Jamaa speakers quoting proverbs in their native language (in most cases this was Tshiluba).

2. In 1939 and 1943 a confrere of Tempels, S. Peeraer, published a collection of admonitions to newlyweds, which, apart from the different social and cultural context, bear a strong resemblance to many Jamaa *mafundisho* (cf. Appendix VI).

MAWAZO: SHARING THE SYSTEM

Myth and Dream

In January, 1967, I participated in a *kilio*—the celebration at the end of a period of mourning—for a deceased Jamaa member at the camp of Kapata. Delegations from all groups in the Kolwezi area had assembled at the house of the widow. The ceremony began with the singing of Jamaa hymns; then a member of the Kapata group welcomed the visitors and gave, in a short speech, what he called the *programme ya kilio,* the program of the *kilio,* i.e., a short instruction about the meaning of this gathering for the Jamaa. Here is the gist of his talk:

> We have assembled to celebrate the *kilio* for the late *baba* Simon. For the *bantu ya inchi* [lit., the people of the land] this would be an occasion to mourn and to lament. For the *bantu ya ndani mwenye kuchunga mawazo* [lit., the "inside" people who guard the *mawazo*] this is a feast of joy. For one of us has preceded us on the way to God. He has become *muntu mawazo,* "thought-man" [cf. the vocabulary, 43]. He is not far away, because he stays in our *mawazo;* we pray that God may receive him and that he will show himself to us.

I have chosen to use this little speech as an introduction because it contains two issues to be discussed in this section. First, the criterion which distinguishes Jamaa people from "ordinary" people (*bantu ya inchi* most often means "natives") is the fact that they "guard *mawazo.*" Second, it is expressed clearly that death means passing into the realm of *mawazo* and that the link between this world and the other is through dreams. This is what the speaker refers to when he expresses hope that the deceased will "show himself." This interpretation is reinforced by the fact that, in Jamaa language, "to dream" is always expressed as *kupata mawazo,* to receive *mawazo.*

MAWAZO AND MYTH-DREAM

The literal translation of *mawazo* (cf. vocabulary [35]) is, according to the *Standard Swahili Dictionary,* "thought, fancy, idea, notion, supposition," but this does not render the complexity of its meaning and function in the doctrinal system. In terms of its function, I have called *mawazo* "a common denominator" in Jamaa teaching. Here I should like to add another suggestion by translating *mawazo* as "communication" and by drawing rough lines of distinction between three major connotations:

1. *Mawazo* may denote the *basis of communication,* that which makes communication possible. Mawazo is a *common substance* between God and man and between man and man: God's nature is *mawazo,* and when he created man he gave him his *mawazo;* man is body and *mawazo.*

2. *Mawazo* and the verb *ku-waza* signify the *act of communication.* "To think," in Jamaa language, means not so much "to reason" but to embrace an idea, a person. *Kuwaza muntu,* think man (said of God), equals *kuumba muntu,* create man. Similarly, Adam induces God to create Eve by "thinking" Eve.

3. *Mawazo* also refers to the *content of communication,* either to a specific idea or proposition (cf. the "three thoughts" in the vocabulary [36]) or the sum total of ideas, beliefs, and norms of Jamaa doctrine.

It is in this last sense that the speaker at the *kilio* employed the formula *bantu mwenye kuchunga mawazo,* people who guard *mawazo.* The best way to conceptualize this consciousness of sharing a common "depository of truth" seems to be the introduction of a term of which we have made little use so far: *myth.*[3] In an earlier attempt to construct an analytical framework for the study of prophetic-charismatic movements (Fabian 1963), I utilized this concept to characterize the pool of symbolic orientations which direct charismatic action via articulation in a prophetic message. I postulated that " 'Myth' does not mean this or that story, but rather the latent (and therefore hypothetical) process, which, in a given society, produces myths (stories) and their variants" (*ibid.,* 797).

Because "myth" is such an all-purpose word and thus has little analytical value, I did not make it a major conceptual tool in this study. But the ethnographic facts, especially the *mawazo* doctrine in Jamaa teaching, all but force one to consider its applicability, especially in the sense it was employed so successfully by K. O. Burridge in his explanation of Melanesian cargo cults. He enlarges

---

3. Elsewhere I have attempted to relate *mawazo* doctrine to a known type in the history of religion: Gnosis. Cf. Fabian 1969b.

the concept somewhat by calling it "myth-dream," which he describes as follows:

> As a concept "myth-dream" does not lend itself to precise definition. Nevertheless, myth-dreams exist, and they may be reduced to a series of themes, propositions, and problems which are to be found in myths, in dreams, in half-lights of conversation, and in the emotional responses to a variety of actions, and questions asked. Through this kind of intellectualization myth-dreams become "aspirations." . . . Eventually, such intellectualizations as are made may become the definitive principles upon which a group of persons may organize themselves into a viable party or movement. And by so organizing themselves the group concerned puts itself into a position from which it may "capture" the myth-dreams by symbolizing and putting into effect the propositions contained in the myth-dream [Burridge 1960: 148].

Let us consider the usefulness of these assumptions for our present purpose. In choosing to conceive of *mawazo* as the myth (or myth-dream) of the Jamaa, we imply, first of all, a distinction between *mawazo* and *mafundisho: mawazo,* the "thoughts guarded by Jamaa people," become *mafundisho* through the intervening activity of a "speaker," of someone who selects out of the common pool of orientations certain aspects by formulating them (or employing ready-made formulae). Such a distinction between a "latent" common pool of orientations (*mawazo*) and a "manifest" system of orientations (*mafundisho*) helps to avoid oversimplified ideas as to how a doctrinal system like the teaching of the Jamaa is shared by its adherents. It is especially useful in handling the following problems.

Even though they appear slight, there are *differences* in teaching between individual speakers and between groups and regions (cf. our remarks on the antagonism between the Lubumbashi and Kolwezi areas in Chapter 2). The strong cohesion of the movement, despite manifest doctrinal differences, is explained by the fact that all followers and groups of followers share a latent common set of orientations which (at least within certain limits) is not affected by differences in emphasis and formulation of teaching. This distinction between *mawazo* and *mafundisho* will also allow us to understand the relationships between "orthodox" and "heterodox" Jamaa groups (cf. below).

Further, the concept of a myth-dream (and this was Burridge's major reason for employing it) may help to integrate the phenomenon of dreaming into our description and analysis of the Jamaa. For the "prophet" (above all, the founder, but also every "speaker" in the movement) is not the only one who articulates latent *mawazo* in a manifest message. In marked contrast to the usage in everyday Swahili (and in Kiluba), Jamaa language has a technical term for "to dream." It is not *ku-lota* (the usual term), but *kupata mawazo,* to receive *mawazo.* Dream and message are both called *mawazo* and may become interchangeable concepts in the Jamaa because of their identical function in relation to what we have called the myth: both articulate and formulate latent orientations in such a way that they become relevant in particular situations and for specific problems. This particular function of dreaming in the Jamaa permits us to understand why a dream may be required as an "initiatory experience" (i.e., as a prerequisite for admission to a degree of initiation; cf. above). It is not so much the contact with "supernatural beings"—Lord Jesus and the Virgin Mary—which the dream is supposed to "prove." In the recorded dreams these beings do not even appear personally but are symbolized by statues (or sometimes by the priest). Nor do they make any important revelations. In the initiatory dream, Lord Jesus and the Virgin Mary "unite" themselves with the dreamer and thus make him participate in the "three big thoughts" (*mawazo*) of life, fecundity, and love. The dream is the proof that the candidate shares the *mawazo* of the Jamaa; he has become *mwenye kuchunga mawazo,* one who guards thoughts.

DREAMING AND AUTHORITY

At this point we have to deal with a possible objection. If we attribute to the dreamer more or less the same function that we attribute to the prophet and speaker, we run the risk of seriously weakening some of our basic assumptions about the nature of the Jamaa. We have employed the concepts of charisma and charismatic authority because they allowed us to trace the emergence of a new and distinct social phenomenon to the formulation of a new system of orientations by a charismatic leader. We have argued that the methodological usefulness of this approach lies in its ability to locate extremely diffuse and complex processes of sociocultural change in the interaction between one or a few charismatic leaders and their followers. If we now say that both the prophet and the dreamer have the same function in relation to the common pool of orientations referred to as the "myth," we must explain how the charismatic authority of a few leaders can be maintained. In a paper on "Dream and Charisma" (Fabian 1966), I argued that Jamaa leaders are able to utilize the charismatic energy which is freed in the dreams of their followers for strengthening their own authority by formulating specific "theories" about the nature and interpretation of dreams and by reserving the application of these theories to themselves. We can now add that this is possible precisely because, in terms of Jamaa teaching, dreams are considered neither as natural nor as supernatural phenomena which "befall" man from some extraneous source but as *mawazo,* the common treasure "guarded" by the movement.

With the exception of one or two cases, no Jamaa leader in Katanga based his authority directly on dreaming. The typical Jamaa leader is not a dreamer or visionary. In part this may be due to the fact that the mission has always counteracted visionary tendencies (cf. the remarks in Sundkler 1961:271). There are, in fact, reports which suggest that Tempels himself had to curb overenthusiastic visionaries in the early phases of the Jamaa. For the present state of affairs, two explanations (probably not mutually exclusive) may be offered. First, dreaming, albeit important and highly esteemed, has not become the sole basis of charismatic authority in the Jamaa, because through its redefinition as *kupata mawazo,* to receive thoughts, it has been placed in a larger context. A dream-*mawazo* is only one of many *mawazo;* the irrational, both threatening and fascinating, aspects of dream life are reduced to a minimum. Second, the attitude toward dreaming among Jamaa leaders may be due to a persistence of the traditional image of the *nganga,* medicine man, among the Luba and related peoples. Let me make clear the terms of comparison. In contrast to the *vidye,* necromancer, whose main function is (visionary) contact with ancestor spirits, the *nganga* is in charge of the *bwanga,* magic "medicines," their production and manipulation (cf. Burton 1961:81). But the *nganga*'s role in the community is by no means exhausted by the material-magic aspects of his profession. As the guardian of *bwanga* he is responsible for the "interpretation" of his medicines and thus becomes one of the major authorities in defining both the ills and problems and their solutions in a Luba community. One of his most important functions is also the "control" of dreams (*ibid.*, 88). Jamaa leaders will, of course, deny any connection with this model (because the Jamaa explicitly forbids consulting *banganga*), but its unconscious use seems highly probable.

In Kikondja, for instance, the local Jamaa group uses Kiluba. There the replacement of "dream" by "thought" exactly parallels the Swahili usage. Instead of *kilotwa,* dream, the term *malango* (sing. *dilango*) is used. This is translated by van Avermaet and Mbuya as *"gedachte,* pensée, idée, concept, supposition, hypothèse, avis" (1954:339); it corresponds exactly to *mawazo.* But a highly interesting connection which cannot be derived from the Swahili terms appears when one looks at one of the meanings of the corresponding verb *ku-langa:* "*Kulanga* also means: explain everything that is related to a *bwanga,* or to prescribe the observances, rites, and tabus connected with it" (*ibid.*). And this is what makes the functions of the *nganga* and the Jamaa leader comparable: both are the interpreters, guardians, and prophets of latent power which for one is the *bwanga,* for the other *mawazo.* This is by no means farfetched if we remember that the Luba society *buyanga* (which is essentially a community of those who participate in the *bwanga* called *buyanga;* cf. Theuws 1962:188) could become a consciously applied model for the Jamaa and for initiation into the movement.

THE ROLE OF TEMPELS

We can now draw some further conclusions regarding Tempels' role as the articulator of a latent myth. If we say that he attracted his followers by formulating a *new* message, we by no means imply that he confronted them with ideas that had no connection with the general cultural context in which he and his followers lived. On the contrary, his success cannot be understood outside this general context, of which he made use and which he "intellectualized" (Burridge). He selected and transformed ideas from the latent myth in such a way that they could be experienced as new and powerful motives for action. The connection between *bwanga* and *mawazo* shows that the transformation which occurred in Jamaa doctrine is one from a predominantly nature-oriented conception of the forces of reality toward a predominantly society-oriented system of ideas. The *nganga* was the prophet of powers materialized in magic symbols and relevant to a society of agriculturists

and hunters. The Jamaa leader is the prophet of powers materialized, above all, in words which give meaning and orientation in an
urban-industrial world. In using the term "transformation," I
wish to imply that the change is between levels of expression and
symbolization, not necessarily of content. It should be remembered
that those basic ideas and values (like the "three big thoughts" of
life/force, fecundity, and love) which became the new "way" of
the Jamaa were first formulated by Tempels as the basic ideas of
Bantu Philosophy, i.e., of traditional Bantu culture.

THE ETHNOGRAPHY OF JAMAA DREAMS

Here I should like to add a brief note on the ethnography of
dreaming in the Jamaa.[4] It was much easier to collect information
concerning Jamaa theories *about* dreams than it was to secure
actual dream accounts. Because dreams are *mawazo,* they are not
considered personal matters; one would thus expect Jamaa members
to be quite eager to communicate their dream experiences. However, this tendency is countered by the intimate connection between
dreams and initiation which, in most cases, makes dreams fall
under the rules of secrecy.

Such generalizations of dream content as the sample at my dis-
posal allows would be more or less the same as those proposed by
Sundkler (1961:265–75). The most important common trait is a
standardization of the manifest content and the formal elements
(symbols, situations, and solutions of conflicts). As in the South
African churches, the most prominent symbolic color is white (a
light; a white gown). The scenery of the dream is usually not a
landscape but the group or the household or sometimes the church.
The most promising line for further research would be to relate the
phenomenon of dream standardization directly to the prophetic-
ritual function of dreams in the Jamaa, i.e., taking dreams as the
enactment of initiation ideology and of typical situations of personal and social conflict (typical because defined in terms of Jamaa doctrine). It goes without saying that dreams could be of
equal importance for assessing the relative impact of traditional
and "new" orientations on individual members of the movement.
The three examples of recorded dream accounts in Appendix IX

---

4. For Jamma classification of dreams I refer to my paper on "Dreams
and Charisma" (Fabian 1966).

were chosen to illustrate the three tendencies just mentioned: initiatory experience, personal conflict, and social tensions.

The Problem of Heterodox Groups

Readers familiar with the ethnography of African prophetic charismatic movements will probably have developed some doubts concerning our presentation of the Jamaa. That this movement is exceptional because it developed in a context previously almost "untouched" by charismatic activities, the Catholic mission, and that it has not been separated from the organization in which it arose are facts established from the evidence available in Katanga. But our description of the Jamaa as an open, universalistic, nonradical, and nonmilitant movement may appear too beautiful to be true. This is the point at which our picture should be made a little more realistic by adding some shadows—or, at least, what supporters of the Jamaa consider to be shadows.

Hardly ever have I had a conversation about the Jamaa in which my informants did not bring up the question of "deviations." During my field work this aspect became one of the most elusive and frustrating problems of research. The difficulties were not caused by the fact that in the group at Musonoi (and presumably in every Jamaa group) there were "devious" individuals: people who utilized the movement for some specific purpose of their own without identifying with its norms and ideas; habitual troublemakers; mentally and emotionally unbalanced types, etc. All this is too "normal" to be problematic. Rather, there were at Musonoi, and in almost all other places where the Jamaa is represented, vague references to a "second group," not in communication with the mission and its local representative and sometimes in open conflict with them. Field work on the Jamaa involves a certain degree of identification with the movement, and this puts restrictions on the possibilities of going beyond the limits of information set by the group one is studying. But as time went on, I was able to collect more and more pieces of the puzzle.

THE RIDDLE OF *KATETE*

The first clue indicating that these "deviations" were more important than most informants suggested was the fact that, throughout the Jamaa of Katanga, they are referred to by the same name, *katete.* This word in itself poses quite a problem. It is apparently not of Swahili origin (although a root, *tete,* soft grain, and *teta,* oppose, backbite, exist). Most of my informants maintained that it does not mean anything at all—that it is just a label. The various explanations that were given can be reduced to one of the following two types:

1. The name *katete* was propagated by one of the prominent members at Jadotville. This man, known in the Jamaa of Katanga as one of the few leaders who tries to base his authority on visionary gifts, once openly claimed to have a "telephone to God." The name was revealed to him in a dream, but its meaning was not explained. I had no occasion to question him personally.

2. Others took their lead from a word *katete* (in Tshokwe, apparently not in Luba) which signifies a bitter herb. In an allegoric application they then would point out that the deviating groups were like a "bitter taste" that permeates the entire Jamaa.[5]

As widespread as the use of the name *katete* are the charges made by "orthodox" Jamaa people. The most current stereotypes are that the *katete* people surround themselves with absolute secrecy; they do things *mpembeni,* in a corner; their meetings and activities always take place at night and in private houses. Second, the *katete* people exchange their women and come together to have sexual orgies. In some regions they are believed to visit cemeteries at night and have ritual intercourse there or in the bush outside the village.

It is almost impossible to verify these charges directly. A more visible indicator of the constitution of a *katete* group is its relationship with the mission and the hierarchy. At Musonoi, during most of the time of my field work, some twenty-five couples of the Jamaa stayed away from church services and did not receive the sacraments. They also refused contact with the local pastor. In late

5. Van Avermaet and Mbuya (1954:669–700) quote a Luba saying in which *tete,* locust, is used as a symbol of moral decay, but my information does not make any such connection. H. J. Greschat mentions in a recent publication on the Kitawala that in Rhodesia, in the early thirties, groups obeying the rules of the white Russelite missionaries were called *achete,* the silent ones, by the dissident Achitawala (1967:41). Since this information was collected only in 1965 and since a linguistic transformation of *achete* into *katete* (replacement of the *a-* through the *ka-* prefix and palatalization of the *t*) is possible, this could be an interesting lead, but at present it cannot be **verified**.

1966, it came, mainly through the mediation of Ignace Kapongo, close to a complete reconciliation. Latest reports from Musonoi indicate that the break has occurred again, this time through severe measures by church authorities. But even at Musonoi these tensions were discussed only in terms of a very general and vague appeal to *umoja,* unity, and *masikilizano,* mutual understanding. Neither references in the public meetings nor conversations with informants revealed the peculiarities of the *katete.* But leaders of the Jamaa (in the clergy and among the lay members) have formed opinions about its origin and "function," some of which I shall mention briefly.

Most sympathizers and the founder himself speak of "exaggerations" and tend to put the blame on individual *katete* leaders. One of the missionaries at Lubumbashi, deeply involved in the movement and at the same time a perceptive observer of its development, suggested an interpretation which seems more likely. The breakdown of controls and, perhaps, a general situation of anomie following independence and the upheavals of the Katanga secession in 1960–61 had left some Jamaa groups in a state of complete *libertinage,* as my informant put it. At that time two Jamaa members who are now the prime *katete* leaders at Lubumbashi went to Kolwezi, presumably in an attempt to get approval for certain practices in conflict with morals as defined by the mission. The same informant maintained that the so-called deviations (i.e., the stereotyped charges quoted here) were present in the Jamaa from the beginning. In his opinion the establishment of *katete* groups must be seen as an attempt to ritualize and therefore *control* these tendencies. There is certainly no lack of models for such ritualization of ecstatic emotional and sexual behavior in the cultural surroundings of the Jamaa.[6]

Other observers point to a very obvious fact: Sexual communism and ritual orgies belong to the traits that can be found in the early stages of all enthusiastic movements (including Christianity, as evidenced in the letters of Paul to the Corinthians), even in those in which they are not an explicit objective founded in the ideology.

Again, others see the *katete* mainly as a psychological phenomenon. The involvement and spiritual intimacy between members

6. Cf. Burton's description of the *bumbudye* society among the Baluba (1961:154–67).

called for by the central values of Jamaa doctrine create emotional tensions which find their outlet in the *katete* practices. All these explanations are plausible, but they are too general to account for the development in the Jamaa. Also, by attributing the *katete* tendencies to some universal psychological mechanism, they are unable to account for the specific orientational problems involved—and these are the ones we are concerned with here.

Let me attempt a more adequate interpretation.

KATETE: A CASE OF NONSEPARATED SEPARATISM

If one does not concentrate on the stereotyped charges of sexual libertinism, the constitution of *katete* groups appears in most cases to be the result of struggles for power among Jamaa leaders. As we have pointed out in Chapter 2, in the section on "Tensions and Trends" in the group at Musonoi, the terms of such struggle are defined by the orientational system of the movement. *Katete* tendencies can be understood as attempts to outdo the "orthodox" Jamaa with respect to the two central values of love/unity and fecundity/filiation. *Katete* people speak of themselves as *maendeleo*, progress, i.e., progress over the "normal" Jamaa. One of the standard accusations is that *katete* leaders "steal" children. This refers to the fact that they recruit their followers, not among the noninitiated candidates, but among those who have reached the second or third degree. In doing this they directly violate the rules of *kizazi*, spiritual kinship, between initiated and initiators. Tempels' letter quoted as an illustration for the concept of *uzazi/kizazi* (pp. 90 f.) clearly refers to such incidents. As an incentive, *katete* leaders usually offer an accelerated program of *mafundisho*, admitting their candidates much earlier than orthodox groups. The power struggle may take on anticlerical overtones; this happened at Musonoi, but it was due to the fact that the local pastor took the side of the "orthodox" leaders. I did not come across any evidence of antiwhite orientations in the *katete* (as there are in the Kitawala and Bapostolo movements).

Power struggle in terms of central Jamaa values is a first step toward an explanation. But it must be taken with caution, because it could lead one to overlook some simple facts of equal importance. First of all, even a glance at the extremely brief account of initiation ideology in the first section of this chapter shows that the so-called deviations are but logical consequences or extensions of Jamaa ideas accepted as "orthodox." The reception of each of the three *mawazo* in the three degrees is indeed phrased or symbolized as an act of "total union," integrating the sexual aspect as its most expressive component (cf. also our remarks on such key terms of Jamaa doctrine as *ku-pata* [57] and *ku-pokea* [58]). Since the founder himself has never clearly determined the limits (and since such a limitation would in fact contradict Jamaa aspirations for complete love, understanding, and unity), it cannot come as a surprise that some Jamaa leaders interpret these ideas less allegorically than others. This question of "interpretation" is the crucial point. It is probably true that *katete* leaders have to some extent changed and developed the ritual of initiation, but all evidence suggests that there are no important *doctrinal* differences between "orthodox" and "heterodox" groups. This was the impression I got from conversations with the leading *katete* member at Musonoi, an impression confirmed by all informants who had been in contact with the dissident groups. Another fact should be noted in this context. Contrary to what the common name *katete* suggests, there is no reason to believe that these groups are organized beyond the local level (which, of course, does not exclude informal relationships between groups, such as visits, letters, etc.). On the local level, relationships between *katete* and orthodox groups may be antagonistic, occasionally to the point of violent clashes, but nowhere have they resulted in a complete separation. Interaction between members of the opposed groups never ceases and sometimes is so frequent that, for a large number of members, it would be quite difficult to decide to which group they belong. Several among the eight or ten major informants at Musonoi admitted participating at one time or another in *katete* practices. So fluid is the relationship that in some cases I could not determine to which group a given informant belonged. In several places I found local pastors completely unaware of the existence of a *katete* in their parish.

The only way to understand this strange situation of a "non-separated separatism" is to see it in the light of the *mawazo* doctrine of Jamaa teaching. At the outset of this section we pointed out that the Jamaa may define itself as "those who guard *mawazo*" and that *mawazo* in this sense can be understood as the shared latent "myth" of the movement, i.e., as a very broad and loosely defined common ideological basis which makes it possible for manifest Jamaa doctrine to embrace considerable differences in emphasis, in choice of means of expression, and in identification with leaders. Furthermore, the closeness of the *mawazo* ideology to the traditional conception of *bwanga* (magical) sources of life/force makes a more direct approach to sexual and fertility rites in the *katete* an insignificant difference between orthodoxy and heterodoxy in the Jamaa, and there are reasons to assume that the present "moiety" division on the local level could continue to exist without causing separation or major changes in the Jamaa. This does not exclude, of course, the possibility that other factors, either internal (such as Weber's "laws" of routinization of charisma) or external (such as open intervention by the mission) may cause the Jamaa to develop in a different direction. The most important open clash between the hierarchy and the movement during the period of my field work occurred in 1966 in the diocese of Bakwanga-Gandajika in the southern Kasai. The local (Congolese) prelate had excommunicated the Katanga-oriented Jamaa *in cumulo,* a measure which involved several thousand people. In an (anonymous) petition to the bishop the writer (or writers) very humbly ask to have the decision reconsidered and propose a meeting in which the controversial issues should be discussed. But the letter ends with a threat:

> Nous ne savons pas si cette malédiction qui nous est frappés signifie implicitement une autorisation de faire fonder une autre Eglise pour un autre Jésus Christ qui n'est pas encore né. [We do not know whether this curse that has struck us implicitly signifies that we are authorized to found another Church for another Jesus Christ yet to be born.]

❧ CONCLUDING SUMMARY

In a way, this study owes its origin to a *horror vacui,* to a discontent with a blank spot on the map of social science. The "blank spot" in question becomes visible—at least in the tradition of social thought to which we feel closest—in the negative position of certain important problems. When Max Weber attempted to formulate a paradigm of types of "authority" (perhaps better: types of social integration), he was compelled by the logic of his initial steps A (traditional) and B (rational-bureaucratic) to add a third category, C (charismatic). A close look at Weber's statements shows that, despite the examples with which he illustrates "charisma" and despite some signs of a conceptual differentiation (leader, staff, congregation, routinization), category C remained a negative and residual concept—the non-A/B, *das Ausseralltägliche,* the extraordinary. We noted in the Introduction that other concepts, such as the unusual "personal qualities" of the leader and the "supernatural" basis of legitimation (both equally negative), have overshadowed later discussion and have discredited much of Weber's vision.

That Weber had touched on a genuine problem becomes evident in the difficulties which a later structuralist-functionalist theory of action had with the explanation of certain problems of social change. Even though we disagree with many of his propositions, I. C. Jarvie made an important contribution when he tried to prove the failure of the structural-functional method by showing that it was unable to produce acceptable explanations of cargo cults. What he accomplished was the demonstration of a "blank spot," the inability of this approach to account for phenomena of social change which are not due to "internal" causes, i.e., the exigencies of the social and personality systems involved (cf.

Jarvie 1964:154–59). But he has left us again with a negative definition of those problems that remain unsolved. (The fact that Jarvie uses the attributes "internal" *vs.* "external" for causes of social change only obscures the issue. "External" cannot have a spatial connotation in relation to a social system; it implies a logical statement of the same kind as the one in Weber's definition of charisma as the extraordinary.)

The point of departure for this study was an attempt to fill these conceptual blank spots with a theory which would allow us to formulate positive propositions to be confronted with a body of empirical facts.

A first step in this direction was to reformulate a *theory of charisma* around the assumption that charismatic authority is based on the perception and formulation (and, therefore, in a sense "creation") of *meaning* for human action. Such a theory implies that charisma must be seen as a dynamic concept in a context of change and innovation. In order to demonstrate that charisma is a "creative" source of social change, one must, first, show that the message as well as the followers of the message constitute distinct entities in their social and cultural environment, i.e., they must be identified as a *system of symbolic orientations* and as a *social movement*. Only then can charismatic phenomena be used as an explanation of sociocultural change in the wider society in which they occur.

The first task, then, was to establish the Jamaa movement as a distinct entity by demonstrating its boundaries. Boundaries are many—spatial, temporal, social, logical. We traced them as we reported on our findings.

In Chapter 1 we were concerned with the historical boundaries, the beginning of the Jamaa in space and time. Our interest was concentrated on the founder, Placide Tempels, a Franciscan missionary who worked in the thirties and early forties among the Baluba Shankadi in southwestern Katanga. We tried to show that the development of both his own personal views and the intellectual climate in the colony caused his conversion from an anonymous missionary in the bush to the prophet of *Bantu Philosophy*. We referred to this event as his "conversion" because it implied, in a way, a reversal of the attitudes expected from a missionary and a colonizer. His most important protest, the publication of *Bantu Philosophy* in 1945, was directed against a majority of "assimilationists," i.e., those (missionaries and others) who thought of themselves as importers of a superior culture and whose professed aim it was to "elevate" the native to their own standing; and this was to be done by an outright replacement of African culture with the ideas and values of European society.

However, what triggered Tempels' conversion was not just the widespread feeling that this approach had failed and that the colonial endeavor was in serious trouble. Its failure resulted in a profound discontent or disappointment with the basic principles of the European world view. *Bantu Philosophy,* albeit written in terms of the categories of Catholic Scholastic philosophy which Tempels had learned in the seminary, is as much an attack against the sterility of "Occidental thought" as it is an attempt to demonstrate the existence and grandeur of the "Bantu soul."

Something distinguished Tempels from other people who spoke out or wrote about similar ideas at about the same time. Its origins are important but difficult to trace, since they lie in the history of his own personality. He himself has often professed that the moving force behind his intellectual efforts was a need for "encounter," a personal, direct communication of his ideas and feelings. Tempels was never content to wait for his writings to have their effect via the usual channels of information. He wanted to break through the bars which separated him from his fellow men, especially from the Congolese he was supposed to missionize. His insisting on an unconventional and uncontrolled relationship as a prerequisite for "understanding" foreshadowed his later role as a charismatic leader. But church hierarchy and colonial administration delayed the effects of his conversion by keeping him exiled in Belgium.

During the period of imposed inactivity (1946–49) his convictions deepened and his ideas developed. In the early fifties the breakthrough to the Bantu soul of which he had dreamed occurred in a small group of followers at Ruwe, a miners' camp of the Union Minière near Kolwezi. This group became the origin of the Jamaa movement.

We may conclude, then, that four events, or chains of events, united and symbolized in the person of the founder, established the Jamaa as a historical entity: (*a*) a situation of intellectual and social discontent with the colonial endeavor at the end of World War II; (*b*) a conversion of the personal attitudes of the founder which made him reject the expectations imposed on him as an official representative of one of the colonizing forces and demand an *ausseralltägliche,* a charismatic definition of the relationships with the colonized; (*c*) a system of thought, formulated in *Bantu Philosophy* as an attempt to define and to solve the problems posed by the situation; and (*d*) acceptance of these ideas as a prophetic message by a small group of followers.

In Chapter 2 we attempted to penetrate the phenomenon Jamaa by describing and analyzing the social manifestations of the response to the founder's person and message. First we gave a picture of the original environment of the Jamaa: the workers' settlement of the Union Minière in south Katanga. Comparing the ideology of the colonizer and the social reality of these "camps," we came to the conclusion that they present a surprisingly successful realization of the "paternalist" vision. Phrased in moral and humanitarian language but dictated by the demands of technical and commercial efficiency, the social policies of the Union Minière had succeeded in "stabilizing" a large labor force through a complicated system of rewards, protection, and control.

We then examined a number of symptomatic situations and cases which allowed inferences to the attitudes of the Congolese inhabitants of these camps. Response to the paternalist dream of the colonizers was found to be ambivalent, to say the least. A certain economic and social security is appreciated, but it is bought at the high cost of a totalitarian limitation of personal freedom and an increasing alienation from the traditional village-centered world. We argued that the orientational problems of this situation culminate in an all-pervading dilemma: the policies of the colonizer defined and organized the settlements as "total societies," the integration of which was phrased in a "moral" language of welfare, cooperation, and attachment to the company; but what was made to appear to the colonized as the ends were only means for the real ends—industrial exploitation. This discrepancy between proclaimed and real ends is a source of constant frustration and confusion.

Against the background of the camp as the original environment of the movement we then presented the Jamaa group at Musonoi as a typical case for the origin, membership, activities, internal organization, and dynamics of leadership at the local level. Concerning the foundation of the Musonoi group, the data led us to conclusions which also apply to the spread of the movement in general: the formation of the group essentially repeated the "pro-phetic event" at Ruwe, i.e., the first congregation of followers around Tempels. Members of the original group found response to the *mafundisho,* the instructions in Jamaa doctrine which they preached among their fellow workers. In the documents we ex-amined, this message is characterized by an emphasis on "know-ing" and "understanding"—understanding, that is, of oneself and of the world in the urban-industrial centers. We did not find any millenarian, nativistic, or separatist motives. Such emphasis on very broad and general problems of "understanding" and the lack of particularistic expectations and promises was thought to cor-respond to two other findings. First, the constitution of the group could not be traced to any specific impulse from the environment, such as an economic crisis, a political event, a natural catastrophe, a sudden change in the population—events which have often been linked with the rise of prophetic-charismatic movements. Second, the recruits to the movement had only one common characteristic that is not shared by the entire population: at one time or another they have been under the influence of the Catholic mission. As far as ethnic origin, professional rank, and economic standing go, Ja-maa membership reflects the makeup of the total population of the camps.

For the outside observer, this inconspicuous character of the movement poses a problem: how does one detect a Jamaa group as a separate entity in a camp? Starting from the observation that membership in the Jamaa has become a recognized social attribute, we investigated, through a survey of the common and public ac-tivities of the movement, the ways in which such an attribute can be perceived. All activities center around the weekly *mafundisho.* This weekly meeting is the model for a number of variants (some involving only part of the local group, others several or all groups in the area). Another field of common activity, mutual economic assistance, was found to stay largely on a symbolic level (expressed in hospitality and occasional collections for members in need). Nothing indicated that the group represents its members for social or political purposes.

The morphology of these activities, i.e., certain externally ob-servable regularities of role differentiation, gave us the clues to an analysis of the internal organization of the Jamaa group. We ob-served three pairs of "contrasts": between (1) the local missionary and the group, (2) prominent members and the rank and file, and (3) the fully initiated and the lower ranks and candidates. The content of these oppositions, i.e., the ideas and norms defining the roles within the movement, was shown to derive from a central concept of Jamaa doctrine, that admission to the movement is by "birth" through initiation. The idea of "birth" implies that the relationship between those who initiate and those who are initiated is one between parents and children. Intimately connected with this definition of relationships is the idea of *uzazi*, fecundity, which allows maximization and therefore provides the (only) avenue to leadership in the Jamaa. Leaders compete in terms of the number and influence of their "children," i.e., the alliance groups formed by those whom they initiated.

Turning from a morphological, static analysis of the intragroup organization to the tensions and trends in the Jamaa of Musonoi, we came to the following conclusions. The tensions (which in their most dramatic form have led to the formation of dissident groups) seem to express an inherent contrast in the ideology of spiritual kinship which provides the organizational matrix of the group. This contrast is between the idea of *kizazi*, spiritual kinship, implying an *ascribed* position for every member, and *uzazi*, fecundity, which allows *achievement* orientation ("the more children, the more authority"). Once the maximization of *uzazi* is no longer balanced by the egalitarian values of *kizazi*, the road is open to the development of authoritarian structures and to various routinizations of charisma. We have stated that the group of Musonoi is on the verge of such developments but that it is not yet possible to determine their direction. Some observations caused us to envisage an alternative to Weber's "economization" and routinization of charisma. Charisma might simply be sealed off against the routinizing factors of reality by becoming a mere means of maximizing power.

Chapter 2 concludes with a survey of urban and rural Jamaa groups in Katanga and in Kinshasa. The presentation was organized in such a way as to serve the double purpose of illustrating a *variety of tendencies* within the movement (such as "dogmatism," "pluralism," "alienation"), and the *patterns of group-transcending integration*. Concerning the second point, our findings can be summed up as follows. The outer limits of the Jamaa movement seem to be coextensive with the "interaction spheres" of the Catholic mission, the large companies of Katanga, and the Luba-Lunda culture. But none of them can sufficiently account for the specific patterns of intergroup integration in the Jamaa. We expressed this by stating that the Jamaa is neither a pious Catholic society, nor an association of industrial workers, nor a cultural movement of "Bantu philosophers." Not only the internal structures of the local groups but the organizational links between such groups can be shown to derive directly from ideas, values, and norms formulated in Tempels' charismatic message. The segmentary tendency implicit in the idea of *kizazi,* alliance through spiritual kinship, is counterbalanced by the principle of *umoja,* unity. One important factor in preserving unity is the founder's continued influence from a distance. Apart from that, prominent local leaders act as advocates of *umoja,* visiting other groups not only to keep up intergroup contact but also to assist in the solution of problems (and by the same token widening their own personal influence). As far as the rank and file are concerned, intergroup communication is kept up through correspondence and visits, mostly along the lines of *kizazi,* i.e., between "parents" and "children," or among those who trace their initiation to a common parent.

In a very general way, then, we may state that description and analysis in the first part of our study did accomplish the initial task of establishing the boundaries of the Jamaa as a social entity and—in a developmental perspective—its impact as a distinct force in the processes of sociocultural change in Katanga. But at the same time our treatment of the data should have made it abundantly clear that analysis could not stop at this point. In our explanation of intra- and intergroup integration we constantly had to point to ideas, values, and norms directly derived from Tempels' prophetic message. The second part of this study, shorter than the first but by no means less important, was devoted to two major tasks. First, we presented Jamaa doctrine as a *system,* in terms of its structural integration, and as a *total ideology,* in terms of the scope of its content. Second, the doctrinal system isolated in such a way was again related to action by a discussion of the ways in which it was internalized, transmitted, and shared by the members of the movement.

In Chapter 3 we first reflected on the theoretical foundations for a "turn to language" in the analysis of a movement. This turn becomes necessary because of epistemological, not just methodo-logical, considerations. A language is the medium which *constitutes* the total intentional context of the Jamaa and, at the same time, permits us to *enter* that context. Formal analysis based on pro-cedures developed in structural linguistics is but a step toward understanding the Jamaa in that it enables us to describe the formal external boundaries and internal structures of the doctrine.

One major document was chosen for the purposes of formal analysis: the *kitabu,* a written catechism of Jamaa teaching, com-piled at Musonoi by members of the Kolwezi area. After a discussion of the history and representativeness of the document, we pro-ceeded to a formal analysis, using a method derived from tech-niques employed in structural linguistics and, in an analogous application, in the structural analysis of limited symbol systems, such as kinship terminologies. In order to define the domain, the structures of which we wanted to isolate, we compiled a basic vocabulary of Jamaa "language," a list of eighty-four important doctrinal terms in Swahili, each with a translation and with a brief comment indicating its function and context in Jamaa teaching. This set of terms was then submitted to componential analysis. Componential classification took its initial clues from morpho-logical and grammatical features of the terms. This led to a distinc-tion of three basic "underlying ideas" or functions of concepts: *projection*—concepts which project basic human values and modes of existence to a transcendental level; *symbolization*—concepts (many of them proper names) which signify prototypes and models for the Jamaa; and *association*—concepts which refer to the enactment of Jamaa ideas, values, and norms in a social group, the movement.

In a second step, the vocabulary was once more rearranged and classified, this time in a paradigm constructed from the permutations of the three basic ideas distinguished above. This made it possible to distinguish seven major structural foci within the system of Jamaa doctrine: an ontology (ultimate sources and principles of being), a theology (the supreme beings), a mystical theory (a direct, nonmediated union with the ultimate principles and supreme beings), a mythology (paradigmatic reali-zation of these ultimate principles by paradigmatic actors), a theory of ritual (standardized and socialized enactment of the mythical models), and a theory of the "movement" (realization and enactment of ultimate principles via membership in the Jamaa). A cosmology defines space and time for all these levels.

What insights are gained from these operations on the vocabulary of Jamaa doctrine? There is, first, the immediate relevance of our findings in terms of the goals of this study. In our analysis of Jamaa doctrine we were able to identify the *systematic integration* of the various doctrinal concepts and propositions contained in our documents. More than that, our attempt to isolate the internal structural foci of this system confirmed one of our initial assumptions: that Tempels' message was not simply addressed to a limited number of specific problems of orientation but that it offers a *total definition* of reality for his followers. It contains all the levels which are usually distinguished in a fully developed *Weltanschauung:* the transcendental and mythological foundations of beliefs, values, and norms, a system of ritual enactments, and the rules for social action.

Apart from these substantive findings concerning the systematic integration and the scope of Jamaa doctrine, Chapter 3 had important methodological implications. First, it demonstrated the applicability of componential analysis to an ideology. The least that can be said for this approach is that it provides a valuable guideline for a contextual interpretation of doctrinal concepts. Second, isolation of structural foci in the doctrinal system established possible units and dimensions for a comparative evaluation of Jamaa doctrine. It was in this context that we touched on the problems of comparative studies in the field of religion in general and of religious movements in particular.

In Chapter 4 we assembled and analyzed data concerning the interrelationships between the "social system" (Jamaa as a "movement") and the cultural system (Jamaa as a system of beliefs, norms, and values). First we studied the ritual of initiation as the major standardized technique of internalization of the doctrine. After a description and interpretation of the ritual, two interesting problems were pursued as a sideline. A comparison between Jamaa initiation and initiation into the *buyanga,* a society of hunters among the Baluba, showed how Tempels had used models from traditional society in organizing his movement. Then we presented data showing various ways in which the ritual of initiation may dramatize or cause conflict, not only for the persons involved but in the integration of the movement as a whole.

Another section dealt with various aspects of "teaching," i.e., the techniques of transmitting the system of Jamaa doctrine. Special attention was given to teaching as a means of exercising charismatic authority, to the "ritual" function of teaching, and to methods and techniques employed.

In a final section of Chapter 4 we discussed the question of how and to what degree the doctrinal system is shared by the followers of the Jamaa. Once more we took our departure from an "ethno-scientific" classification which contrasts *mafundisho,* the manifest system of orientations, with *mawazo,* the latent common pool of orientations. This classificatory distinction was found to correspond to the one between "myth" and "myth-dream" employed by K. Burridge in his study of Melanesian cargo cults. With the help of these conceptual tools we were able to integrate two important sets of data in our analysis: the role of dreams and dreaming, and the moiety-like coexistence of "orthodox" and "heterodox" Jamaa groups.

✿ EPILOGUE

Luabo, June 12, 1966: For days we have been rolling through dust and green confusion. Every now and then a stream crosses our road and offers a moment of clarity. . . . Somehow, this reminds me of my work: I still seem to traverse, rather than follow, insights.

When I wrote these lines after a long drive through the marshes of southwest Katanga, I had been with the Jamaa for less than six months. Today, after more than three years, they still describe my feelings, perhaps even more so. This book represents a first step in an endeavor of understanding. Trying to disentangle the Jamaa from the complicated and ever-changing world of which it is a part, I had to dissect analytically what, in the life of the prophet and his followers, is one: origin and growth, organization and doctrine, life and thought, logic and message. The main effort was directed toward mapping the structures of Jamaa teaching. Whenever I was tempted to follow the meaning of its tenets—the idea of *umuntu,* the "three big thoughts"—in their proper course, I had to move on with the task of formal description. This means that my understanding remains painfully incomplete. In a way, it was a hidden purpose of this exercise to demonstrate exactly that. Analysis in terms of established approaches in current anthropology *is* incomplete. Reduction of empirical realities to clear, formal relationships between structures of thought and action is not the end.

We shall have to progress to the level of ideational content of Jamaa "behavior." This will involve, first of all, an adequate documentation of the doctrinal content.[1] Then there will arise

1. A volume of selections from Jamaa teaching and other documents is scheduled for publication in the near future. The selection was made accord-

the necessity of ideological critique. This last step, no matter how difficult and unprecedented it may be, is a direct consequence of the epistemological principles that have been guiding my work on the Jamaa (and which have become clarified in its course, I should add). If the study of charismatic action is possible only from within a common context of communication—i.e., common to participants and observers—then the intellectual encounter cannot stop at a formal reduction of a movement to "scientifically" manipulable size. It must confront its message in terms of the intent and content of ideas. Tempels' vision of *umuntu* is a direct challenge to the idea of man implicit in anthropological theory; it must be reflected upon, interpreted, and criticized.[2]

Clearly, once anthropology has developed to that level, the division between scientific observer and "subjects," around which so much discussion concerning the ethics of the discipline revolves, will reveal itself as a false and obsolete problem. The cultural anthropologist produces knowledge only insofar as he participates in the processes which he studies. I cannot think of a more appropriate ending for this book than the greeting of the Jamaa: *Yambo yetu*—which means, literally, "Our concern."

---

ing to a method which allows adequate illustration of doctrinal content as well as representation of the literary genres of instruction. The text will appear in both the original Swahili and a translation into English.

2. Anthropology must transcend its scientistic *esprit borné* at a boundary which it has in common with current efforts in the philosophy of the social sciences: with hermeneutics and dialectical epistemology. Since these efforts are both numerous and somewhat outside the horizon of technical anthropological literature, I shall limit myself to two references: Habermas 1967 and Radnitzky 1968. Both contain excellent surveys of these attempts. The argument was developed in a reflection on our investigations into the Jamaa, in Fabian (forthcoming).

Appendixes

I ✿ Kolwezi Mine Workers: Some Statistics

In interpretating the following tables,[1] which incorporate data about mine workers in the Kolwezi area, one must take into account several possible sources of error:

1. Population statistics (Table 1) are based on a census of "official" inhabitants. It does not include wives of polygamists (polygamy is officially banned), more or less permanent "visitors" (relatives, children of relatives attending school at Kolwezi), and the usual hosts of parasites following wage-earners into the cities. The administration tries to supervise population movement in the camps and goes so far as to employ private spies and plainclothes policemen, but it is not able to exercise perfect control, nor does the *chef de camp* always have the means to enforce his orders. Since independence, public and private (Union Minière) administrations no longer work in close collaboration.

TABLE 1—Population of the Camps of the Union Minière Organized in the "Groupe Ouest–Kolwezi"* (December, 1966)

PLACE	MEN	WOMEN	CHILDREN	TOTALS
Kolwezi	2,194	1,803	6,492	10,489
Musonoi	3,478	2,989	11,024	17,491
Luilu	1,447	1,242	4,202	6,891
Ruwe	428	398	1,524	2,350
Kapata	1,210	1,063	3,546	5,819
Total "Groupe Ouest–Kolwezi"				43,040

* "Groupe Ouest" is an administrative term for Union Minière operations in the Kolwezi area.

1. With the exception of Table 2b, which was obtained at the local office at Kolwezi, information was furnished by the Office of the Directeur Général de la Gecomin, Lubumbashi, whose cooperation is gratefully acknowledged.

2. The official report on the ethnic composition (Tables 2a and 2b) must be taken *cum grano salis*. First, the categories chosen are much too broad; boundaries—e.g., between any of the seven tribal subdivisions listed for Katanga—are extremely fluid. Dembo will often call themselves Lunda. Second, some of the categories, e.g., "Luba-Kasai," refer to language groups rather than to social or political entities. Still, on the whole, Table 2b reflects fairly accurately the ethnic situation, especially if taken as a document for self-identification rather than ethnological or linguistic classification in the technical sense.[2]

TABLE 2a—Ethnic Composition of the Workers in the Camps of the "Groupe Ouest–Kolwezi" (December, 1966)

	KOLWEZI	MUSONOI	RUWE	LUILU	KAPATA
Katanga	920	1,521	189	675	374
Kasai	1,102	1,707	206	648	485
Rwanda	11	54	12	11	291
Zambia	97	100	12	54	34
Angola	56	89	9	56	25
Others	8	16		3	1
Total	2,194	3,487	428	1,447	1,210

3. Table 3 is based on the *cote,* i.e., the official scale of professional ranking applied to Congolese workers of the Union Minière. It does not contain the very small number of Congolese who are considered *personnel de cadre* and who are in theory on an equal basis with white employees, many of whose privileges they share (e.g., housing in the core city, special food rations, etc.); but they are not paid in Belgian money, and, to my knowledge, all of them occupied the bottom of the scale applied to white personnel, since none of them had had access to higher technical education. The top-ranking Congolese officials of the Union Minière at the time of my field work were one or two *chefs de camp.* The process of ranking is a fairly complicated one. A memorandum (dated February, 1967) lists six separate instances of evaluation (three superiors at work, the local personnel manager, the *chef de camp,* and a

2. Cf. Biebuyck's main criterion in his paper "On the Concept of Tribe," based on Congolese material. He states that "tribe" is "first and foremost a device used by rural people for classifying themselves" (1966:510).

TABLE 2b—Tribal Affiliation of Workers in the Camps, in Percentages
(December, 1964)

	KOLWEZI	MUSONOI	LUILU	KAPATA	RUWE	GROUPE OUEST
Katanga						
Lunda	14.83	11.10	14.64	9.50	18.49	12.74
Dembo	9.35	8.85	10.40	8.57	8.07	9.15
Tshokwe	3.34	2.72	4.48	4.33	1.56	3.33
Sanga	1.42	1.81	2.20	0.85	2.34	1.66
Yeke	1.38	2.28	1.37	1.44	1.82	1.76
Bemba	1.07	1.03	1.21	1.02	0.53	1.05
Luba	11.00	13.26	11.38	6.70	8.86	11.26
Total	42.39	41.05	45.68	32.41	41.67	40.95
Kasai						
N. Kasai	2.72	3.08	2.81	3.14	2.61	2.93
Songe	7.75	9.56	8.73	7.29	11.20	8.71
Luba	17.68	16.06	17.37	12.30	14.32	16.07
Kanioka	8.46	8.28	6.90	5.00	8.59	7.68
Lulua	9.79	10.92	6.37	8.74	7.55	9.46
Kete	1.86	2.13	1.52	2.12	3.39	2.02
Total	48.26	50.03	43.70	38.59	47.66	46.87
Other						
Congolese	0.18	0.33	0.07		0.26	0.20
Foreigners						
Rwanda	0.58	2.19	1.21	21.20	3.65	4.32
Others	8.59	6.45	9.34	7.80	6.76	7.66
Total	9.17	8.64	10.55	29.00	10.41	11.98

representative of the central *service de qualification professionnelle*)
before the candidate's final ranking is established. A series of
tables defines the qualification for each of the technical functions,
not all of which go up to the highest rank (e.g., a chauffeur cannot
get higher than *cote* 15).

4. Table 4 indicates seniority of workers in terms of contract
periods and illustrates the success of the policy of "stabilization"
(cf. above, pp. 56 ff.). The latter is also expressed in the following
rates of total turnover in the labor force of the Kolwezi area: 9
per cent in 1950, 10 per cent in 1959, 24 per cent in 1964, and
7 per cent in 1966.

TABLE 3—Professional Ranking of Congolese Workers
(December, 1966)

Cote*	Kolwezi	Musonoi	Ruwe	Luilu	Kapata
6	223	471	43	168	526
7	385	590	85	368	92
8	495	354	77	237	83
9	297	927	83	259	267
10	185	220	31	87	29
11	185	340	35	121	69
12	74	87	14	39	36
13	162	279	32	75	29
14	30	28	2	30	15
15	52	89	15	26	17
16	48	61	6	20	8
17	16	10	4	6	0
18	24	12	0	14	4
19	5	7	1	4	1
20	10	3	0	3	1
21	2	0	0	0	1
22	1	0	0	0	3

* A scale of 22 ranks (*cote d'emploi*) is divided into three major categories: unskilled (*manoeuvres*): 6–9; semiskilled (*semi-qualifiés*): 10–13; skilled (*qualifiés*): 14–22.

TABLE 4—Seniority of Workers in Terms of Contract Periods
(Issued December, 1966)

YEAR	KOLWEZI	MUSONOI	RUWE	LUILU	KAPATA
1966	54	44	2	38	54
1965	75	181	6	40	140
1964	202	398	58	135	143
1963	351	587	40	242	275
1962	224	219	22	139	82
1961	149	176	35	137	68
1960	118	159	26	134	57
1959	45	43	9	34	19
1958	51	141	22	56	28
1957	16	81	14	6	17
1956	32	63	5	26	44
1955	52	102	7	37	41
1954	69	88	8	32	22
1953	82	94	11	40	31
1952	41	95	11	37	21
1951	72	101	10	24	23
1950	61	156	7	30	25
1949	34	38	3	17	9
1948	26	61	8	14	6
1947	53	82	16	31	16
1946	30	76	16	27	2
1945	8	27	3	11	4
1944	17	21	3	6	2
1943	27	36	4	24	3
1942	67	97	23	21	17
1941	62	116	19	22	21
1940	61	80	10	32	9
Before 1940	105	196	30	59	29
Total	2,194	3,478	428	1,447	1,210

II ❧ The Outgroup Image of the Jamaa

In the course of field work one cannot help but notice outside reaction to the Jamaa. The mere fact that one becomes known as "the anthropologist who does the Jamaa" constantly provokes questions and comments, most of which find their way into the notebook. But such reactions hardly permit systematic investigation of the way in which the movement is perceived by nonmembers. The major obstacle is the difficulty in finding a group or category of outsiders unified and large enough to produce responses which can serve as a basis for generalizations. Among those whom I questioned about the Jamaa were political leaders, government officials, the local police, teachers, Union Minière administrators, traditional chiefs, businessmen, workers, houseboys, and hitchhikers. Apart from the fact that almost all of them had some knowledge of the existence of, or even personal contact with, the movement, the answers were so vague and general as to yield little information about the impact of the Jamaa on its environment. One might be inclined to take this as a proof for the apolitical and otherworldly character of the Jamaa claimed by many observers. In my opinion, it reflects only an attitude of Congolese politeness on the part of these "random" informants—a tendency to please the inquirer and to avoid controversial issues.

The picture changes quite radically as soon as one seeks information within a group or category of nonmembers, such as the majority in the mission clergy. As people who are involved and who have frequent occasion to communicate their experiences and opinions, most of them showed a keen interest in the movement, and some a very profound understanding. "Reaction" among the clergy and in the hierarchy has led to conferences, workshops, and official declarations about the Jamaa, some of which are accessible in printed or mimeographed form and constitute important documents on the change in attitudes and expectations after independence in 1960.[1] The over-all tendency is a somewhat reluctant acceptance of the movement based on the (questionable) assumption that it is a kind of revival inside the organizational and doctrinal boundaries of the mission church. "Deviations" too visible to be overlooked are explained as "exaggerations." Generally, there is a lack of understanding of the prophetic-charismatic processes

1. Since a systematic investigation into the reaction to Tempels' writings and to the foundation of the Jamaa is part of a project to follow the present study, I shall limit myself here to a very few references. As far as reactions from the clergy and leading laymen are concerned, there is first a series of short papers in the periodical *Christ to the World:* Gérard (1964a, b), Moysan (1964), Mulago (1964), and Piette (1964). More important are some attempts to understand the Jamaa published in *Orientations pastorales* (the periodical in which most of Tempels' catechetic writings appeared): Meert (1961), Mulago (1960, 1961), Theuws (1960). Others are Déchanet (1962) and Jomier (1963). Cf. also Noirhomme *et al.* (n.d.), De Craemer (1965), Janssen (1967), and Pirotte (1968).

To illustrate the attitudes taken in official statements from the hierarchy, I include the following quotation from a pastoral letter by Archbishop Mels of Luluabourg:

"We must confess that it is often with some astonishment and even mistrust that we regard the birth of spontaneous and charismatic movements like the Jamaa, which arise in our parish or our mission, without our direct intervention and outside our 'hierarchical' organization. It would be dangerous to bear them a grudge because we did not stimulate or organize them ourselves. On the contrary, we must take an interest in them and assume the place they reserve for us, as a Father 'giving birth' to them in grace, by transmitting divine life to them, through the Sacraments, as a prudent guide in the investigation of the mysteries of our faith and also as a real brother in Christ participating in the same divine life as they, without wishing to suffocate happy initiatives, and without wishing to regulate and over-organize. . . . It is true, however, that these movements present certain dangers and are subject to easy deviations. . . . It is a question of trying to explain to the greatest possible extent and in Bantu style, the deepest mysteries of our faith and to live them intensely. If we watch over them with prudence, but also with fatherly comprehension, we shall also be able to correct errors or faults in time" (Mels 1964:503 f.).

This document is perhaps somewhat unusual for its tolerance and self-criticism. In a personal encounter at Luluabourg in 1966, I found Msgr. Mels much less tolerant. He gave me a rather icy welcome and made it quite clear that an anthropologist traveling around could only make the situation worse—implying, of course, that it was already "bad." His attempts to establish a benevolent supervision of the Jamaa had failed.

which have led to the emergence of the Jamaa. Only a few of the mission clergy are aware of the fact that involvement and leadership in the movement call for the same profound change of attitudes that marked the "conversion" of the founder.

On several occasions during my field work I observed a tendency among missionaries to misjudge the notoriety of the Jamaa among nonmembers. An attempt to check on some of these preconceptions has yielded most impressive data on the outgroup image of the Jamaa. In a conversation one of the missionaries at Kolwezi who taught at one of the local high schools maintained that the movement was unknown among his students. After some preliminary inquiries I decided to conduct a survey, which yielded some surprising results. Later consideration led to the conclusion that high-school students constitute an excellent test case indeed for an "outgroup":

1. High-school students come from the same environment in which the Jamaa operates, the camps of the Union Minière and the C.E.C. at Kolwezi. Since they live with their families, they have ample opportunity to observe the activities of the movement; a number of those who responded are children of Jamaa parents.

2. Because they are too young, and are unmarried, they are excluded from membership in the movement.

3. In terms of their cultural and social orientations they are removed from the generation to which most Jamaa members belong. Most of them no longer speak an autochthonous language; all of them aspire to higher social positions than their parents have achieved.

4. They have lived most of their formative years after independence and do not share their parents' experience of the mission (and colonial administration) as an uncontested factor in the social situation.

The survey was conducted in the simplest possible way. Students at the Lycée Jean XIII (and subsequently at three other institutions) were asked to write a short essay responding to two questions: What is the Jamaa? What do you think about it? So far I have evaluated 232 of these essays (the total number exceeds 700), written by students of eight classes representing all age groups and branch specializations at the Lycée. In his instructions to the students, Father Peeters, who administered the test between

March 14 and 23, 1966, laid much emphasis on actual knowledge and personal impressions—not on "good" performance.[2]

A preliminary evaluation reveals a number of traits that deserve our attention. Most striking at first glance are two facts. First, more than half the students proved to be well informed about the Jamaa. Second, a large number (101 out of 232) express an unequivocally positive opinion. But comparison of the figures between the different classes (i.e., age groups) reveals another dimension for which we have to account. The frequency of negative or negative/positive judgments seems to be correlated with age of the informants and the quality of their information. That is, of course, not surprising in itself. An 18- or 20-year-old student is more likely to form and express an opinion than a boy of 15 or 16. And the fact that his opinion is more likely to be negative may just reflect a tendency to contradict the presumed expectations of the teacher who conducted the test. But this is probably not a sufficient explanation. Among working people of the same age group as the students, I have encountered similar reactions which cannot be ascribed to the teacher-student situation. This became very clear, for example, when a group of social workers at Musonoi began to promote a family association among the more educated younger people (especially elementary school teachers and other white-collar employees of the Union Minière). Almost all of those who were approached wanted a guarantee that this association had nothing to do with the Jamaa or with "religion." On the whole, the trend toward a negative attitude among younger and better-educated Congolese confirms the opinion of M. Ndala at Lubumbashi about the "reactionary" character of the Jamaa in the Kolwezi area (cf. above, Chapter 2). Since I concentrated on the significance of the test as an accurate picture of the Jamaa (and not as a picture of the questioned students), we shall not comment on the value judgments contained in the list of quotations. The factual information may be summed up as follows:

1. The most surprising outcome of the test was the quality and

2. A thorough analysis of the survey is planned. Here I shall report only first impressions concerning its over-all results. Essays in the sample that was examined were graded on two points: amount and quality of information and opinion. More information concerning this procedure, as well as documentation of responses, may be found in Fabian MS.

quantity of information available to the students as a group. If one assembles the scattered pieces of information, the result is a quite accurate and interesting ethnography of the Jamaa in the Kolwezi area. Methodologically this constitutes an important test and a confirmation for one of the major aims of this study: to separate from the complex network of changing reality the Jamaa as a distinct social entity. It is my impression that observers of prophetic-charismatic phenomena, especially those without direct field experience, have often tended to create "movements" out of a few pieces of available information without being able to demonstrate their existence as separate, boundary-maintaining units of observation.

2. As regards definitions and concepts, I found 26 different attempts to conceptualize the Jamaa as a social entity. In practically all of them the attributes "Christian" or "Catholic" define, quite correctly, the "outer limits" of the movement. But its specific character and organization are experienced in such a way that none of the usual, everyday labels for social groups seem to fit. It appears that this uncertainty must be taken as an indicator for the charismatic, i.e., noninstitutional, character of the Jamaa.

3. As a consequence of these difficulties of conceptualization, ideas about the spread and numerical importance of the Jamaa are vague: it occurs "in the Congo," in the Congolese sections of the industrial centers of Katanga. One statement refers to the constitution of a local group; another, "The Jamaa is widespread throughout most of the world," is either made up or is an echo of Jamaa teaching.

4. Concerning membership, recruitment, and organization, the most prominent trait observed by the students is the barrier which separates them from the Jamaa: age and marital status. Much less emphasis is laid on the social status of Jamaa recruits: they are "workers" and "simple people." Only one response reflects a tribal prejudice and maintains (incorrectly) that people from the Kasai make up the majority of Jamaa members. The localized character of the movement (i.e., the association between the parish and the local group) is recognized and also the basic facts about its leadership. In only one of the statements are Jamaa leaders said to be autocratic. One student makes a very perceptive observation that most recruits to the movement have gone, as Christians, through a second conversion. There are several hints at "deviations" (cf.

the section about heterodox groups in Chapter 4), such as the formation of dissident groups, exchange of women, and excessive proselytizing. Apparently, the fact that membership is exclusively Congolese (at least as far as lay people are concerned) is accepted without question. Only one student expresses his surprise that whites do not participate in the Jamaa. At least one statement contains an unmistakable allusion to the parent-child relationship between initiating and initiated in the Jamaa.

5. The origin and history of the movement are well known. As a whole, the statements in this category contain all the essential facts concerning the person of the founder, the development and aim of his message, and the time and place of the beginnings of the Jamaa.

6. Very differentiated are observations on the activities of the movement. I merely list some major points: (*a*) emphasis on communal prayer and participation in the rites of the mission church; (*b*) instruction in the doctrine; (*c*) exchange of "counsel" (cf. our remarks on *shaurio* in Chapter 4); (*d*) singing of Jamaa hymns; (*e*) mutual economic assistance, lodging of visitors, and occasional parasitism; (*f*) a special greeting and special terms of address between husband and wife; (*g*) rules of secrecy; (*h*) the importance of dreaming.

7. Most interesting, finally, are statements about motives, goals, and effects of the movement; many contain or imply value judgments which we decided to exclude from our considerations since they contain information about the respondents rather than the movement. But in many cases the reasons given for those judgments show that the aims and functions of the Jamaa are surprisingly well understood.

The most prominent issue is the change brought about by the movement: a new definition of the relationship between husband and wife and, consequently, a new definition of the (nuclear) family as an emotional and economic focus. Redefinition of old orientations results in "conversion" and change of attitudes. As far as the function of the movement is concerned, the students point either to "instruction," i.e., orientation, or to some form of "mutual aid" in a difficult situation. One student sees the Jamaa in the context of other charismatic movements in the same environment; another takes it as a revival within the church. Only a few think of it as just another ecclesiastical organization. Traditional African elements in the new doctrine are recognized. Perhaps the most perceptive definition of the movement is given in the following statement: They "met to form their movement to satisfy not only the church but also the Christians."

III ❧ Sources and Documents

TEMPELS' WRITINGS

1. The foundations of Tempels' later teaching were laid in *Bantu Philosophy,* which was completed, according to the Dutch edition, between June, 1944, and June, 1945, at Kamina. (The first French translation was published in 1945.) Until some years ago, Tempels pursued the theme of this book in replies to critical reviews and in several papers in which he tried to clarify his views; most of them appear in the bibliography.

2. The line which leads to Jamaa ideas is taken up by the essay "Catéchèse bantoue" (published in 1948). The first part of this document was used to illustrate the conversion of the author—his change from missionary to prophet. The second part contains an outline for a reinterpretation of Christian teaching in terms of Bantu (i.e., Baluba-Katanga) thinking.

3. Tempels resumes the (public) discussion of his ideas in 1960 with a series of "Etudes de catéchèse" in the periodical *Orientations pastorales,* published at Léopoldville/Kinshasa. The papers that appeared between 1960 and 1962 were then printed as a collection under the title *Notre rencontre* (1962). A second collection of essays (some of them previously published), planned as Volume II of *Notre rencontre,* was deemed too controversial to be printed. The Centre d'Etudes Pastorales at Kinshasa, however, put mimeographed copies into circulation. I found them in the hands of most people interested in, or directly concerned with, the Jamaa.

4. From one of Tempels' confreres I received a carbon copy of a typewritten manuscript in Dutch (46 pages). The undated

paper bears the inconspicuous title, "Hoe Godsdienstonderricht ontstaat en groeit"—"How Religious Instruction Originates and Grows." Yet it is by far the most systematic and explicit outline of Jamaa teaching by the founder of the movement. To my knowledge it has been neither published nor otherwise widely circulated.

5. We should include, finally, Tempels' correspondence, even though only fragments are available at the moment.

If we want to evaluate these documents in terms of our problem, we must keep in mind that none of them was written primarily for the use of Tempels' immediate followers. They face outward, as it were; many are explanatory or directly apologetic, often discussing the compatibility of Tempels' ideas with traditional Catholic dogma. Others represent Tempels' attempts to spread his message beyond the limits of his movement in Africa. None of this is of immediate concern for Jamaa people. (The only exception I noted was *Notre rencontre,* which I saw in the hands of several members of the Jamaa and to which Tempels himself refers in one of his letters dealing with the organization of the *mafundisho.*)

We must conclude, then, that Tempels' writings, albeit accessible for analysis, cannot be included in the limited body of orientations we need to isolate for the purpose of formal analysis. Because of their scope and—for most people in the Jamaa—because of their form (they are written and published in Dutch and French), they are largely irrelevant as sources of orientation.

MAFUNDISHO

Jamaa people themselves have objectified and isolated the body of their orientations as *mafundisho.* The most adequate translation of this term would be "teaching," denoting the two aspects of "doctrine" and "instruction." In Jamaa language, the term (with the verb *ku-fundisha*) is used in a number of different contexts:

1. An observer probably first hears the term in expressions like *mafundisho ya mu kazi inne, mafundisho* on Thursday; this refers to the regular weekly *mafundisho* meeting. In this sense it is used interchangeably with *réunion,* as exemplified by phrases like *kwenda ku mafundisho,* go to the meeting.

2. *Kuleta mafundisho,* give a *mafundisho* (actually the prefix

ma- denotes the plural form, but in Katanga Swahili the term is used as a *plurale tantum*). This is the speech, or recitation of doctrine, which is made by one or several members during a public reunion or in a private meeting.

3. *Kipande ya mafundisho ya Jamaa,* a chapter, part, of the *mafundisho* of the Jamaa (or about the Jamaa). In this context, the term refers to the body of standardized, organized doctrine.

4. Related to the preceding category is the use of the term in expressions like *mafundisho moja ya Jamaa,* which is best translated as "the unity of teaching in the Jamaa." The difference between categories 3 and 4 may be conceived of in terms of the distinction between doctrine and dogma or as doctrine *vs.* metadoctrine, i.e., a system of teaching *vs.* the rules and principles which constitute such a system.[1]

5. Tempels' axiom *ukubwa inaua mafundisho,* power kills *mafundisho,* was quoted earlier. A simple translation is impossible; we shall comment on this category later.

6. If a member takes instructions as a candidate for initiation, he is said to *kufwata mafundisho,* to follow the *mafundisho.* This does not simply mean "to learn the instruction" (that would be *kufunza mafundisho*); it is also in clear contrast to "learning" and "education" in general (e.g., *kufwata masomo,* go to school). It might be more accurate to take the literal sense of *kufwata* and translate the expression as "to be a follower."

7. With the preceding category corresponds the expression *mwenye kufundisha,* a participial form meaning "the one who gives *mafundisho*" or "the one who has the power, is authorized, to give *mafundisho.*" This refers to the persons we called "speakers" and later identified as leaders in a local group. Interestingly enough, I have never heard the term *mwalimu,* "teacher."

The various meanings of *mafundisho* and *kufundisha* can be arranged on two axes:

1. The integration of a system of doctrine shared by a group of individuals (categories 3 and 4);

---

1. This distinction was first suggested to me by the material on dreams and dreaming in relation to charismatic authority. I found that a "theory of dreams" in the sense of an accepted and more or less standardized doctrine is applied by Jamaa leaders, even though such a theory is *not* part of the *mafundisho* in the sense of category 3 (cf. Fabian 1966:555).

2. Various aspects of internalization and institutionalization of this system (categories 1, 2, 6, and 7).

Somewhere between those two axes lie all the problems one would wish to solve in terms of a Weberian-Parsonian theory of action—with one very significant exception. Category 5 does not really fit into the schema. Here *mafundisho* is seen in contrast or opposition to *ukubwa;* it is an instance of the ageless philosophical and moral problem of cognition *vs.* volition, intellect *vs.* power. This, however, should not disturb us. On the contrary, it is evidence for the charismatic character of Jamaa action, i.e., action which is far from being fully institutionalized and has not settled down, so to speak, in a balanced system.

We may conclude that the property space of the concept *mafundisho* offers a valid frame of reference and a practical guideline for analysis of the intentional content of Jamaa behavior, and we can now give a brief general outline of available information:

1. Information directly relevant for the aspect "integration of the doctrinal system":

a) An untitled, typewritten manuscript of 53 pages at Musonoi, most often referred to as *kitabu* (the book). This document is the result of the *pulan* meetings of the early sixties. It contains a rough outline of the themes of instruction leading toward the first degree of initiation. It is the only written source of any length that has been formulated by members of the movement.

b) More comprehensive but less valuable as an original document is a mimeographed compilation of Jamaa teaching at Kinshasa (118 pages, in French, with frequent citation of important concepts in Lingala, Kikongo, and Swahili). The author is Father Frank de Waele, one of the supporters of the movement in the capital.

c) A few letters by Tempels (in Swahili) directly addressed to Jamaa groups, containing outlines for *mafundisho.*

d) About fifty *mafundisho* (in the sense of categories 2 and 3), recorded in the field, most of which have been transcribed and translated (about 260 typewritten pages).

e) Field notes on ten initiation sessions at the C.E.C. at Kolwezi.

f) Notes about other unrecorded *mafundisho,* outlines of instructions, topics, meetings, discussions.

g) Texts and recordings of Jamaa hymns.[2]

2. Information directly relevant for the aspect "internalization and institutionalization of the doctrinal system" (some of which has been used in the first part of this study):

a) About 40 tape-recorded conversations, interviews, and dreams (i.e., discussions *about* teaching, dreaming, cases, history of the movement, personal accounts of conversion, experiences, etc.). Most of this material (about 220 pages) has been transcribed and partly translated.

b) Letters from Tempels containing directions in matters of discipline.

c) A few letters, or written statements, from Jamaa members.

d) Field notes recording information and observations about the internalization and institutionalization of doctrine.

e) A copy of a handwritten "autobiography" of a Jamaa member at Lubumbashi (in Swahili, translated into French by one of his relatives; 19 typewritten pages).

2. Throughout this study we have paid little attention to hymns. Apart from my own limitations in time and energy, I should like to point to the following reasons for this apparent gap: during the period of my field work in the Kolwezi area, singing of hymns was not practiced during the regular *mafundisho* meetings. The hymns that were sung at more festive occasions or in more private gatherings belonged to a very limited "popular" stock—a fact which contradicts the observation of others, who have reported an unusual creativity and proliferation of singing in the Jamaa. As documents for the doctrinal system, Jamaa hymns will be utilized only after a thorough study of their function in the movement. Thematically they appear to be much more limited than the *mafundisho*. The prominence of songs addressed to the Virgin Mary and Lord Jesus points to their primarily ritual character. There are other reasons which suggest that singing in the Jamaa is above all an expressive activity. A great number of the hymns are in languages other than Swahili and are therefore not understood by some members, but they are nonetheless appreciated, and sung, by the entire congregation. The text of these hymns is usually the creation of an individual author (but I do not recall any references to authorship), and the same is claimed for the melody. However, as far as I can judge, the great majority of these songs are imitations of hymns heard in mission churches. An interesting point would be to look for the influence of Protestant and sectarian hymns on the "Catholic" Jamaa.

IV ❧ From the *Kitabu* of Musonoi

The following selections from the *kitabu*, which we have used as the principal document for a formal analysis of Jamaa doctrine, are samples meant to illustrate style and content. They represent only a small portion of the document. Concerning the origin, organization, and importance of the *kitabu,* cf. our remarks on pp. 126 ff. For the sake of a more uniform presentation of the Swahili texts, the selected passages were transcribed according to the standards adopted for the transcription of tape-recorded texts (cf. Fabian 1966:547; 1967:134). Instead of punctuation marks, three signs are employed to signify the three intonation patterns used most frequently to separate syntactic units:

: = "open" or sustained clause
/ = full clause
? = question

I have tried to make the translation as literal as possible; explanatory remarks are kept to a minimum. Whenever it seemed useful, key concepts of Jamaa teaching were given the numbers in our basic vocabulary to facilitate cross-reference.

1. *MAFUNDISHO* ABOUT THE CATHOLIC JAMAA—PART ONE

Wakristiani wa dunia muzima wanatafuta kuwa na umoja wa ukristiani wao: wanapata kintu kimoja/ wanasema tukuwe Jamaa moja duniani muzima: sawa

The Christians of the entire world seek unity in their Christian faith so that they may be one thing (76). They say: Let us be one Jamaa [or: one family]

vile Mungu alisema: nikuwe na Jamaa moja mu dunia muzima na mu mbinguni/ kwa sababu mwanzo wa ukristiani wetu tulikuwa na mawazo mbali-mbali/ tulianza kuregea: na kuachiliana pasipo kukumbushana tena kwa ukristiani wetu/ tuliteswea pale: hatukuwa na njia: tulikuwa na upeke wetu/

wamapadri wanasema: ni sisi ndiyo wakubwa wa eklezia: hatutake muntu mwengine kufundisha neno ya Mungu/ sisi wakristiani tuliwaachilia ukubwa wao aseme: ni kazi yao: na wao wanatubatiza wanasema: ni kazi yao/

pale wababa na wamama palikuwa njia? ya kutafuta umoja wetu?

ao sisi wababa na wamama wa ndoa: tuliachiliana mu ukristiani wetu/ tunalala pamoja pasipo kujua kazi yetu ya ukristiani tulipata/

hata sasa Mungu ametukumbusha mawazo yake: tupate kujua ukristiani wetu: ndio tukuwe Jamaa moja/ ni kintu cha nguvu sana kuwa na ile mawazo ya kuwa Jamaa moja/ kwa sababu wandugu wetu wakristiani tulibatizwa nao wanakatala kutafuta masikilizano ya kuwa Jamaa

in the entire world, as God has said: I want to have one Jamaa in the entire world and in heaven. Because, in the beginning of our Christian life we were separated in our thoughts (35). We became indifferent, and we neglected each other, without reminding (28) each other of the matters of our Christian faith. At that time we suffered and had no way (50): we were living in our isolation (80).

The priests said: We are the lords (74) of the church and we do not want anyone else to teach the word of God. We Christians let them have their power, telling ourselves: It's their business. And they who baptized us said: That's their business.

Bababa and *bamama*, did we then have a way to pursue our unity?

Or take us married people. We neglected each other in our Christian life. We slept together, but we did not know the duties (26) of the Christian faith we had received.

Now God has made us think about his thoughts (28) so that we may understand our Christian faith, that is: that we become one Jamaa. But to be with this thought of becoming one Jamaa is very hard. For our Christian brethren (49) with whom we were baptized refuse (25) to

moja/ wanaanza kutucheka: wanasema: sisi hatuna wa Jamaa/
paka wale wanafwata mafundisho ya Jamaa: ndio wa Jamaa/

come to an understanding with
us and to be one Jamaa. They
begin to ridicule us and say: We
do not belong to the Jamaa (22),
only those who follow the *mafundisho* (14) of the Jamaa are
Jamaa people.

wababa na wamama: wale wandugu ni wanani? si wakristiani?
ao si wa Jamaa wa Kristo? ni wa
jamaa wa Kristo/ kile wanakatala ni kutumikia Kristo: kwa
kutafuta jamaa yake/ wanafa-
nana na watu wanapata *ticket*
ya kazi pasipo kutumika/ wanakuwa paka na jina ku *liste:*
alafu watawalipa/ namna gani
pasipo kutumika ule bwana wa
kazi atafurahi kwa watu wa kazi
yake? namna gani wale walio-
andikisha kwake pasipo kutumika?

Bababa and *bamama,* who are
these brethren? Are they not
Christians? Do they not belong
to the family (Jamaa) of Christ?
They do belong to the family of
Christ. What they refuse is to
work (26) for Christ, to search
for his family. They are like people who get their punchcards without working; they only had their
names on the list and still get (or:
expect to get) paid. How can the
employer be pleased with workers who do not work even though
they are on his payroll?

kwetu kazi yetu ni hii/
1. kusali kila siku na kila
mara/
2. kusumbulia na wantu mafundisho ya Mungu/ wapagani
na wakristiani wanakuisha kua-
cha njia yao ya ukristo/ na ku-
endelesha watoto wote wana-
muke na wanaume: kwa sababu
ni wao watakuwa wapadri na
wamabikira/

Among us: these are our duties:
1. Pray every day, again and
again;
2. Discuss (67) God's *mafundisho* with the people, with
pagans and with Christians who
have left the way of Christianity, and to see that all children,
girls and boys, are well brought
up; because they will be priests
and sisters.

2. *MAFUNDISHO* ABOUT THE CATHOLIC
JAMAA—PART TWO

wababa na wamama: tunataka
kusumbulia pa kipande cha ku-
anza cha Jamaa/

Bababa and *bamama,* let us discuss about the first chapter on
the Jamaa.

ni mafundisho yenyi kutuletea uzima: na uzazi: na mapendo/ kwa sababu tuliisha kupoteza ile uzima wetu ulituletea Mungu na Jamaa yake/ kwa sababu kama muntu anakuwa na uchafu: atafanya nini? hatakimbilia ku maji? ni pamoja na sisi/ tunaanza kukimbilia mu mwanzo ya Jamaa kule ilikuwa/ ni wapi?

mwanzo yake ni hivi/ Jamaa ni nini? Jamaa ilianza wapi? Jamaa ilianza kwa Mungu yee mwenyewe/ hii vyote tunaona havikuwako: dunia: mbingu: Jamaa ilikuwako/ ilikuwako wapi? kwa Mungu mwenyewe/

pale Mungu alikuwa peke yake: aliwaza: sitaki kuwa miye moja: nitakuwa na Jamaa yangu/ ni pale Mungu alianza Jamaa yake katika mawazo/ na Jamaa ilianza kuwako paka pale katika mawazo yake: na yeye alianza kuwa katika mawazo wa Jamaa yake/

Jamaa yake alikuwa naye mu mawazo ni nani? Jamaa yake alikuwa naye mu mawazo ni sisi wantu/ ni wantu gani? ni siye: bwana na bibi/ ni wa Jamaa/ ilikuwa ku mawazo ya Mungu/

It is the *mafundisho* which brings us life (82), fecundity (81), and love (32). Because we lost this our life which God had given to us and for his Jamaa. For, if someone is dirty, what is he going to do? Will he not run to the water? So we, too, begin to run to the beginning (45) of the Jamaa. Where is it?

This is its beginning. [We have to ask] what is the Jamaa? Where did the Jamaa begin? The Jamaa began with God himself. All the things we see were not there yet, earth and heaven, but the Jamaa was there. Where was the Jamaa? With God himself.

When God was alone (80) he thought: I do not want to be alone, I shall be with my Jamaa. This was when God began his Jamaa in [his] thoughts (35). And the Jamaa began to be in his thoughts and he began to be in the thoughts of his Jamaa.

Who was this Jamaa with whom he was in his thoughts? His Jamaa in his thoughts was: We people. Which people? We, husband and wife, we are the Jamaa that was in the thoughts of God.

The *mafundisho* goes on to describe how God's thoughts were forgotten by men on earth and concludes as follows:

Mungu pa kuona ile Jamaa yake aliweka mu dunia inaharibika kwa bwana na kwa bibi/ hamuna

God saw that the Jamaa he had put on earth was being destroyed by husband and wife. There was

masikilizano: hamuna masaidiano: na tena hamuna mapendo/ ni pale Mungu alisikilizana na ule Jamaa yake alikuwa naye mbinguni: Bikira Maria/ ni vizuri utatangulia dunia/ kwa sababu: anagalia ile mawazo yetu tulileta mu dunia kwa wale watoto wetu wawili bwana na bibi: inaharibika/ hawana tena na njia ya kufika kwetu/ kumbe tuende tukawaonyeshe mfano ya kutumikia Jamaa: vile sisi tunatumikiana/

no mutual understanding (34), no mutual help (33), no love (32). Then God came to an agreement with the Jamaa with whom he was in heaven, the Virgin Mary (5): It will be good that you stay on earth, because look, our thoughts we gave to our two children on earth, husband and wife, have been destroyed. No longer do they have a way to come to us. Therefore, let us go and show them how to live for the idea of the Jamaa the way we do it among ourselves.

ni pale yeye mwenyewe alishuka mu nyumba ya Joseph na Bikira Maria: sawa mutoto kiloko pa kati ya ule bibi na ule bwana/ kwa kuonyesha mufano ya ndoa yao: kuwatosha mu kabila yao: na kwa kuwatosha tena ku mawazo yao ya ukabila wa ubibi na ubwana/

This is when he himself descended (66) on the house of Joseph and the Virgin Mary, as a small child between this wife and this husband, in order to make visible the meaning of their marriage by taking them away from their tribe(s) (73) and from the idea of a separation between wife and husband.

wababa na wamama: tukumbukeni muzuri ile mafundisho/ hatuwezi kuisoma vile tulisoma mu vitabu vya zamani/ ile kabila aliwatosha ni kabila gani? ni kabila ya mwili: kuwaunganisha/ roho na roho/ wababa na wamama: humu dunia mwanamuke na mwanaume muzuri tunamuchagua ku mwili/ kama anafika ku nyumba: tunaona mawazo yake ni mubaya: tutapenda tena mwili wake?

Bababa and *bamama*, let us carefully think about this *mafundisho*. We cannot read in it the way we used to read in the books of old. What is the tribe from which he took them away? It is the separation caused by the body. He united them: soul and soul. *Bababa* and *bamama*, in this world we choose a woman or a man according to the beauty of his [her] body. But when he [she] arrives in our household and we realize that his [her] thoughts are bad, are we then still going to love his [her] body?

mafundisho pale ni hivi/ na sisi Mungu anaisha kushuka mu nyumba yetu: kwa kutuunganisha na mawazo yake ya ule Jamaa yake Bikira Maria/ alikuwa mu mbinguni zamani/ na sisi tutafanya vitendo yenye kuachana na kabila yetu/

The meaning of the *mafundisho* is this: God has descended on our house, too; to unite us with the thoughts of his Jamaa, the Virgin Mary. She was in heaven from the beginning. Let our actions be such that they are different from our tribe [i.e., our tradition].

3. *MAFUNDISHO* IN PART FOUR— THE JAMAA AMONG THE APOSTLES

Pale Mungu aliingiza mafundisho yake mu nyumba ya Joseph na Maria: pale alitengeneza: akaona: asema haina shaka kwao na kwa wantu wale waliwaona vile walikuwa wanatumika kazi yao ya Jamaa yao/

When God had introduced and realized his *mafundisho* in the house of Joseph and Mary, he saw that there was no doubt in them, nor among the people who saw how they did the work of their Jamaa.

alipenda kuingiza kwa dunia muzima ile mawazo yenyewe: kwa bwana na bibi yote/ wababa na wamama: tusikilize pale vile Mungu mwenyewe aliwaonyesha mufano wake kwa sisi wantu wa dunia/ ni mufano wa mawazo yake yenye [or: ienee] dunia muzima/

Then he was inclined to introduce this thought to the entire world, to all husbands and wives. *Bababa and bamama,* let us listen how God himself showed his example to us, people of this world, the example of his thought for the entire world.

wababa na wamama: pale ni Yezu alifwata ao ni wantu walimufwata/ tukaone vitendo vya huyu muntu ni vizuri sana: na sisi tupate vitendo yake/ hii anatumika namna yake: na sisi tutumikiane na wamama wetu vile yeye anatumikia/

Bababa and bamama: this is Jesus who followed, or rather the people who followed him. When we see that what a certain person does is good, then we want to have part in his doing. He does it in his way—we and our wife are going to do it the same way.

wababa na wamama: kwa sisi kuingiza Jamaa kwa wantu we-

Bababa and bamama, how are we going to introduce (21) the

ngine: tutaingiza namna gani? ni vile Mungu anaingiza kwetu: ni kule wantu wataangalia vitendo vya sisi wababa na wamama/ pale watasema tufwate vitendo vyetu sisi waJamaa: kwa sababu: muangalie wale wantu vile wanakala mu mandoa yao/ pasipo matata hata kidogo/ hata kati yetu hatuwaone vile sisi twiko/

Jamaa to other people? To the degree God enters us, people will see our actions, *bababa* and *bamama,* and they will say: Let us follow the example of the Jamaa. Look, how they live in their marriages, without the slightest trouble. You don't see people like this among us.

wanageuka/ ni wantu wa Mungu/ kweli: kumbe tuwafwateni: tugeuke vile wao wanageuka/ bibi yao ataanza kufwata mama wetu kwa kusumbulia naye: kwa bwana wake ageuke sawa baba wa Jamaa/ na bwana pale atafwata baba wa Jamaa: kwa bibi wake ageuke sawa mama wa Jamaa/

They changed (18), they are truly people of God. So let us follow them, let us change the way they changed. Their wife will begin to follow our *mama* to talk with her so that her husband may change and become like a *baba* of the Jamaa. And the husband will follow a *baba* of the Jamaa so that his wife may change and become like a *mama* of the Jamaa.

wale wantu wanatufwata sababu gani? wababa na wamama: ni vile Bwana Yezu alisema na wantu: muacheni kazi yenu: munifwate/ wale wabwana waliitwa na Yezu walienda kusumbulia na wa bibi wao: sisi tunataka kumufwata Yezu/ wabibi walipenda sana/

Why do these people follow us? *Bababa* and *bamama,* it is like the Lord Jesus told the people: Leave your work and follow me. Those husbands who were called by Jesus went to talk it over (67) with their wives: we want to follow Jesus. The wives were very much in favor of it.

kumbe na sisi tutakala vizuri sana mu nyumba yetu: sawa Yezu na Bikira Maria/ wababa na wamama: amri yangu ni kupendana/

Therefore, let us, too, live in harmony in our households, like Jesus and the Virgin Mary. *Bababa* and *bamama,* my commandment is to love each other.

4. *MAFUNDISHO* IN THE PART ABOUT *UMWANA* [BEING CHILD] OF GOD

wababa na wamama: ile umwana ni hivi/ ule umwana wake ulikuwako tangu zamani: mbele ya vintu vyote hivi tunaona/

Bababa and *bamama,* this is what *umwana* [being child (78)] means: His *umwana* existed before eternity, before all the things we see [came into existence].

Mungu baba pa kueneza umwana wake: alikuja kuzaliwa kwa mama/ alijishusha/

In order to realize his *umwana* he came to be born by a mother; he humiliated himself (66).

wababa na wamama: umwana wake unaisha? hapana/ anakuja kutuonyesha vile iko mwana kwa Mungu na muntu/ ule umwana wake: alitaka kuwa nao yeye moja? hapana/ ametupao na sisi wababa na wamama/ na sisi tuwe na jina la umwana/

Bababa and *bamama,* was this the end of his *umwana?* No, he came to show us [his *umwana*] as the child of God and man. Did he want to have his *umwana* for himself alone? No, he gave it to us, *bababa* and *bamama;* we, too, should have the name (30) of *umwana.*

kwa sisi tufanye nini kwa kueneza umwana wetu sawa yeye mwenyewe ameneza umwana wake? sisi tujishushe vilevile sawa yeye mwenyewe: tupate kuzaliwa/ bwana azaliwe kwa bibi: na bibi azaliwe kwa bwana/ sawa vile aliita mwanamuke mama: anaita mwanaume baba/

What are we to do in order to realize our *umwana* in the same way God realized his *umwana?* Let us humiliate ourselves as he did so that we may be born (84): the husband shall be born to his wife and the wife to her husband [as it is expressed] in the way he called the woman mother and she the man father.

kwetu ile umwana ikuwako namna ile? wababa na wamama: Bwana Yezu Kristo alisema ile kintu: kwa kupata ufalme wa mbingu: paka uzaliwe mara ya pili/ ni pale utaitwa mwana wa Mungu/

Is *umwana* among us in this way? *Bababa* and *bamama,* the Lord Jesus Christ said this: In order to gain the kingdom of heaven, be born a second time; then you'll be called child of God.

na sisi wababa na wamama: tu naanza kufwata ile maneno polepole: twiko mu njia/ sasa yee mwenyewe alisema/ tuliisha kuzaliwa mara ya pili/ tutafute kwa kujua ya kama tuliisha kuzaliwa: tuliisha kuzaliwa namna gani?

And we, *bababa* and *bamama,* begin to follow this matter step by step, we are on the way (50). He himself has said so. We were born a second time. Let us try to understand how we were born.

alafu pale unamuita bibi mama: pale tunamuita bwana baba/ wababa na wamama: amri yetu ni kuzaliwa/

[Is it not] the moment you call your wife mother, and we call the husband father? *Bababa* and *bamama:* Our commandment is to be born.

5. *MAFUNDISHO* IN THE FIRST PART ABOUT ADAM AND EVE

Wababa na wamama: tunataka kusumbulia mu kipande cha Adam na Eva/

Bababa and *bamama,* let us discuss the chapter about Adam and Eve.

sawa vile tulisikia mu kipande ya umuntu: mawazo vile alikuwa kwa Mungu mu mawazo ya Mungu/ sasa Mungu anataka kumuweka ule muntu alikuwa kwake mu mawazo akuwe muntu wa mwili wa dunia/

In the chapter about *umuntu* [being man (77)] we have heard the thought how he was with God in the thoughts of God. Now God wanted to put the man with whom he had been in his thoughts, in a body on earth.

pa kuumba ule muntu: Mungu aliwaza mawazo yake ya kumuumba nayo/ akasema: mimi nitafanya nini? kumbe niumbe mwili wa udongo/ mule ndani ya mwili ya udongo tutawekamo mawazo yetu/ hata ni udongo: tutafanana nao ku mawazo yetu/ Mungu anaisha vile: akashuka yeye mwenyewe mu dunia pa fasi penye udongo mwekunda/ mwenyezi Mungu akabeba udo-

In order to create this man, God thought of a plan according to which he might create him. [This was the result:] He said: What shall I do? I shall form a body out of clay. Into this body of clay we shall put our thoughts. Even though it is clay we shall be similar to them in our thoughts. After that God himself descended on earth, on a place where there was red clay. Al-

ngo mwekunda na mikono yake:
akafanya mwili ya muntu/ ule
mwili ulisimama sawa muntu:
pasipo mawazo ndani/

mighty God carried red clay in
his hands and made the body
of man. This body stood up like
a man, but it was without
thoughts inside.

Mungu akaona vile: akawekamo
mawazo yake: akasema: paka tufanane naye ku mawazo yetu/

When God saw this, he put his
thought into him and said: We
shall be similar to him in our
thoughts.

huyu ni mwili wa muntu mwa-
naume/

This is the body of a man.

kiisha kuwekamo mawazo yao:
muntu anaanza kutembea/ Mungu anamuacha mu dunia: ana-
kwenda/

As soon as he had put his
thoughts inside, the man began
to walk around. God left him
on earth and went away.

wababa na wamama: tunasikia
ile kipande ya Adam: inatua-
mbia nini?

Bababa and *bamama:* We listen
to the chapter about Adam—
what does it tell us?

ile mwili ya udongo iliumba
Mungu ilikuwa ya kabila gani?
ile mwili ilikuwa ya mweusi? ao
ya muzungu? ao kabila gani? ilikuwa ya *président:* ao ya wakubwa wote wa dunia muzima?
ilikuwa ya mutajiri ao ya maskini?

This body of clay which God
created—to which tribe did it
belong? Was it the body of a
black man, or the body of a
white man? Of which tribe? Was
it the body of a president, or of
all the powerful in the world?
Was it the body of a rich man,
or was it the body of a poor
man?

wababa na wamama: sababu gani? sasa tunakabula ule mwili
kwetu: unakuwa mbali-mbali/
kila muntu anajivuna: anashu-
sha mwili wa mwenzake: ana-
pandisha yake/

Bababa and *bamama,* why [do
we ask this]? Today we take
this body as a means of discrimi-
nation and it separates us. Everyone is proud of himself; he down-
grades the body of his fellow
man and upgrades his own.

siku moja mwili huyu tunaweka
nayo majivuno: itarudia mu

One day, this body in which we
put our pride will return to clay.

udongo/ kwa Mungu tutakwenda
na nini na majivuno?

With what shall we go to God,
having nothing but our pride?

6. *MAFUNDISHO* IN THE SECOND PART ABOUT THE ANGELS: GABRIEL: THE CONVERSATION BETWEEN GOD AND THE VIRGIN MARY

wababa na wamama: usiku ule Bikira Maria aliona mwangaza wa nguvu unamushukia mu nyumba mule alikuwa/

Bababa and *bamama,* that day the Virgin Mary saw a strong light come down on the house where she was.

ndani ya ule mwangaza sauti: ao alisikia sauti ya muntu mwanaume inamuuliza: wee Maria habari gani? ulisikia nini leo? Maria akasema: niliona malaika/ sauti ikamuuliza: mulisungumuza naye nini? yeye akajibu: tulisungumuza ile mambo Mungu alimutuma/ tena sauti ikasema: uliitika ile mambo? na yeye Maria akasema: ni paka vile Mungu anapenda/ tena ile sauti ikamuuliza: wewe Maria: ile sauti unasungumuza nayo ni nani? yeye akasema: ni sauti ya mwenyezi Mungu/

In this light was a voice; she heard the voice of a man asking her: How are you Mary? What did you hear today? Mary said: I saw the Angel. The voice asked her: About what did you talk with him? She answered: We talked about the matter for which God had sent him. Then the voice said: Did you agree to these things? And Mary said: It is as God wants it. Then this voice asked her: You, Mary, who is the voice you are talking to? She said: It is the voice of God Almighty.

Mungu akasema: ni mimi Mungu: nakuja kwako kwa kusungumuza na weye/ tena ni mimi Mungu mwenyewe nilikuumba/ nilikuwaka na weye tangu mwanzo mu mawazo/ hii vyote vintu unaona hii havikuwako: weye ulikuwako na mawazo tatu/ ulikuwa mama kwangu: tena mwana kwangu: na tena ulikuwa bibi kwangu/ sasa tu-

God said: It is I, God, and I come to you to talk with you (67). I am also God who created you. From the beginning I have been with you in the thoughts (35). All those things that you see were not there yet, but you were with the three thoughts (36, 30): You were my mother [lit., mother with me], my child, and my wife. Now we shall real-

nataka kueneza na weye ile mawazo yote tatu: hata weye wiko
na mwili: miye roho tupu/

sasa ujitayarishe: ujitengeneza
sawa bibi anataka kumupokea
bwana/ mama Maria akasema:
ile ni namna gani? weye hauna
na mwili wa umuntu mwanaume:
nitakupokee namna gani? Mungu
akasema: mwenye kuumba ule
mwili wa mwanaume ni miye/
nitakosa kuwa nao namna gani?

pale Maria alisikia vile: alianza
kujitayarisha sawa bibi anataka
kumupokea bwana/ alisikia nguvu ya umuntu mwanaume ina-
anza kushuka kwake/ ama ile
nguvu ilianza kuingia kwake: sawa bwana na bibi/ uzima wa
Mungu unaanza kuwa kwake:
uzazi wa Mungu unaanza kuwa
kwake: na tena ubwana wa
Mungu/ Roho Mutakatifu ulii-
ngia kwake: wakaisha kazi yao/

Mungu akamuambia: sasa hauna
tena mutoto mwanamuke: wiko
bibi/ naisha kukupa mimba/
ule mutoto iko mu mimba yako
ni mukombozi wa dunia/ uta-
mupa jina Yezu/ tena ule mutoto mutakuwaka kueneza naye hii
mawazo tunafanya na weye/
yeye na mwili: weye na mwili/
hii maneno unapata: usimua-
mbie muntu hata nani: hata nani/
uchunge mu roho yake: utaenda
kuikuta Elisabeth/

ninyi wababa na wamama: wenye kusikia hii mawazo: musie-

ize together with you all those
three thoughts, even though you
have a body and I am pure
spirit.

Now, get ready; prepare yourself
like a wife who is going to receive (58) her husband. Mother
Mary said: How shall that be?
You do not have the human
body of a man, how shall I receive you? God said: I am the
creator of the male body, how
can I lack it?

When Mary heard this she began
to prepare herself like a wife
who is going to receive her husband. She felt the male force
descending on her. This force
began to enter her: like husband
and wife. The life/force (82) of
God began to be with her, his
fecundity (81), and his *ubwana*
[being husband (30)]. The Holy
Spirit entered her and they finished their work.

God told her: Now you are no
longer a girl, you are a wife. I
have made you pregnant. The
child you carry is the savior of
the world. You'll give him the
name Jesus, and together with
this child you will realize those
thoughts as we did it with you.
He has a body, you have a body.
Do not tell anyone about these
things you experienced. Guard
them in your soul, go and meet
Elisabeth.

Bababa and *bamama,* now that
you have heard these thoughts,

nde kuisema-sema/ ni mambo ya
baba yetu na mama yetu/
mwenye kwenda kusema-sema:
atakuwa na mukoshi yake/

do not go and talk a lot about
them. They are matters of our
baba and our *mama*. Whoever
goes and talks shall be cursed.

ile maneno ndio asili ya njia yetu
ya Jamaa/ ni kule tunapata uzima wetu wa kuendelesha nao/
musilete na muntu pasipo katika
Jamaa yetu/

This is the origin of our way,
the Jamaa. From there we get
the strength to make progress
(12). Do not give it away to anyone who is not a member of
our Jamaa.

V ✵ Mafundísho [Public Instruction]

The following selection contains about half of the full text of a public *mafundisho*. The speaker is Monica Kabole of the C.E.C. at Kolwezi. The recording was made by Monsignor Malunga in 1963. As in the excerpts from the *kitabu* in Appendix IV, key concepts of Jamaa doctrine are given the numbers of our vocabulary. Underlined words in the text mark responses from the audience. These, as well as the stereotyped Jamaa greeting *yambo yetu,* are not included in the translation.

TEXT

Bababa na bamama yambo yetu—*yambo yetu*/ leo tunataka kujikumbusha mambo ya jamaa yetu/ tujue vile jamaa alianza/

wantu mingi wataona ya kama pengine jamaa anaanza na muntu wa dunia/ si vile/ jamaa haianza na muntu wa dunia hata moja/ jamaa haianza hata hapa pa Kolwezi: hapana/

kintu hata kimoja: jamaa ilikuwa/ kumbe jamaa ilikuwa ni ku mawazo ya Mungu yee mwenyewe peke: pasipo kuwa jua: mwezi: nyota: dunia: hata kiumbe kimoja/ alafu jamaa ilikuwako/

Mungu si maskini: hapana/ Mungu ni mutajiri wa vyote/ Mungu ni mwenyi kuweza kila kintu yoyote/ ni ule alianza mawazo ya kusema: mimi nitakuwa na jamaa yangu/

kumbe ule jamaa Mungu alianza kukumbuka mu mawazo yake/ hakukuwa na kabila yake hapana/ ule jamaa pengine tunaanza kuwaza asema: ni muzungu/ maneno tunaona muzungu ndio muntu wa mayele mingi/ si vile? pengine tunawaza ni muntu mwanaume: kwetu tunaona muntu mwanaume anazidi kusema mingi: ao anazidi kufanya vintu mingi/ si vile? ule jamaa Mungu alikumbuka si mwanamuke/ kumbe alikuwa nani? alikuwa paka jamaa mawazo/ ni muntu tu mawazo/ vile Mungu mwenyewe alikuwa yee mawazo: vile ule Jamaa yake ni muntu alikuwa paka mawazo/ yambo yetu bababa na bamama—*yambo yetu*/

kumbe Mungu alianza mawazo makubwa kabisa pamoja na ule jamaa yake/ Mungu alifanya kazi ya nguvu/ pengine tuliona ni kintu kipesi Mungu alifanya paka hivi maneno ni mwenye vintu vyote: hapana/ alitafuta alifanya kazi/

kumbe Mungu alikumbuka namna gani? sasa minaisha kuwa na jamaa yangu/ kintu kikubwa minakumbukia ndio ni nini? nimuingijie hii jamaa yangu mu butajiri yangu/ na yeye na miye tufanane tukuwe kintu kimoja/ mimi sitakuwa mukubwa mbele ya jamaa yangu/ mimi sitaona jamaa kwa kusema pengine ni kintu kidogo: hapana/ minatafuta kwa kusema ingie ndani ya utajiri yangu/ na yeye na miye tufanane/ kumbe Mungu alitafuta mawazo makubwa matatu yenyi kuunganisha pamoja na ule jamaa yake/

Mungu alitafuta mawazo makubwa matatu ile ya kusema wazo ya kwanza: miye pamoja na jamaa yangu tusikilizane/ maneno tunaona kama masikilizano hakuna: hapana kwa wantu wawili: hakuna kintu kingine kinaweza kupita kati yao: hapana/ kumbe kintu ya kwanza masikilizano/

Mungu na jamaa alibakia na ile masikilizano miaka milele na milele siku mingi/ si ni siku moja vile sisi tunaanza kutafuta pengine tunaanza kuskilizana leo: kesho itaisha: hapana/ ile masikilizano ilianza miaka milele na milele/

wazo ya pili: Mungu alianza kusaidiana na jamaa yake/

na wazo ya tatu: Mungu balipendana na jamaa ya—*yake*/

ndio vile mawazo makubwa matatu ndio iliunganisha Mungu na jamaa: Mungu: ni paka ile mawazo makubwa tatu/

kumbe pale Mungu alikumbuka ule jamaa yake ni kusema: alikatala wazo ya upeke/ kwa kusema: mimi niko wa vyote: niko wa furaha yo—*yote*/ kumbe mi sitakuwa upeke: hapana/ nitakuwa na jamaa yangu/ kumbe yeye na miye tuungane tukuwe kintu—*kimoja*/

kumbe tunaona pa ile fasi ya kama Mungu alifanya hapa kintu kikubwa sana/ kama pa kati pa Mungu na jamaa yake palikuwa majivuno: kama ile mawazo makubwa tatu kuwa kati yao—*hapana*/
kumbe Mungu alituonyesha kama majivuno ni kintu kizuri hapana:
ni pale Mungu alituonyesha minakatala majivuno/ minakatala mawazo yote/ kumbe nikuwe paka na mawazo makubwa tatu ni ile
inaunganisha mi Mungu na jamaa—*yangu*/ yambo yetu bababa na
bamama—*yambo yetu*/

kumbe pa ile fasi Mungu alilaka jamaa yake kwa kumuambia ya
kama unaona sasa pa kati ya weye jamaa na mi Mungu tuko na
mawazo makubwa—*tatu*/ kumbe minakulaka kama sitaweza ku-
tumika kazi ya upeke pasipo wee jamaa yangu kujua—*hapana*/ kazi
yoyote mi Mungu nitaweza kufanya tutatweza kuwa na wee jamaa—
yangu/ tutatumika ile kazi sisi wote wawili pamo—*pamoja*/ kumbe
ile mawazo ibakie kwako miaka milele na-*milele*/ pasipo kushindwa
pale ile mawazo makubwa ilibakia kwangu ni kusema: tunaona pengine pa kati ya Mungu na jamaa yake: chuki hapana/ bishilani
hapana/ majivuno hapana/ wote wawili wanakuwa kimo—*kimoja*/
kumbe ni vile jamaa ilianza pamoja na Mungu mwenyewe. . . .

Mungu alisema na jamaa ya kama sitabakia na wee mawazo: na mi
mawazo: hapana/ Mungu alitutuma mu dunia/ alituma ule jamaa
yake mu dunia/ pale ule jamaa anakuwa mu dunia Mungu alimu-
fanya nakuwa muntu wa mwi—*wa mwili*/ na Mungu alimuambia ya
kama hata vile minakufanya nakuwa muntu wa mwili: utafananana
na miye Mungu wako ku mawa—*ku mawazo*/ ni paka ku ile mawazo makubwa yake ta—*tatu*/ kusikilizana: kusaidiana: na mape—
na mapendo/

ni vile Mungu alitutuma sisi wantu mu dunia kwa kusema: mwende
sasa mu dunia: mutafanana na mi Mungu wa—*wako*/ mwanze kutumikia ile mawazo vile mi mwenyewe minaitumikia kwako/ kumbe
tunaona ile mawazo: sisi wantu wa dunia tunakuja kuisahau/ hatue-
ndelea tena na ile mawazo vile ilianza Mungu mwenyewe tangu zamani: hapana/

kumbe ni vile Mungu anatupa kazi/ tuweze kufanya ile kazi vile yee
mwenyewe alifanya/ tunaona pale muntu alikuwa kwa Mungu pasipo
kabila/ muntu alikuwa na Mungu pasipo na bufupi burefu: hata pale
tunafika ku dunia ile mawazo inakuwa mbali mbali. . . .

muangarie vile huyu muntu pale alikuwa kwake alikuwa paka muntu
huyu moja/ muntu tu mawazo/ hata pale Mungu anakuja kumuweka

mu dunia: tunaona huyu muntu: Mungu alimupa nyumba mbali-
mbali/ nyumba muke na nyumba mume/ ni pahali pa kusema na
sisi tufanye kazi/ tutafute kile kintu kilikuwa na Mungu tangu za—
zamani/ kama Mungu alitufanya wantu wa kimo kimoja: pengine
tulitaka kushindwa namna ya kufanya kazi. . . .

musione ni bule: hapana/ kumbe pa ile fasi Mungu anatupa kazi/
ni pahali pa shee kufanya kazi tufanane na Mungu we—*wetu*/ vile
yee alitulaka ya kama: mi nitakutuma mu dunia alafu utafanana na
mi Mungu wako hata unakuwa muntu—*wa mwili*/

kumbe pa ile fasi tutafuteni: ni kazi Mungu anatupa ya shee kwa
kufanya/ tutafanya namna gani?

baba aanze kutafuta ile mawazo ilianza nayo Mungu tangu za—
zamani/

mama aanze kutafuta ile mawazo ilianza nayo Mungu tangu za—
zamani/

kumbe ile mawazo tuanze kuiunganisha ndani ya nyumba yetu/ ni
mawazo gani? paka ile mawazo makubwa matatu Mungu alianza nayo
pamoja na jamaa ya—*yake*/ masikilizano: masaidiano: na mapendo/

muangarie hiyi mawazo tuliikumbuka baba pasipo kumuona mama na
mwili/ ile mawazo inamutesa baba ndani mwake/ mama pasipo
kumuona baba na mwili ile mawazo ilimutesa mama ndani mwa—
mwake/ tunaanza kuitumikia ile jamaa ao hatuiona na ma—*na
macho*/ pale baba anafanya ile kazi nguvu paka vile jamaa yake/
mama alifanya ile kazi nguvu paka vile ule jamaa ya—*yake*/ alafu
sisi tunakuwa kuonana na mwili: ile mawazo inatukumbi—*inatuki-
mbia*/

pa kati yetu kunakuwa nini? majivuno: chuki: bishilani na mambo
mabaya yo—*yote*/ ni juu ya nini? kwa sababu tunapoteza ile mawazo
makubwa tatu ilianza na Mungu mwenyewe tangu za—*zamani*/ masikilizano: masaidiano: na mape—*na mapendo*/ . . . tutakuwa na ile
mawazo yote tutaweza kutendeana/ kumbe tuangarie vile mawazo
ilianza na Mungu wetu ni vile alitupa sisi wantu wa dunia kwa kusema
tufanana naye/

kumbe ile kazi bababa na bamama banatupa kwa kusema: tutafute
mu manyumba ye—*yetu*/ . . .

TRANSLATION

[Greeting.] Today we will meditate (28) together about the matters concerning our Jamaa. We want to know how the Jamaa began.

Perhaps, in the opinion of many people, the Jamaa was started by a human being from this world. This is not so. The Jamaa did not begin with any man from this world; nor did the Jamaa begin here in Kolwezi.

The Jamaa began in eternity with God himself. Before anything existed, there was the Jamaa. The Jamaa was in the thoughts (35) of God alone—the sun, the stars, the earth, not one creature was there yet, but the Jamaa was there.

God is not poor, God is rich in everything. God is the Lord of everything. He had the thought: I shall be with my Jamaa (22).

The Jamaa whom God began to think (28) in his thoughts had no distinction (73). Perhaps we are inclined to think that this Jamaa was a white man. Because we see that the white man is a man of great intelligence. Is it not so? Maybe we think [this Jamaa] is a man. Because we see that in our society the man has a lot to say and can do a lot. Is it not so? [But this is not true]; nor is this Jamaa God had thought out a woman. So who was [this Jamaa]? It was just thought-Jamaa, thought-man (43). Just as God himself was thoughts, this Jamaa of his was just thought-man. [Greeting.]

So God began a very great plan together with this Jamaa of his. God accomplished a difficult task. Perhaps we regard it as something easy which God did just like that, because he is almighty. No, he sought to accomplish a difficult task.

How did God think? Now that I am with my Jamaa, what is going to be the big plan I am thinking about? I shall take my Jamaa into my wealth. The Jamaa and I shall be similar (13), and we shall be one thing (76). I shall not dominate (74) my Jamaa, nor look down on it. It shall enter my wealth, and we shall be similar. Then God sought the three big thoughts (36) which were to unite him (79) with this Jamaa.

Among these three big thoughts the first one was: I and my Jamaa shall understand each other (34). Because we see that if there is no mutual understanding between two people, nothing at all is going to happen between them. Therefore, the first thing is mutual understanding.

God and the Jamaa lived with this understanding through eternity. It was not the way it is with us: One day we begin to look for mutual understanding—the next day it's over. Their understanding began in eternity.

The second thought: God and his Jamaa began to help each other (33).

And the third thought: God and his Jamaa loved each other (32).

These are the three big thoughts which united God with his Jamaa. The big thoughts which made the Jamaa participate in God's wealth are these three.

Therefore, when God thought his Jamaa, he rejected (25) the thought of being alone (80). [He told himself]: Even though I am the Lord of everything and I have every joy, I shall not stay alone, I'll be with my Jamaa. The Jamaa and I shall be united, and we shall be one thing.

At this point we see that God accomplished a great thing. If, between God and his Jamaa, there had been pride and envy, the three big thoughts would not have been realized by them. So God showed us that pride is a bad thing. He showed us: I reject pride and everything else; I only shall be with the three big thoughts. They will unite us, me, God, and my Jamaa.

[Greeting.] At this point God made a promise to his Jamaa: Between you, Jamaa, and me, God, there are the three big thoughts. Therefore I promise: I shall not do my work alone without you, my Jamaa, knowing about it. You, my Jamaa, will be with me in every work I do. The two of us will do this work together. This thought shall be with you forever, and it shall not fail. We see what this means: Between God and his Jamaa there is no hatred, no evil thoughts, no pride. Both are one thing. This is how the Jamaa began with God himself. . . .

God told his Jamaa: I shall not stay with you in thoughts [only]. God sent the Jamaa on earth. When this Jamaa was on earth, God made it a human being with a body. And God told him: Even though I made you a human being with a body, you shall still be similar to me, your God, through the thoughts—through your three big thoughts: mutual understanding, mutual help, and love.

This is how God sent us people into the world: Go into the world; you shall be like me, your God; begin to work for (26) these thoughts the way I did it with you. [But] then we see that we people of this world forgot these thoughts. No longer do we live according to these thoughts which originated with God in eternity.

God gave us a task, and we can accomplish it the way he himself did it. We see that [thought-]man was with God without distinction, neither short nor long. Only once we arrive on this earth the thoughts get separated. . . .

Look: As long as he was with God, this [thought-]man was just the same: just thought-man. But when God put him into this world—

this is how we see this man—he gave him different houses, male and female. This is where our task comes in: to search for the thing which was with God from eternity. If God had made us people of one and the same kind, perhaps we would have failed to accomplish our task. . . .

Don't regard this as nonsense. This is the point where God gave us our task to accomplish so that we may be similar to our God. He has promised us: I send you into the world, but you shall be similar to me, your God, even though you are a man with a body.

Therefore, let us search (68). This is the task God gave us to accomplish. How are we going to do it?

Baba [the husband] shall search for the thoughts which God began in eternity.

Mama [the wife] shall search for the thoughts which God began in eternity.

Let us begin to be united in those thoughts in our household. Which thoughts? The three big thoughts which God initiated with his Jamaa: mutual understanding, mutual help, and love.

Look: *Baba* has been moved by these thoughts before he actually saw *mama* [lit., before he saw *mama* in her body]. *Mama* has been moved by these thoughts before she actually saw *baba*. [This proves that] we start to live this Jamaa before we see it with our eyes. Then *baba* did this difficult work [of realizing the three big thoughts] like his Jamaa, and *mama* did her difficult work like her Jamaa. But as soon as we look at the body (46), those thoughts flee from us.

And what is between us? Pride, hatred, evil thoughts, and all sorts of bad things. Why? Because we lost the three big thoughts which began with God himself in eternity: mutual understanding, mutual help, and love. . . . If we have these thoughts, we shall be able to realize them for each other. Therefore, let us see how these thoughts began with God, how he gave them to us, people of the world, so that we may be similar to him.

This is the task, *bababa* and *bamama,* we are to accomplish in our households. . . .

VI ❧ Mashaurio [Counsel]

The following is a typical example of the *mashaurio* variant of instruction. Even though we present only an excerpt from the text, the basic tendencies are sufficiently illustrated: doctrinal statements give way to direct, practical admonitions and applications, and the style of *mashaurio* is rambling, full of digressions and repetitions. The text was taped on May 6, 1967, at Musonoi in the house of Adolphe Lubala. The speaker is his wife, Sidonie, who was asked to give a *mafundisho* about marriage to my sister and brother-in-law, who were then about to get married—a situation that came as close as possible to an actual session of marriage counseling in the Jamaa.

TEXT

mama M: na baba N/[1] banataka kuingia mu ndoa/ tuko tunaiomba: banaikala ku ndoa yenu muzuri/ kuikala mu ndoa muzuri ni hivi/ wee mama utaweza kuchunga baba/ baba nayee ataweza kumu-chunga/

. . . mu chipande ya kwanza ya ndoa: mama: alikuwa ku mikono ya bazazi yake/ asikuanza asema mi huyu batanifwata kwiko baba N/ hapana/ N nayee: aliikala nayee ku mikono ya bake bazazi/ pasipo kuyua asema: mi huyu nitafwata M ku nyumba ya bazazi yabo: hapana/ kumbe mu muunganisha Mungu yee moya: vile ali-waza asema: N: atafwata M ku nyumba ya bake bazazi/ M nayee atafwata N ku nyumba ya bake bazazi/

kufwata ni hivi/ vile bazazi ya zamani balikudya bwarafiki yabo: balikuwa: huyu asema: huyu muntu ni rafiki yangu/ kumbe wabo

1. *Mama* M and *baba* N are the two marriage candidates.

banaikala mukati ya bwarafiki yabo muzuri/ banaona bitendo yabo
bya kuikala mukati ya rafiki muzuri/ ao huyu anazala wake mutoto
mwanaume/ huyu naye wake: mwanamuke/ kumbe pale banaikala
mu bwarafiki yabo muzuri: mi: atasema: mi wangu mutoto mwanaume: anapenda wako huyu mwanamuke/ huyu naye anasema: kumbe
vile wako anapenda wangu mwanamuke: bataweza kuungana kwa bo
benyewe/

ndio vile: baba N alifwata mama M: ilikuwa sawa bwarafiki bwa
bazazi yabo/ bale balipendana mu bwarafiki yabo/ ndio maana
batoto na batoto balikwenda kuoana bo benyewe/ ndio vile batoto
balipendana bo benyewe: vile N alipenda M: M nayee asema: minamupenda M: ni wangu/ tutaweza kuikala nayee hata mukati ya
ndoa yetu: kwa mapendo yetu: vile shee wawili: tunapendana/ kupendana kwetu kulitoka sawa bwarafiki kwa bazazi yetu/ vile bazazi
yabo balipendana/ baliunga bwarafiki yabo: bwa kuikala asema wee
uko rafiki yangu/ na mi naye niko rafiki yako/ sasa pale banazala
batoto yabo: na vile batoto yabo banakuya kupendana mukati yabo:
vile ni bwarafiki mukubwa ya Mungu/

kumbe na mukati ya ndoa yabo: bataweza kupendana sawa vile
bazazi balianza bwarafiki/ bwa kupendana/ bataikala mukati ya
ndoa yabo: vile balipendana bo benyewe/ asema: N asema: minamupenda M/ M nayee asema: minamupenda N/ kumbe na mukati ya
ndoa bataweza kuikala muzuri: kati ya nyumba yabo/ kwasipo bishawishi mubaya: kwasipo nini/ vile balipendana: vile N alifika mu
baM asema: minapenda wangu moya M/ M nayee: bwana N asema:
minamupenda wangu moya N/ kumbe mapendo yetu inakuwa sawa
bwarafiki ya Mungu/ tutaweza kuikala mukati ya ndoa yetu: muzuri/
kwa kupendana mukati ya nyumba yetu/ kwasipo bishawishi mubaya/
kwasipo mateso mubaya. . . .

TRANSLATION

Mama M and *baba* N are about to get married. We ask them:
They should live right in your marriage. To live right in marriage
means this: You, *mama*, shall guard *baba*, and *baba* will guard
her. . . .
   In the first chapter about marriage [let us reflect on the following]:
Mama was in the arms of her parents. She did not first tell herself:
The relatives of *baba* N are going to ask for me. Also N, he was in
the arms of his parents. And he did not know: I am going to follow

this M in the house of her parents. So God alone brought you together. He thought: N shall follow M into the house of her parents; M shall follow N into the house of his parents.

"To follow" means this: Long ago their parents had made a pact of friendship, declaring: This man is my friend. They lived well in their friendship and saw the good that came out of their friendship. Now one of them had a child, a boy. The other one also, a girl. Because they were such good friends, the one of them would say: My girl loves your boy. And the other one said: My boy loves your girl; so they themselves will get together.

And that is what happened. *Baba* N followed *mama* N, and it was like the friendship between their parents. They loved each other in their friendship. So the two children finally decided themselves that they were going to get married. This is how the children themselves loved each other; how N loved M, and M said: I love N, he is mine. We'll live together in marriage, in the love with which we two love each other. Our mutual love began like the friendship between our parents. Their parents loved each other and became friends and lived as friends, telling themselves: You are my friend, and I am your friend. When they had children, they, too, came to love each other. This is the great friendship that comes from God.

So, in their marriage they will be able to love each other like their parents began their friendship. They'll live in their marriage, and they themselves will love each other. N says: I love M. M says: I love N. So they'll live right in their marriage and in their household, without evil intentions and what not. This is how they came to love each other: N came to M's people and said: I love my only M. And M, too, said to N's [father]: I love my only N. Our love is like friendship from God. We'll live well in our marriage, and we'll love each other in our household, without evil intentions, without unfortunate suffering. . . .

REMARK

Concerning the content of this passage, see *rafiki* (60) in our vocabulary. There the theme of personal friendship was contrasted with the "social" character of marriage arrangements in traditional society. Free, sentimental love (as between friends) is one of the most important points in Jamaa teaching about marriage. This does not preclude the use of models from tradition. In the text just quoted, the expression used for "make a pact of friendship," *kudya bwarafiki,* points in that direction. *Kudya* is a Luba, not a Swahili, word and literally means "to eat." It is used in a large number of expressions, one of them being *kudya bulunda,* "recevoir qqn. par amitié réciproque" (van Avermaet and Mbuya 1954:106); according to my information, this refers to a formal pact of friendship.

VII ❀ Arísi [The Parable]

The following is an example of the type of stories, fables, and parables employed in Jamaa teaching. Jamaa people refer to it as an *arisi* (the Katanga version of *hadithi* in classical Swahili). The informant is Ignace Kapongo; the recording was made in a small meeting at the C.E.C. at Kolwezi on January 7, 1967.

TEXT

Ile arisi minasema ni hivi/ pa ile mambo ya Mungu sisi tuko tuna-zungumuza: hata na arisi tunatega: ni juu paka ya kuonyesha vile tunajirudia sisi nayo mambo ya Mungu/ tuliona hapa baba anatuambia: kwa kama: sisi bababa: na sisi bamama: nguvu yetu ni kwa saserdos/ nguvu yetu ni kusaidiana: kusikilizana: na tena kupendana/ na Mungu mwenyewe alipenda paka ile kintu/

baba moya alikuwa na safari yake/ anatoka mu mugini yao: anaanza kwenda ku fasi ingine ya mbali/ alitembea: alitembea: alitembea/ alisikia hata na muchoko: mu kutembea kwake/ alikutana tena baba mwenzake: ku nyumba yake/ yee alimuonyesha na baba mwenzake asema: mwenzetu minachoka sana/ unipeko mayi ya kunywa/ ule mwenzetu alimukaribia alimuita ku mulango yake: anakamata chilasi moya: anamupa/ ule baba anakula ile chilasi: anasikia nguvu/ ule anamupa tena mayi: yee anakunywa tena mayi: anasikia nguvu/ sasa anamulaga ule mwenzake: baba ubakie muzuri: minapata nguvu sasa/ ule asema: ni kweli: wende muzuri baba/

ule baba anakwenda ku safari yake: anakwenda kufika/ kule alirudia kwabo ku mugini: wakati ilipita murefu: na tena ule baba alikuja kufa/ paka anakuja kufa: alikuwa muntu mwema sana kwa Mungu/

Mungu alimubeba ule baba: anamuweka pahali paka patakatifu/
anaikala mu mbinguni/

lakini tu anaikala wakati murefu sana/ ule baba tena aliletaka chilasi
na ule baba: wakati yake tena inaenea/ Mungu anamubeba/ kiisha
ule baba alikuwa mwenye kutangulia zamani kwa Mungu: ana-
muomba Mungu wake: anasema: Mungu wangu: ule baba ni baba
moya mwema sana/ minakuomba ile baba anapashwa kuja kuikalako
karibu na wee Mungu wake: na sisi benyewe: beko banaikala hapa/
Mungu wake anasema: yeye ni mwema namna gani? asema: ilini-
ponyeshaka sana/ mu njia nilitembea nilichoka sana: yee aliniponye-
sha: alinipa chilasi: minakula: ananipa mayi ya kunywa: minaku-
nywa: minapata nguvu ya kwenda kule nilikuwa nakwenda/ Mungu
anasema ni kweli/ vile alimuponyesha na chilasi/ lakini na miye minatafuta kumuponyesha na wee na chilasi/

Mungu anamuonyesha lukamba ya chilasi/ sema: ukate lukamba
hiyi/ yee anakata lukamba ya chilasi/ asema: utupe ile lukamba
chini: wee mwenyewe ukamate ku lukamba/ ule baba akamata ku
lukamba yako ile: tena unaanza kumukokota: na vile atafika hapa
twiko/ ni kweli: ule baba mutakatifu alikamata ile lukamba/ ana-
mwekea mwenzake/ mwenzake na yeye anakamata ku lukamaba/

kiisha: ile wakati: kulikuwa tena muntu mwengine: wakati yake inae-
nea: naye Mungu tena alimubeba/ ule muntu angaliki naye paka pale
chini/ anaangaria asema: mwenzetu huyu anapanda/ miye nibakie
hapa: hapana/ tutapanda paka pamoya sisi wote haba mbili/ sasa
ule mukwetu anakuya nayee: anakamata ku mukulu ya mwenzake:
asema batukokote sisi wote twende kwa Mungu/ pale ule baba:
mwema: ule alileta na kilasi: anaona vile: asema: huyu mukwetu
akuja tena kunikamata ku mukulu/ ile kilasi balinileta juu ya mi
moya: maneno ya mi kupanda kwa Mungu/ sababu gani: yee nayee
akuja ku mukulu? anatupa mukulu ingine ya ngambo ingine: ile ilibakia yasipo kukamata ule baba: anatwanga ule baba paka mu nsula:
kápù/ baba ule yee iko chi—*iko chini*/

ndio Mungu asema na ule mutakatifu asema: unaona?
wee ulisema: huyu baba mu dunia ni mwema sana/ iko baba moya wa
huruma sana/ mwenzake anamukamata ku mukulu asema: twende sisi
wote kwa Mungu/ sababu gani yee anapenda paka yee moya kuja huku
kwangu? sasa ule mwenzake abakia chini: anamupiga mwenzake
mukulu: anamuongosha na chini/ kumbe ile bwema yenu mulifansiana
mwee mwenyewe: kwa sababu mulijuana ku mambo ingi—*ingine*/

kwa hapa sasa minamukatala na yee mwenyewe: kwa sababu yee ku-penda muntu mwenzake: hapana/ Mungu anakamata kisu: anakata luka—*lukamba*/ na ule muntu anaanguka/

TRANSLATION

The *arisi* I am going to tell you goes like this: When we talk about the matters of God—even with the *arisi* we put together—we have only one purpose: to show how this turns our minds back to the things of God. We have seen how this *baba* [i.e., the one who spoke before him] has spoken to us, saying, *bababa* and *bamama*, that our strength comes from the priest. Our strength is to help each other, to understand each other, and to love each other. God himself loved only that.

A *baba* was traveling. He left his village and set out for a place far away. He walked, and walked, and walked. Then he got tired from walking. He met another *baba* near his house. He explained to him [his distress] and said: Friend [lit., a term of address for equals in age, kinship category, or for fellow tribesmen], I am very tired, give me water to drink. This man told him to come closer and enter his house. He took a sweet potato and gave it to him. The *baba* ate the sweet potato and felt strengthened. The other one also gave him water. He drank the water and felt strong. Then he took his leave from the other one: Goodbye, *baba*, I have regained my strength. The other one said: Truly, have a good trip, *baba*.

This *baba* continued his journey and finally arrived. From there he returned to his village. A long time went by, and this *baba* came to die. In the eyes of God he had been a very good man. God carried this *baba* away and put him in a sacred place: he lived in heaven.

There he stayed for a very long time. Then the time to die also came for the *baba* who had given him the sweet potato. God carried him away. The *baba* who already had been a long time with God asked God: My God, this *baba* is a very good man. I ask that this *baba* should come and live close to you, his God, and to us who are staying here. His God said: In what way is he good? He said: He once helped me a lot. I was traveling and got very tired. He re-freshed me. He gave me a sweet potato, and I ate it. He gave me water to drink, and I drank. So I gained strength to go where I in-tended to go. God said: Truly, so he strengthened you with a sweet potato. I, too, will see to it that you help him with a sweet potato.

God showed him a string [vine] on which sweet potatoes grew and said: Cut this string. He cut the sweet-potato string. [God] said:

Let this string down. You hold the string, and this *baba* shall hold onto your string. Then you start to pull him up, and this is how he will arrive in our place. Truly, this holy *baba* took the string, let it down to his friend, and he held onto the string.

It so happened that at the same time another man came to die, and God carried him away. This man was left down on earth. Then he saw [what was going on] and said: This fellow is going up, shall I stay where I am? No. Let the two of us go up together. Now he came, too, and grabbed a leg of the other one, telling himself: They'll pull both of us so that we can go to God. Then the good *baba*—the one who had given the sweet potato—saw what was happening. He said: This fellow comes and grabs my leg. They let the string down for me alone so that I could get to God. Why is he now holding onto my leg? He stretched the leg that was free and kicked the other *baba* on his head—bang; the other one was on the ground.

Then God said to this holy *baba:* You see? You said: This *baba* on earth is very good, he is a man full of compassion. Then his fellow man held onto his leg, saying: Let us both go to God. Why did he want to come alone to me? Now his fellow man remains on the ground; he kicked him with his leg and left him on the ground. Therefore, the good you did each other was done because you had some other arrangement [lit., because you knew each other in terms of other things]. So I reject him now, because he does not love his fellow man. God took a knife, cut the string, and this man fell down.

REMARK

The key to the *arisi* must be sought in the "other arrangement" between the two men. Mutual love, preached by the Jamaa, is not based on any links of kinship, tribe, or other mutual obligation.

VIII ☙ *Mufano* [The Short Example]

Jamaa people differentiate (terminologically) between full-length stories meant to illustrate the point of a doctrine (*arisi,* cf. Appendix VII) and *mifano,* short illustrations, comparisons, etc. Here are two examples of the latter.

1. In a *mafundisho* about *umuntu* (being man [77]), S. Mutombo depicts the following scene of postindependence everyday life in order to illustrate conceit and lack of respect for *umuntu.* In this particular example, intonation and gestures are extremely important and make a translation very difficult. The passage is taken from a text taped on February 17, 1967, at Kolwezi:

sawa vile mufano/ sawa vile ba Commissaire: banavwala: unaona: banavwala kasemisi hivi kaloko na kamupila: ah: iko mwanetu [laughs]. . . . leo: ah banakuwa ku *commissaire* . . . *ma-Officier:* ingine: banakuya/ unaangaria bale banavwala mupila: na semisi yabo/ *allez allez:* yote: *ceder:* iko nini? ile muntu iko bule/ sasa anaangaria kintu gani? ule *commissaire:* anaangaria kintu gani? aweze tena kuangaria ule muntu? angaria ile muntu iko ndani? ya mwili wake? sasa anaanza kuangaria paka *uniforme* yake/ anaanza kumuletea nini? kiburi/ anaanza kumupa majivuno/ sasa/ hajue tena

Here is an example. Just as you see the police dressed in neat shirts and sweaters [uniform coats?]. [They walk by and everybody is supposed to say] *mwanetu* [devout greeting in Luba]. Ah, there they come, the officers and the others. . . . Look at them in their shirts and sweaters, yelling: Move, move! What's the matter? This idiot there! Now, what does such a police officer look at? Is he still able to see this man [as a human being]? Can he still see what is inside his body? He just sees his [own] uniform and lets him feel his pride and arrogance. He no longer recognizes his hu-

bumuntu bwake/ haweze kujua tena muntu mwenza—*mwenzake*/ hata kiloko/ anashindwa kuyua bumuntu bwake/ kama aliyua bumuntu wake: kama alitaka kuwaza: ule muntu iko mawazo ya Mungu/ na huyu muntu iko ndani: ya mwili wangu/ ni muntu paka mo—*moja*/

man dignity. He no longer recognizes his fellow man. He fails to know his own *bumuntu* [human dignity]. If he knew his *bumuntu*, he would think: this man is thoughts (35) from God. And this man who is inside my body [and his] are the same.

2. The *kitabu* illustrates with the following *mufano* that a Jamaa member who failed to "unite" himself with his fellow men on earth will not be accepted by the Jamaa in heaven. As is often the case with the *mifano*, the logic of the case derives from ideas and values of traditional society, even though it is supposed to prove a point of Jamaa teaching.

Wababa na wamama: kwa mufano/ humu duniani kama muntu anazaliwa mu kizazi yao: yeye hapendi wanduku yake hapana: iko anawaua ku ulozi/ kama anakufa wale wenye kubaki watasema nini?

Bababa and *bamama*, for example: A man here on earth is born into his kinship group. But he does not love his relatives and kills them through sorcery. What are his survivors going to say when he dies?

wataanza kumuchekelea: asema anakufa tena namna gani? tena wale alikuwa anaua: watasema namna gani? hapana pale watamuona watachekelea? kusema anakuya tena uku namna gani? pale si watamufukuza?

They will begin to laugh at him: How did he finally die? And those whom he killed, what are they going to say? Are they not going to look down on him and laugh at him, saying: How is he going to come to this place? Will they not chase him away?

IX ❦ Mawazo [Dreams]

The number of dreams recorded in the field does not allow classification based on quantitative analysis of the material. I have chosen three accounts of dreams representing types, or tendencies, which seem characteristic of the Jamaa. The first is clearly connected with the initiatory experience expected from the candidates upon admission to the first degree (cf. above, Chapter 4). The second has a much more personal character and contains such universal themes as color symbolism, paternal authority, and guilt, but its setting reflects the specific environment of the dreamer: the Jamaa and the camp. The third example deals with tensions between a local priest and the movement, a topic that occurs quite frequently in Jamaa dreams (for a similar account see Fabian 1966:557 ff.).

The accounts are presented in the original, transcribed from tape recordings made by Father B.; the identity of the informants is, for obvious reasons, not disclosed. Each text will be followed by some remarks on the manifest content. On the role of dreams and dreaming in the Jamaa see the section on "Sharing the System" in Chapter 4.

FIRST DREAM

Recorded May 14, 1966, at Musonoi. The dreamer is a woman.

Tulipata mawazo siku ya kazi tano takatifu/ tuliona baba M. . . . alikuja na komunio hivi: anakamata ku mukono anasema:	We dreamed on Good Friday and saw *baba* M. . . . He came with the communion, took it in his hand, and called me: You,

ananiita: wee mama X: minaiti-
ka/ anasema: kamata hii kintu/
minaangaria minaona ile komunio ku mukono minasema: baba
hiyi kintu: unionyeshe mufano
yake/ mimi sijui vile iko kama
iko namna gani: hapana/ alafu
unionyesha mufano yake ndio ni-
jue asema ni kintu fulani/

kumbe alirudia mara ya mpili:
alikuja na msalaba wa Bwana
Yezu: na Bwana Yezu pa msalaba mwanzo anafanya kichwa
hivi/ anakuja naye: anasema:
kamata Bwana Yezu huyu umu-
chunge/

na mi nilimujibu minasema: baba: sasa unanipa Bwana Yezu:
alafu baba wangu atabakia paka
hivi pasipo Bikira Maria?

na yee alisema: minakwenda kubeba Bikira Maria/ anakwenda
anakuja na sanamu kiloko hivi:
na mwangaza mingi sana/ kiisha
pale alikuja na ile sanamu anasema: Bikira Maria yee huyu minakuja kuleta kwa baba wako/

mama alikuwapo/ ule mama P.
alisema: mi nibebe hiyi: huyu
Bikira Maria ni wangu/ wende
ukaletee wabo/

tena minasema mara ya mpili:
mama: baba wangu atabakie hivi pasipo Bikira Maria? ali-
kwenda alikuja na sanamu ingine
mukubwa sawa: iko mwangaza
ku maungo sana/ inakuja na ile

mama X! I answered. He said:
Take this here. I looked and
saw this communion in his hand.
I said: *Baba,* explain to me what
this means. I do not know what
it means, I really don't. Explain
it to me so that I know what
sort of thing it is.

So he came back a second time
with the cross of Lord Jesus;
and Lord Jesus on the cross held
his head like that [she makes a
gesture]. He came with the cross
and told me: Take this Lord
Jesus and guard him.

And I answered him and said:
Baba, now you give me the Lord
Jesus; shall my *baba* [husband]
stay just like that, without the
Virgin Mary?

And he said: I hurry and get the
Virgin Mary. He went and came
back with a statue about that
small [she gestures] full of light.
When he arrived with the statue,
he said: I come to give this
Virgin Mary to your husband.

Then there was a *mama*. This
mama P. [wife of *baba* M.]
said: I'll carry her, this Virgin
Mary is mine. [? Her husband
says:] Go and give her to them.

So I said again: *Mama,* is my
husband going to stay just like
this, without the Virgin Mary?
She went away and came back
with another statue about that
big [indicates] shining with light.

sanamu anasema: Bikira Maria yee huyu minakuja kuleta kwa baba wako/ alisema: wee mama: siku ya Pasaka kama wakati ya kupeleka komunio utatangulia kwenda mbele ku kibasa ya komunio/

She came with this statue and said: I come to bring this Virgin Mary to your husband. He [she?] said: You, *mama,* on Easter Sunday, when they distribute communion, you shall go up to the communion rail.

kiisha anakuja kusimama: anasema: sala sala ya majuto/ nisala sala ya majuto: sala sala ya kusadiki/ minasala sala ya kusadiki/ kiisha alikuja kusema: hiyi huyu Bwana Yezu minakupa mweye mutazalia Mungu batoto/ hiyi ni ukombozi mutakomboa dunia/

Then he stood [before me] and said: Say the prayer of contrition. I said the prayer of contrition. Pray the confession of faith. I said the confession of faith. Then he said: I give you this Lord Jesus so that you may bear children for God. This is the salvation with which you will save the world.

kiisha anakuja kusema: alleluja: alleluja: alleluja/ na minasema: bwana: bwana: bwana: ukuje kwangu/ kiisha nilikuwa kusema baba wangu: minasema baba: huyu Bikira Maria banakuja kukuletea/ umuchunge muzuri katika mawazo yako/ wee baba usitoshe sauti mubaya mu kinywa yako/ wee baba usizungumuze mazungumuzo mabaya/ usitembee mwendo mubaya/ minasema na baba vile/

Then he said: alleluia, alleluia, alleluia. And I said: Lord, lord, lord [or: husband . . .], come to me. Then I talked to my husband and told him: *Baba,* they gave you this Virgin Mary; guard her well in your thoughts. You, *baba,* do not speak evil, do not tell bad things, do not go evil ways. This is how I spoke to my husband.

kiisha minakuja kushituka: niko ku mawazo/

Then I woke up and found myself in thoughts.

Remarks

The actors are an initiating couple (*baba* M. and *mama* P.) and their candidates (the dreamer and her husband). Union (symbolized by "communion") between the wife and Lord Jesus

and between the husband and the Virgin Mary is the basic theme
of the first degree of initiation; the allusion to fecundity ("you may
bear children for God"), however, anticipates ideas of the third degree. The dreamer is a fully initiated member of the Jamaa. Interesting
are the moralizing admonitions at the end of the account. They
seem to confirm the opinion of many outsiders that women of the
Jamaa use the movement and its ideology to dominate their husbands.

SECOND DREAM

Recorded March 26, 1965, at Musonoi. The dreamer is a woman.

Kwanza minaona tunekala na bababa na bamama/ tuko tuna-
sali/ alafu: kuangaria ku mu-
kongo hivi: tuona paka baba
yangu mwenye kunizala/ baba
pale anakuja: anapita mbele yetu: anageuka muzungu/

First I see: We are together with
the *babababa* and *bamama* [of the
Jamaa], and we are praying.
But looking behind me I see my
own father. Father comes for-
ward, passes us, and as soon as
he is in front of us he changes
into a white man.

bamama na bababa banasema:
banasema: eh: angarie huyu mu-
zungu/ pale anakuwa pa mu-
kongo: tunaona muntu mweusi/
anapita mbele yetu: anakuwa
muzungu/ minasema hapana:
bakwetu muangarieni huyu muntu ni baba yangu mwenye kuni-
zala/

The *bamama* and *bababa* say:
Look at that white man. As soon
as he is behind us, we see [him
as] a black man; when he passes
us and is in front of us, he is a
white man. I say: No, my
friends; look, this man is my own
father.

baba anageuka pale anatuanga-
ria anasema: hapana: mimi niko
baba yake/ ni kweli vile anasema: niko baba yake/ alafu
ananiita baba anasema: angaria
pale pa fasi/ minakuja minasi-
mama minaangaria minaona paka masanamu mbili/

Father changes [again], looks at
us, and says: No [do not have
any other thoughts], I am her
father. What she says is true: I
am her father. Then father calls
me and says: Look over there.
I stand up and look, and I see
two statues.

baba asema: mbele twanga magoti chini: maneno unazidi kulialia siku yote unasema: ni hiyi maladi inanikamata mi sijue/

Father says: First get on your knees, because every day you are complaining; this illness has taken hold of me, I don't know what it is.

siku yote benzetu beko banatembea/ paka banakwenda pa fasi ya mbali/ beko banabeba bintu bya buzito mu kichwa/ tena beko banazalia batoto ku mulango/ mimi maladi mwanzo inanikamata: pasipo kubeba kintu kya buzito: pasipo kutembea fasi ya mbali/ alafu abo batoto niko nabo batakula nini?

My friends walk around all the time, even make trips far away. They carry heavy loads on their heads and give birth to children in their houses. But I, since the illness got me, I cannot carry heavy loads or walk long distances. What are my children going to eat?

sasa: masanamu ile utaona mbele: utwange magoti chini: ubelezee/ alafu usielezee nguvu hapana/ ubelezee paka ku masikio/ pasipo kusikia muntu mwingine/ useme mateso yako yote: muishe yote sawa vile uko unateswa/ bo benyewe ndio banajua: paka ile masanamu mbili/

Now [father says]: look at those statues, fall on your knees and tell them. Don't talk in a loud voice, just speak into their ears so that no one else can hear it. Tell them all your misery, everything you suffer. They know, those two statues.

na vile minasema minasema minasema: bakwetu mi huyu minateswa/ sijui hiyi maladi: kama ni bantu bananitumiayo: kama ni Mungu yee mwenyewe/ pale penyewe niko nisema na sauti tu kiloko sana baba alinielezea/ paka ku masikio ya ile sanamu mbili/ na vile minasema mambo yangu yote: mateso yangu yote: minasema/

So I talk and talk and talk. Friends [lit., people from my own village or country], this is what I suffer from. I don't know about this illness, whether people sent it to me or God himself. I tell them about this in a very low voice, as father had told me, just into the ears of the two statues. So I tell them everything, all my misery.

asema: *bon:* ni kweli/ alafu we mwenyewe kaukubebake franga? minasema hapana/ mimi sikubeba franga/ kama minabeba fra-

[Then father] says: Okay, this is it. But you, didn't you steal money? I say: No! I did not steal money. If I stole money, you

nga: unibebe mi: nikufe/ na yee anasema hapana/ kweli kweli sema tu kintu moja kintu ya kweli kweli: haubeba franga? minasema: mi sikubeba franga/ kama minabeba franga: unibeba baba mi nikufe/ baba ananiuliza mara na mara: mimi minajibu paka vile asema hapana/ mi kama nilibeba ile franga mi ni-kufe/

can carry me away and I'll die. He says: No [let's not talk like that]. Just tell the truth. You did not steal the money? I say: I did not steal money. If I did it, you carry me away and I'll die. Father asks again and again. I answer the same way: No, if I did it, I'll die.

asema ni kweli/ minaona mu roho yako haukubeba franga ha-pana/ kama utabeba franga: kama minakubeba: unakufa pa-ka leo paka leo/ alafu hauku-beba franga ile hapana/ na hivi minakuja kushituka/

Then he says: Truly, in your soul I see that you did not steal the money. But if you steal money, I'll carry you away, and you die today. But you did not steal that money. With that I wake up.

Remarks

Typical of Jamaa dreams is the presence of the group in the dream scene. The appearance of the deceased father of the dreamer is a very common traditional element; this is also true for the ambivalent attitude toward the dead: the father appears both as a benevolent helper (he introduces his daughter to the statues) and as a threat (he accuses her of stealing money). It is interesting to see that this double quality is symbolized in his change from a black to a white man. The "misery" of the dreamer reflects the typical situation of a housewife in a camp: care for the children, long marches to the markets in the company of other women, the importance of money (cf. our description of camp life in Chapter 2). The two statues are not explicitly identified, but we may assume (cf. preceding dream) that they represent the Lord Jesus and the Virgin Mary. This connects the dream with the ideas of Jamaa initiation. However, the attitude the dreamer is expected to assume toward the statues is not typical for the Jamaa. In the term used to address them (*bakwetu,* people from our village), one may see a clue for the fact that the dreamer takes them as ancestor statues. Another theme typical of the general cultural context is the fluid boundaries between physical illness and moral wrong. The dreamer is told to confess her sins, presumably in order to be relieved of her suffering. Notice also her reflection about the origin of her illness (whether people sent it, or God himself).

THIRD DREAM

Recorded July 25, 1965, at Musonoi. The dreamer is a man.

Tulilala ndani ya nyumba yetu/ na mama na watoto wetu/ tulisali: tulimuomba Mungu na Bikira Maria na Bwana Yezu na Roho Mutakatifu/ kwa kwitushushia amani: tubakie na huruma katika nyumba yetu/

We were sleeping in our house, together with my wife and our children. We prayed and implored God, the Virgin Mary, Lord Jesus, and the Holy Spirit to let peace descend on us so that we may live with mercy in our house.

alafu kulala minapata mawazo/ minaandika mukanda: minasema hiyi mukanda: nitamuletea baba B: asikie kwanza mambo hiyi iko hapa petu/ na hivi minatoka na hiyi mukanda: minasema minakwenda kuletea kwa baba B/

But falling asleep I receive thoughts. I write a letter, and I say: I am going to bring this letter to Father B. so that he may understand our affairs here. So I leave with this letter and say: I go and get it to Father B.

kutoka kule minashuka ku chimbotelo: minakutana baba B iko anakuja mu njia na *voiture* yake mweupe/ sasa baba G ilikuja na *camion* yake ya *bleu* ku mukongo/ minasema: baba B: unasimamisha/ kisimamisha sema baba: ile mukanda ni yetu? minasema: baba mukanda ni yetu/ minakuya nayo minasema: nikamuletee baba B na yee asikie/

From there I descend into the [open-pit] mine, and I meet Father B. approaching on the road in his white car. At that moment *baba* G. came behind him in his blue truck. I say: Father B., stop [your car]. When he had stopped the car he said: *Baba,* is this letter for us? I say: *Baba,* this letter is for us [i.e., for you]. I brought it along telling myself: I'll give it to Father B. so that he may understand.

ule baba namujibu asema: ndio ule mukanda unaandika? mimi minasema: eheh/ ndio ile nili-

The other *baba* said: Is this the letter you wrote? I say: Yes, this is the one I wrote in order to

kuwa minaandika kwa kwenda kumupa baba B/ sasa minakwenda na mukanda/ minasema: alafu wee baba: mwiko munakwenda wapi? yee anasema: minakwenda kumuonyesha baba B fasi ile yee bado kufika/ ndio wananituma wanasema: wenda na kumuonyesha/ . . .

sasa na vile minajibu minasema: baba: hiyi mukanda minaandika sawa sababu pale ulifwata wee mafundisho ya Mungu: ya nkundi ya eklezia katolika/ ulikuwa unatuma bantu asema: wenda mukaandike/ ndio unipe mi nifunze/ wee unajibu asema: baba: mwenye kusema sawa: mukoshi wake/ mukoshi wake/ mi nilikuwa minaandika sikupati kintu/ ni paka vile baba B na baba Placide alinitolea ya kama na wee utatafuta baba na mama ba kukuendelesha hiyi mafundisho ya Mungu utaipata/

angaria kakibasa yangu haka: ni kale nilikuwa nakwenda kuikala mu nyumba ya baba na mama baiko bananiendelesha/

sasa ni nani anasema?
minasema: nduku yako ndio anasema bakaandika kwiko bantu bakuje banipe/ sasa wee usikia vile: ni kutosha muzabibu kwanza kufinga nayo unaipiga chini anasema mukoshi yake na kule atakwenda na kule atatokea ha-

go and give it to Father B. Now I am on my way with the letter. I say: But you, *baba*, where are you going? He says: I go and show Father B. a place he hasn't seen yet. This is what they sent me for, telling me: Go and show him [around].

Then I say: *Baba,* I wrote this letter because [people tell] when you followed the *mafundisho* of God, of the group of the Catholic church [i.e., initiation into the Jamaa], you ordered people to write it down, telling them: Give it to me so that I may learn. You answer [the dream is told to Father B.]: Whoever said this be cursed; he be cursed. If I had written, I would not have gotten a thing. This is what Father B. [a mistake, refers to someone else] and *baba* Placide handed down to me: Look for a *baba* and a *mama* who can initiate you so that you may receive the *mafundisho* of God.

Look at my stool here; I sat on it in the house of [my] *baba* and *mama* who initiated me.

Now who brought this up?
I say: It was your confrere who said the people should write it down and come and bring it to him. As soon as you hear this, you take off [?] the rope with which you gird yourself and beat the ground with it, swearing: He

taona mama Bikira Maria: hataona Bwana Yezu: hataona
Roho Mutakatifu/ kweli amani
hataishuka kwake: hapana/

be cursed, and where he comes
and where he goes [i.e., whatever he tries] he shall not see the
mother Virgin Mary, nor Lord
Jesus and the Holy Spirit. Truly,
peace shall not descend upon
him.

na ule baba anijibu anasema:
baba X/ minaitika/ unaona?
ule anafinga ni nani?

And the other baba said: *Baba
X* [the dreamer]. I answer:
Yes. [He says] Do you see?
Who is the one who curses?

kama shee tunasema: bababa
tuangarieni hatuna mu umoja na
baba wetu: mwee mutasema: ooh
iko anatafuta busultani/ sasa ule
iko anafinga ni baba B, ao ni
muntu ingine?

When we say: *Bababa*, look, we
are not united with our priest,
then you'll say: Oh, he is looking
for power.
Now, the one who curses, is that
Fr. B. or someone else?

pa kusema vile mimi minakuwa
kushituka: niko ku mawazo/

Saying this I wake up: I am in
thoughts.

Remarks

Two short passages were left out: one of them is incomprehensible, the other could reveal the identity of one of the participants.
The dreamer comes from a camp near Kolwezi where the Jamaa
group was in endemic conflict with their local pastor. He appeals
to Father B. from Musonoi (as many of the groups in the Kolwezi area do). In his dream he causes a violent reaction by Father
B. This is more or less the way the impulsive missionary would
have reacted, even though it appears somewhat distorted and larger
than life. It must be emphasized that the setting of the dream is
perfectly realistic. In other words, if it were not for the introductory
and concluding formulas, it could be taken as the account of an
actual event. The dreamer has to cross the mine in order to get to
Musonoi, and he might very well have met Father B. in his white
Volkswagen, followed by *baba* G. in a blue-grey Peugeot pickup
truck of the Union Minière. Both Father B. and P. Tempels often
spent their free time driving or walking through the open-pit mines

around Musonoi, which offer a spectacular view, very much in contrast to the dull savanna of the surrounding country. Finally, the excitement about someone trying to "write down" Jamaa doctrine is something with which I became very familiar (cf. the account of my abortive attempt to take a census of the group at Musonoi in Chapter 2).

Bibliography

The following list includes only material referred to in the text.

ANDERSSON, EFRAIM
  1958 Messianic popular movements in the lower Congo. Uppsala: Almquist & Wiksell.
APTER, D. E. (ed.)
  1964 Ideology and discontent. New York: The Free Press.
ASHTON, E. O.
  1961 Swahili grammar. London: Oxford University Press.
BALANDIER, G.
  1955 Sociologie actuelle de l'Afrique noire. Paris: Presses Universitaires de France.
  1957 Afrique ambigue. Paris: Plon.
BANTON, M. (ed.)
  1966 Anthropological approaches to the study of religion. New York: F. A. Praeger.
BARRETT, D. B.
  1968 Schism and renewal in Africa. London: Oxford University Press.
BARTH, FREDERIK
  1967 On the study of social change. American Anthropologist 69: 661–69.
BAUMANN, H., and D. WESTERMANN
  1948 Les peuples et les civilisations de l'Afrique. Paris: Payot.
BERTIEAUX, RAYMOND
  1953 Aspects de l'industrialisation en Afrique centrale. Brussels: Institut des relations internationales.
BIEBUYCK, DANIEL P.
  1966 On the concept of tribe. Civilisations 16:500–515.

BIRNBAUM, NORMAN
1960   The sociological study of ideology (1940–60)—A trend report and bibliography. Current Sociology 9:91–172.

BOONE, O.
1961   Carte ethnique du Congo. Quart Sud-Est. Tervuren: Musée Royal de l'Afrique centrale.

BOULAGA, F. E.
1968   Le Bantou problématique. Présence Africaine No. 66:4–40.

BURLING, R.
1969   Linguistics and ethnographic description. American Anthropologist 71:817–827.

BURRIDGE, KENELM
1960   Mambu—A Melanesian millennium. London: Methuen.

BURTON, W. F. P.
1961   Luba religion and magic in custom and belief. Tervuren: Musée Royal de l'Afrique centrale.

CAPRASSE, P.
1959   Leaders africains en milieu urbain (Elisabethville). Elisabethville: Edition CEPSI.

CHAPELIER, A.
MS   Elisabethville, Jadotville et Kolwezi: Etude de géographie urbaine comparée. Thesis, University of Liège, 1956.

COLLE, R. P.
1913   Les Baluba. Brussels: Institut national de bibliographie.

COMHAIRE, J.
1956   Some aspects of urbanization in the Belgian Congo. American Journal of Sociology 62:8–13.

DEBRA, A.
1949   La femme noire dans les C.E.C. et les camps de travailleurs au Congo. Bulletin CEPSI 9:131–41.

DE BRIEY, P.
1952   L'industrialisation de l'Afrique centrale et les problèmes sociaux qu'elle pose. Bulletin CEPSI 14:13–59.

DECHANET, J. M.
1962   En marge du monachisme africain: La Jamaa. Parole et Mission 5:429–36.

DE CRAEMER, WILLY
1965   Analyse sociologique de la Jamaa. Léopoldville: Centre de Recherches Sociologiques.

DE HEMPTINNE, J. F.
1929 La politique des missions protestantes au Congo. Elisabethville: Edition de "L'Essor du Congo."

DENIS, JACQUES
1956 Elisabethville: Matériaux pour une étude de la population africaine. Elisabethville: Edition CEPSI.
1958 Le phénomène urbain en Afrique centrale. Brussels: ARSC.

DETHIER, ROBERT
1961a Les citadins Katangais et leur jardin: Aspects psycho-sociaux de la vie en milieu africain urbain. Liège: Travaux de l'Institut de Sociologie de la Faculté de Droit.
1961b Une famille de citadins du Katanga. Liège: Travaux de l'Institut de Sociologie de la Faculté de Droit.

DE WAELE, FRANK
MS La catéchèse dans les Jamaas à Léopoldville. Kinshasa, n.d. [1965].

DOUCY, A.
1954 Le rôle des influences coutumières sur les travailleurs du Congo Belge. Revue de l'Institut de Sociologie (Solvay) 27:817–30.

DOUCY, A., and P. FELDHEIM
1951 Problèmes du travail au Katanga. Revue de l'Institut de Sociologie (Solvay) 3:393–461.
1952 Problèmes du travail et politique sociale au Congo Belge. Brussels: Librairie encyclopédique.
1958 Travailleurs indigènes et productivité du travail au Congo Belge. Brussels: Institut de Sociologie Solvay.

DOW, T. E.
1968 The role of charisma in modern African development. Social Forces 46:328–38.
1969 The theory of charisma. Sociological Quarterly 10:306–18.

D'YDEWALLE, CHARLES
1960 L'Union Minière du Haut Katanga—De l'âge colonial à l'independence. Paris: Plon.

EPSTEIN, A. L.
1959 Linguistic innovation and culture on the copper belt, Northern Rhodesia. Southwestern Journal of Anthropology 15:235–53.

FABIAN, J.
1963 Führer und Führung in den prophetisch-messianischen Bewegungen der (ehemaligen) Kolonialvölker. Überlegungen zur Methode. Anthropos 58:773–809.
1965a Ideology and content. Sociologus 16:1–18.

1965b   Kung Bushman kinship—Componential analysis and alternative interpretations. Anthropos 60:663–718.
1966   Dream and charisma. "Theories of dreams" in the Jamaa movement (Congo). Anthropos 61:544–60.
1967   Tod dem Propheten: Ein Dokument zu eine prophetischen Situation. Sociologus 17:131–46.
1969a   Charisma and cultural change: The case of the Jamaa movement in Katanga (Congo Republic). Comparative Studies in Society and History 11:155–73.
1969b   An African gnosis: For a reconsideration of an authoritative definition. History of Religions 9:42–58.
1970a   Religion and change. *In* PADEN, J., and E. SOJA (eds.), The African Experience, pp. 381–99. Evanston: Northwestern University Press.
1970b   *Philosophie bantoue:* Placide Tempels et son œuvre vus dans une perspective historique. Etudes africaines du CRISP. Brussels: Centre de recherche et d'information socio-politiques.
MS   Language, history, and anthropology. Journal for the Philosophy of the Social Sciences 1 (in press).
MS   Charisma and cultural change: A study of the Jamaa movement in Katanga. Ph.D. dissertation, University of Chicago, 1969.

FIRTH, R.
1959   Problem and assumption in an anthropological study of religion. Journal of the Royal Anthropological Institute 89:129–48.

FISHMAN, J. A., C. A. FERGUSON, and J. DAS GUPTA (eds.)
1968   Language problems of developing nations. New York: John Wiley & Sons.

FORDE, D. (ed.)
1956   Aspects sociaux de l'industrialisation et de l'urbanisation en Afrique au sud du Sahara. Paris: UNESCO.

FORTHOMME, GEORGES
1951   Un aspect de l'évolution de la mentalité indigène en contact de centres industriels. Elisabethville: Edition Imicon.
1957   Mariage et industrialisation. Evolution de la mentalité dans une cité de travailleurs d'Elisabethville. Liège: Travaux de l'Institut de Sociologie de la Faculté de Droit.

GEERTZ, CLIFFORD
1964   Ideology as a cultural system. *In* APTER, 47–76.
1966   Religion as a cultural system. *In* BANTON, 1–46.

GERARD, O.
1964a   Christian life in the "Jamaa." Christ to the World 9:22–32.

1964b   A remarkable case of fruitful adaptation in Africa. Christ to the World 9:119–31.

GERARD-LIBOIS, JULES
1966   Katanga secession. Madison: University of Wisconsin Press.

GHILAIN, J.
1968   A propos de la formation du capital autochtone en Afrique noire; le *likilimba*. Revue de l'Institut de Sociologie (Solvay) 3:443–46.

GLUCKMAN, MAX
1963   Order and rebellion in tribal Africa. London: Cohen & West.
1968   The utility of the equilibrium model in the study of social change. American Anthropologist 70:219–37.

GOODY, J.
1961   Religion and ritual: the definition problem. British Journal of Sociology 12:142–64.

GRESCHAT, H. J.
1967   Kitawala—Ursprung, Ausbreitung und Religion der Watch-Tower-Bewegung in Zentralafrika. Marburg: Elwert.

GREVISSE, F.
1951   Le centre extra-coutumier d'Elisabethville. Brussels: Institut royal colonial Belge.
1956   Le centre extra-coutumier d'Elisabethville. *In* FORDE, 182–87.
1958   Notes ethnographiques relatives à quelques populations autochtones du Haut-Katanga industriel. Elisabethville: Edition CEPSI.

GUEBELS, L.
1952   Relation complète des travaux de la Commission Permanente pour la Protection des Indigènes au Congo Belge. Elisabethville: Edition CEPSI.

GUMPERZ, J. J. and D. HYMES (eds.)
1964   The ethnography of communication. Menasha, Wis.: American Anthropological Association.

HABERMAS, J.
1967   Zur Logik der Sozialwissenschaften. Tübingen: J. C. B. Mohr (Paul Siebeck).

HAMMEL, E. A.
1965   Formal semantic analysis. Menasha, Wis.: American Anthropological Association.

HELM, JUNE (ed.)
1964   Symposium on new approaches to the study of religion. Seattle: American Ethnological Society.

HODGKIN, THOMAS
1956 Nationalism in colonial Africa. London: Muller.

HOLTON, GERALD (ed.)
1965 Science and culture. Boston: Houghton Mifflin.

HORTON, R.
1960. A definition of religion and its uses. Journal of the Royal Anthropological Institute 90:201–26.

HUNTER, W. F.
1959 A manual of Congo Swahili grammar. Goma-Bunia: n.p.

HYMES, D.
1964 Introduction: Toward ethnographies of communication. *In* GUMPERZ, J. J., and D. HYMES (eds.), 1–34.

JACOBSON, DAVID
1968 Friendship and mobility in the development of an urban elite African social system. Southwestern Journal of Anthropology 24:123–38.

JANSSEN, TH. M.
1967 Religious encounter and the "Jamaa." Heythrop Journal 8: 129–51.

JARVIE, I. C.
1964 The revolution in anthropology. New York: Humanities Press.

JOHNSON, FREDERICK
1963 A standard Swahili-English dictionary. Oxford: Oxford University Press.

JOMIER, J.
1963 Un prêtre africain parle. Parole et Mission 6:593–602.

JOYE, PIERRE, and ROSINE LEWIN
1961 Les trusts au Congo. Brussels: Société Populaire d'Editions.

KOPYTOFF, IGOR
1964 Classifications of religious movements: Analytical and synthetic. *In* HELM, 77–101.

LEBLANC, MARIA
1960 Personnalité de la femme Katangaise. Contribution à l'étude de son acculturation. Louvain: Nauwelaerts.

MANNONI, O.
1950 Psychologie de la colonisation. Paris: Editions du Seuil.

MARCUSE, HERBERT
1965 Remarks on a redefinition of culture. *In* HOLTON, 218–35.

MEERT, J.
 1961   Quelques considérations sur la "Jamaa." Orientations Pastorales 13:17–28.

MELS, B.
 1964   An example of fruitful adaptation in Africa—The "Jamaa" at Luluabourg. Christ to the World 9:500–504.

MINON, P.
 1960   Katuba. Etude quantitative d'une communauté urbaine africaine. Liège: Travaux de l'Institut de Sociologie de la Faculté de Droit.

MOTTOULLE, L.
 1946   Politique sociale de l'Union Minière du Haut Katanga pour sa main-d'œuvre indigène et ses résultats au cours de vingt années d'application. Brussels: Van Campenhout.

MOYSAN, N.
 1964   Apropos the "Jamaa"—A wonderful and feasible experience. Christ to the World 9:239 ff.

MULAGO, VINCENT
 n.d. [1960]   Autour du mouvement de la "Jamaa." Orientations Pastorales (Léopoldville), Cahier No. 1, pp. 3–28.
 1961   Quelques jalons pour une catéchèse bantoue. Orientations Pastorales 13:1–10.
 1964   A visit to the "Jamaa." Christ to the World 9:17–19.

MWEPE KYABUTHA, GASPARD
 1967   Quelques aspects des conséquences sociales de l'industrialisation au Katanga. Civilisations 17:53–69.

NOIRHOMME, G., W. DE CRAEMER, and M. DE WILDE D'ESTMAEL.
 n.d.   L'église au Congo en 1963. Rapport d'une enquête socio-religieuse. Léopoldville: Centre de Recherches Sociologiques.

ONWUMELU, JOHN A.
 MS   Congo paternalism: an isolationist colonial policy. Thesis, University of Chicago, 1966.

PARSONS, TALCOTT
 1961   The structure of social action. Glencoe: The Free Press.
 1963   The social system. Glencoe: The Free Press.

PARSONS, TALCOTT, and E. SHILS (eds.)
 1959   Toward a general theory of action. Cambridge: Harvard University Press.

PARSONS, TALCOTT, EDWARD SHILS, KASPAR D. NAEGELE, and JESSE R. PITTS (eds.)
 1961   Theories of society. Glencoe: The Free Press.

PEERAER, SERVAAS
1939   Toespraken tot jonggehuwden bij de Baluba (Katanga). Kongo-Overzee 5:241–76.
1943   Toespraken tot jonggehuwden bij de Baluba (Katanga). Kongo-Overzee 9:1–59.

PIETTE, A.
1964   Fruits yielded by the "Jamaa" in Luluabourg. Christ to the World 9:19–21.

PIKE, K. L.
1966   Etic and emic standpoints for the description of behavior. In SMITH, A. G. (ed.), 152–63.

PIROTTE, JEAN
1968   Une expérience chrétienne au Congo: La Jamaa. Neue Zeitschrift für Missionswissenschaft 24:282–83.

POLOME, E.
1963   Cultural languages and contact vernaculars in the Republic of the Congo. Studies in Literature and Language 4:499–511.
1968   The choice of official languages in the Democratic Republic of the Congo. In FISHMAN et al., 295–311.
MS   Lubumbashi Swahili.
MS   Multilingualism in an African centre: the Lubumbashi case.

RADNITZKY, G.
1968   Continental schools of metascience. Göteborg: Akademiförlaget.

RUBBENS, ANTOINE (ed.)
1945   Dettes de guerre. Elisabethville: Editions de "L'Essor du Congo."

SACLEUX, C.
1939   Dictionnaire Swahili-Français, I. Paris: Travaux et Mémoires de l'Institut d'Ethnologie.
1941   Dictionnaire Swahili-Français, II. Paris: Travaux et Mémoires de l'Institut d'Ethnologie.

SCHUYLER, P.
1963   Jungle saints. New York: Herder.

SMITH, A. G. (ed.)
1966   Communication and culture. New York: Holt, Rinehart & Winston.

SPIRO, M. E.
1966   Religion: Problems of definition and explanation. In BANTON, 85–126.

SUNDKLER, BENGT G. M.
  1961   Bantu prophets in South Africa. London: Oxford University Press.

TEMPELS, P.
  1944–45   Le mariage indigène et la loi. Kongo-Overzee 10/11: 265–82.
  1945   La philosophie de la rebellion. *In* RUBBENS, 17–23.
  1945   Justice sociale. *In* RUBBENS, 71–75.
  1945   La philosophie bantoue. Elisabethville: Lovania.
  1946   Bantoe-filosofie. Antwerpen: De Sikkel.
  n.d. [1948]   Catéchèse bantoue. Bruges: Abbaye de Saint-André.
  1959   Bantu philosophy. Paris: Présence Africaine.
  n.d. [1962]   Notre rencontre. Léopoldville: Centre d'Etudes Pastorales.
  n.d.   Notre rencontre, II. Léopoldville: Centre d'Etudes Pastorales.

THEUWS, TH.
  1960   Naître et mourir dans le rituel Luba. Zaire 14:115–73.
  1961   The "Jamaa" movement in Katanga. London: Mission Press.
  1962   De Luba-mens. Tervuren: Musée royal de l'Afrique centrale.

THIRD INTERNATIONAL AFRICAN SEMINAR
  1965   African systems of thought. London: Oxford University Press.

TUCKER, ROBERT C.
  1968   The theory of charismatic leadership. Daedalus 1968:731–56.

TURNER, H. W.
  1966   Problems in the study of African independent churches. Numen 13:27–42.

TURNER, VICTOR W.
  1966   Colour classification in Ndembu ritual—A problem in primitive classification. *In* BANTON, 47–84.

TYLER, S. A. (ed.)
  1969   Cognitive anthropology. New York: Holt, Rinehart & Winston.

UNION MINIERE DU HAUT KATANGA
  n.d.   Monograph 1950. Liège: G. Thone.
  n.d. [1957]   1906–1956. Brussels: L. Cuypers.

VAN AVERMAET, E., and B. MBUYA
  1954   Dictionnaire Kiluba-Français. Tervuren: Musée Royal du Congo Belge.

VANNES, J.
  1959   De l'évolution de la coutume d'Elisabethville. Elisabethville: Edition CEPSI.

VANSINA, JAN
n.d. [1966] Introduction à l'ethnographie du Congo. Kinshasa: Editions Universitaires du Congo.
1966 Kingdoms of the savanna. Madison: University of Wisconsin Press.

VERBEKEN, A.
1965 Petit cours de Kiswahili pratique suivi d'un vocabulaire Français-Kiswahili, Kiswahili-Français et de phrases usuelles. Elisabethville: IMBELCO.

VERHAEGEN, PAUL
1962 L'urbanisation de l'Afrique noire: Son cadre, ses causes et ses conséquences, économiques, sociales et culturelles. Brussels: CEDESA.

VERHULPEN, EDMOND
1936 Baluba et Balubaisés du Katanga. Antwerp: L'Avenir Belge.

VERSTRAELEN, F. J. J.
1964 Le patrimoine religieux des Baluba et de quelques autres peuplades dans le sud-est du Congo. Fribourg: n.p.

WEBER, MAX
1964 Wirtschaft und Gesellschaft. Cologne and Berlin: Kiepenheuer & Witsch.

WORSLEY, P. M.
1957 The trumpet shall sound—A study of "cargo" cults in Melanesia. London: Macgibbon & Kee.

YOUNG, CRAWFORD
1965 Politics in the Congo—Decolonization and independence. Princeton: Princeton University Press.

Index

[With few exceptions, Jamaa doctrinal terms in Swahili are not listed in this index. The reader will find an extensive glossary of these terms in our "basic vocabulary of Jamaa language" on pages 132–49.]

Initiation: and dreams, 169, 186, 258;
and filiation, 11, 167, 168, 175; and
organization (*see Kizazi*); prerequisites for, 160; and research, 16–
17, 124–25; and ritual, 168–70,
204; and rules of secrecy, 166–68,
172; traditional models for (*see
Buyanga*)
Institutionalization: and charisma,
110–11; documentation of, 226,
227; and ritual, 174
Integration: documentation of, 225,
227; structural, of Jamaa language,
149, 204; systematic, and totality,
125–26
Interaction: spheres of, and integration of Jamaa movement, 112–15,
201; symbolic *vs.* instrumental, 180

Jamaa:
—activities: definition of, 76, 200;
group meetings, 77–79; intergroup
meetings, 79–81. *See also* Dreams;
Initiation; *Mafundisho;* Ritual;
Teaching
—doctrine: and *Bantu Philosophy*,
29; componential analysis of, 149–
60; deviations from, 193–94; and
historical origin of the Jamaa, 46,
71 (*see also Baba saba*); and language, 130–31; and leadership, 179;
and mission church, 162–63; as
model of and *model for*, 51; and
propagation of the movement, 72,
112; property space of, 155; and
secrecy, 126–27; sources and documents of, 124–29, 223–27; structural components of, 160–65; as a
system, 125, 149
—groups: at C.E.C. Kolwezi, 93–96;
at Kikondja, 108–10; at Kinshasa,
99–102; at Lubumbashi, 96–99; at
Musonoi (*see* Musonoi, Jamaa
group at); at Muteba, 106–7; at
Ruwe, 37–40,112, 198; at Samutoma, 107; at Sandoa, 104–6; members and candidates of, 84–85; and
the missionary, 82–83 (*see also*
Priest); orthodox *vs.* heterodox,
85–88, 185; speakers and audience
in, 83–84
—language: basic vocabulary of,
132–49, 203; and Swahili, 130–31

—leaders, 66–72, 73, 74, 76, 83–84,
87–88, 94–95, 96–99, 100–102,
176, 178, 179, 180
—movement: cultural background of,
11–15, 115; descriptive definition
of, 9–11; as a historical entity, 46,
198–99; origin of, at Ruwe, 37–40,
198, 200; patterns of group-transcending integration of, 110–16,
201–2; patterns of spread of, 70–
72; social environment of, 51–66,
72, 75, 113–14, 199, 211–15
—outgroup image: among the clergy,
216–18; among high-school students at Kolwezi, 218–22
Jarvie, I. C., 196, 197

Kabondo-Dianda, 21, 113
Kafakumba, 114
Kamina, 21, 113, 223
Kapanga, 107–8, 113
Kapata, 52, 183
Kasai, 10, 15, 103, 108, 113, 175, 195
Kasaji, 103, 113
Katete (heterodox groups): charges
against, 191–93; and initiation, 193;
interpretation of, 193–95; and
mawazo, 194–95; origin and mean-
ing of the term, 190–91
Kayeye, 21
Kikondja, 108–10, 113, 188
Kinshasa (Léopoldville), 45, 99–102
Kinship ideology: as foundation for
leadership, 88–89, 99; offenses
against, 89, 193; as principle of
organization, 91–92, 115–16; and
ritual, 175
Kipushi, 41
Kisenge, 104, 106
Kitabu (book): as main document,
126–29, 166–67, 203; selections
from, 228–40
Kitawala, 72, 191*n*, 193
Kizazi (unit of filiation), 11, 88–92,
99, 103, 112, 115–16, 175, 193, 201
Kolwezi, 10, 12, 15, 22, 39, 45, 51–55,
79, 93–96, 103, 116, 218, 256
Kopytoff, I., 163–64

Language: and context, 121, 203; as
epistemological criterion, 121, 124;
philosophy of, and cognitive anthropology, 122–23; the "turn to,"